The painted towns of **Shekhawati**

21/1/05

Eric

best wishes

GW00630569

Beyond the rush and bustle of the old princely capitals of Jaipur, Jodhpur and Bikaner with their rajas and palaces lies a desert region long overlooked by the tourists who visit Rajasthan.

Shekhawati comprises an area bounded by Jhunjhunu, Sikar and Churu. Here, in little towns set against an impoverished landscape, are startling murals, gracing the outer and inner walls of mansions and memorials. Covering any subject that caught the artist's fancy, from aeroplanes to childbirth to religion, these murals became the synthesis of Western and Eastern idioms.

Here, for the first time, is a book that not only provides an insider's guide to this painted world, but traces the genesis, history and development of the pictures, their painters, their patrons, and the buildings they decorate.

With 98 colour photographs, 11 guide maps, 11 black and white illustrations, and advice for the traveller.

MAPIN GUIDE TO INDIA

The painted towns of Shekhawati

Ilay Cooper

Mapin Publishing Pvt. Ltd., Ahmedabad

First published in the
United States of America in 1994 by
Grantha Corporation
80 Cliffedgeway, Middletown, NJ 07701
in association with
Mapin Publishing Pvt. Ltd.
Chidambaram, Ahmedabad 380 013 India

ISBN: 0-944142-80-X (Grantha)
ISBN: 81-85822-17-4 (Mapin)

Distributor for Asia:
Mapin Publishing Pvt. Ltd., India

Distributor for North America:
University of Washington Press, Seattle

Distributor for UK and Europe:
Gazelle Book Services, Lancaster

Editor: Gouri Dange
Design: Subrata Bhowmick & Mapin Studio

Typeset in Berkeley Bold by
Akar Typographics Pvt. Ltd., Ahmedabad

Printed and bound by
Tien Wah Press, Singapore

Jacket:
Lakshmangarh (13): Two carriages cross the
south wall of Shyonarayan Kyal Haveli. The
rath drawn by bullocks is driven by
Hanuman, Rama's monkey ally. Rama and his
brothers are passengers. A European carriage
follows with two ladies under guard. (c1900)

Full title page:
Bissau (13): Two merchants, their beards
neatly protected against the dust, set out on a
camel. Perhaps the horseman accompanies
them as a guard. In a room of Nathuram
Poddar Haveli. (c1890)

DEDICATION

To my mother

Mary Loveday Cooper

Born Kasauli 1917

Died Farnham 1989

With Thanks

Contents

Foreword

In the autumn of 1972, I went to stay with Suresh Bansal in his village of Narnaund, in Haryana. The surrounding countryside is flat, so we often chose to cycle some distance to neighbouring towns either to visit his friends or to see the latest Hindi film. Usually the evenings were spent at his small shop in the bazaar gossiping with whoever turned up. During one such session, inspired by a day out cycling, I announced my intention of touring the adjoining state of Rajasthan by cycle. That caused sufficient effect to become a commitment. The following day Suresh and I went to Jind, the nearest town, and returned with a second-hand bike, a solid, black upright. So I came to spend that winter riding across much of North India, from Jaisalmer in the west, to Gaya in Bihar in the east. That was how I came to Shekhawati.

I entered Rajasthan by route even now unfamiliar to tourists, passing through Rajgarh, Taranagar and Sardarshahr on my way westwards. One feature of these three small towns stirred my imagination. Here, for the first time, I saw great mansions covered with murals. Continuing towards Bikaner, I quitted that painted region. Nothing I saw throughout the rest of my long journey compared with those painted *havelis*.

Later, in Delhi, I was asked to write an account of my tour for the Indian Tourism Development Corporation's magazine. In those days I carried no camera so I had to draw on their collection of photographs to illustrate my text. They had no pictures showing paintings such as I had seen and no one seemed aware of their existence.

In 1975, returning with a camera, I made straight for Taranagar. My arrival coincided with an outing. The grain merchant who had put me up during my previous visit had just purchased a truck and he was off with his family and friends to have it blessed at the Hanuman temple at Salasar. I made the trip with him. It was from my perch on top of the cab of that truck that I first set eyes on true Shekhawati and discovered that there were far more, similar paintings in Sikar, Fatehpur and Ramgarh. When I left Taranagar it was in that direction.

The more I explored the area and talked to its people the more interested I became in the phenomenon which had given rise to this explosion of colour in such an impoverished land. So I decided to work on a book, basing myself in the district town of Churu and from there getting to know the three painted districts, Churu, Jhunjhunu and Sikar.

I travelled alone or with local friends, sometimes by cycle, sometimes on foot, sometimes cadging a lift from a passing camel-cart. I rode on the roofs of tough little buses plying the tracks between villages, or in the slow, convenient train that still puffs its way out of Churu each morning, passing some of the best painted towns as it heads south for Sikar.

Meanwhile, interest in the murals grew. I wrote several articles and a book was published in 1982. In December 1984, a seminar was held in Mandawa Fort, funded by the newly-formed Indian National Trust for Art and Cultural Heritage (INTACH). I heard of it by chance, through friends in England. By that time I had passed a total of three years living in the region so, feeling that I had something to offer, I gatecrashed and was invited to stay. As a result, I was asked to undertake a survey of Shekhawati, listing the buildings of interest as a first step towards their conservation.

I selected a local teacher, Ravindra Sharma, to assist me in the project. Together, we spent two years touring those three districts on a small motorcycle, mapping each town and describing and photographing no less than 2260 buildings. The work is due to be published by INTACH under our names.

The spelling of Shekhawati – with a 'w' or a 'v' – is one of those pointless arguments that so enrich human life. I have always followed local usage, since it seems best to express the local Marwari pronunciation, thus Shekhawati,Mandawa, Nawalgarh etc.

Another note on spelling concerns the names of deities. I have followed the accepted form – i.e. Rama, Shiva, Krishna. This is misleading in conversation since the final 'a' is not pronounced. People speak of Ram, Shiv and Krishnan.

Throughout the text there are references to local towns followed by a number (i.e. Fatehpur 17). These refer to some building listed in that section of the guide under the number given.

Acknowledgements

My thanks are principally due to all those people in Churu, Jhunjhunu and Sikar districts who made my prolonged stay possible. First amongst these, Nand Kishore Choudhary and his family who, from the day I first arrived in Churu, provided me with hospitality and friendship. 'Nandu' later moved to Jaipur, so I had a pied-a-terre in that city, too. Sri Girish Chandra Sharma ('Masterji'), his wife and children became my substitute family through the eighties. His sons Arvind, Ravindra ('Rabu') and Ram Ratan ('Munji') helped in my work and all three travelled with me in search of murals at different times. Arvind took up Shekhawati tourism professionally and has been involved with several of the local facilities. 'Munji' helped me launch the survey of monuments at a period when, discouraged by problems, I was at my most ungracious. To 'Rabu' must go the greatest credit. He agreed to take leave from his teaching post to become my assistant throughout the rest of the survey. He rapidly became indispensable. Without his help and support I should not have persisted with my final two years work, that same survey.

Lakshmikant Jangir, proprietor of Hotel Shiv Shekhawati, and Arvind again, then its manager, provided board and lodging whenever I was in the vicinity of Jhunjhunu. They also put me up while I wrote and corrected much of this book.

I am grateful to Sri Govind Aggarwal of Churu, the authority on the local merchant families. It was he who took me to meet old mason/painters for the first time and showed me the interiors of some of the havelis in the town. Those of his writings which appear in the bibliography were all gifted to me. In Jhunjhunu, Sri Yusuf Hakim helped with the deciphering of some Persian inscriptions. Thanks are also due to many local masons, especially the late Sri Jhabarmal Chejara of Mandawa, for information on techniques.

After a seminar on the murals, held in 1984, where I was asked to carry out the survey, I am indebted to Dr. F. R. Allchin and Sir Bernard Feilden for their support at various times. In 1985, the Ancient India and Iran Trust provided funds which allowed me to spend several weeks in Cambridge, consulting the collection of Dr. Jan van Lohuizen and other libraries.

The British Council contributed money and air fares, which made my participation in the survey possible when INTACH was compelled to drastically cut the agreed funding. I should also like to thank Smt. Harshad Kumari Sharma of INTACH for her support and co-operation during this project. My thanks go also to those who, when my work was completed, paid my pension contributions out of their own pockets.

I am always dependent on good friends to soften the blows of my frequent migrations. In Delhi my thanks to Amrit and Goodie Vohra for their friendship and hospitality; in London, to John Pickford who, apart from providing me with occasional lodging, read through part of this book and made suggestions; in Langton Matravers, to Trev and Sue Haysom, always ready with a transitory room and often with employment in their quarry when I have been broke.

No one who has had occasion to work at the India Office Library in London can fail to be grateful for the help its staff provides. Thanks, also, to those at the National Archives in New Delhi.

Amongst the many others who have earned my gratitude at different times are Jo Darrah (then of the Victoria and Albert Museum, London) and Karen Groen (of the Hamilton Kerr Institute, Cambridge) for tests on pigments; Andrew Topsfield of the Ashmolean Museum, Oxford; Richard Blurton of the British Museum; John Gillow for support in Cambridge and India and Annie Davis.

Lastly thanks to my parents. Both carried out little bits of research for me. They provided moral support with their regular correspondence and their willingness to help with the odd chore.

Unfortunately, there is also a negative side. The Government of India Tourist Department has published a booklet on Shekhawati the format and text of which is largely copied from sections of an earlier edition of this book. This without acknowledgement, payment or permission.

North India showing Bikaner and Jaipur States and the painted region

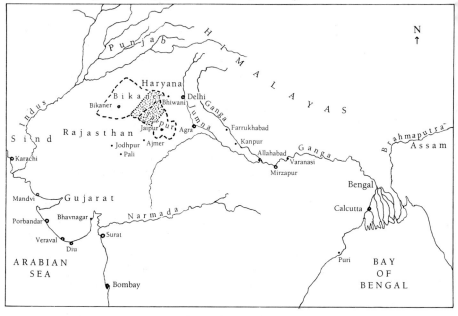

Introducing The Murals

The murals of Shekhawati were painted in an impoverished corner of an arid land. The place was the border between two desert kingdoms, Bikaner and Jaipur, the time no less of a border, for the 18th century formed an interregnum between two great Empires. As the Mughals declined the British rose, and the first fine paintings in Shekhawati appeared between the two.

The genesis for those early murals came in the late 16th Century in the ateliers of the court painters of that greatest of Mughals, Akbar. He had encouraged them to abandon their homes in Persia in favour of Agra. When he shifted his capital to Fatehpur Sikri the new school produced some of its first murals. From there the new style reached Amber, some 225 km to the west, capital of what was to become Jaipur State. The journey was simply accomplished since the Raja, Man Singh, was a pillar of the Emperor's court, one of his finest generals. It is appropriate that the earliest murals of Mughal descent in Rajasthan seem to be in his city in his memorial.

If the Muslim Mughals created the seed for the Shekhawati murals, they equally prevented its germination. As long as their regime held sway, it supported local Muslim barons, prohibited by their faith from depicting man or beast. Such indictments might be flouted by the Emperor if he so chose, but smaller men were more careful. Two barons held all that territory which was destined to produce the greatest concentration of painted buildings.

A century passed. The Empire embarked on its prolonged decline. There were more profound problems to be considered than the fate of a group of minor barons surrounded by Hindu-ruled territory. Amongst the Hindu rulers were Shekhawat Rajput barons forming a loose federation allied, but not subject, to the Amber/Jaipur throne. Sharing common descent from a 15th century warrior, Rao Shekha, they held lands east of the Aravalli Hills.

Even in the lifetime of the last great Mughal, Aurangzeb, the Shekhawats had begun to encroach through the hills, enlarging their holdings at the expense of Muslim nobles. With the decline of Mughal authority the encroachment accelerated, and by 1732 the conquest was complete. The Nawabs of Fatehpur and Jhunjhunu had been evicted and two Shekhawat barons, Sardul Singh and his distant cousin Shiv Singh, shared most of the usurped land.

However, the triumph was not untarnished, for it was about this time that the Shekhawat federation was compelled to recognize the Raja of Jaipur, Jai Singh 11, as its overlord. From then on, Shekhawati was in theory, though often not in practice, a tributary of Jaipur.

It was the Shekhawat barons who summoned the first muralists to the region to decorate some of their buildings with fine figurative paintings. They had probably seen such work during their visits to the court at Amber and Jaipur and the painters almost certainly came from there. The brrons' increased revenues gave them the wherewithal to construct handsome temples and memorials.

In their desert estates, the barons had two main sources of revenue. They taxed the farmers on their often-pathetic harvests and they imposed duties on the merchandise crossing their borders. Camel-borne trade was an important feature of Rajasthan's economy and a small merchant community oversaw local commerce.

In the era of strife which was the 18th century, each prince found it very difficult to fill his treasury. The Rajas of Bikaner and of Jaipur tried every means to raise funds. Along with other rulers they increased tariffs on trade. Together, their kingdoms spanned the whole of the north of Rajasthan, except for narrow corridor, the land of the Shekhawats. The barons were tributaries, but each set his own rates of duty. This meant that a caravan crossing that way might have to pay several times, but the total sum was so much lower than that levied in Jaipur proper that it was worth making a long detour. From the turn of the century until 1822 a vast amount of trade was diverted through Shekhawati and more merchants were attracted into the region.

These men and their descendants were to finance the vast majority of the murals which, by their synthesis of eastern and western idioms, are so characteristic of the Shekhawati style. Their prosperity had been enhanced by the deflection of trade through the region, not merely by inflated tariffs but also, earlier, by a shift in the route followed by much of the traffic between Delhi and the coast. Some of the money they earned went towards building temples, memorials and mansions. These might contain paintings, but the great era of merchant patronage was yet to come. When it did, the fortune it represented would owe little to the caravan trade.

The days of flourishing cross-desert commerce were numbered. If it had merely been disrupted by growing banditry then its repression by the Shekhawati Brigade during the 1830s should have brought relief. It did not. The British had profoundly affected the traditional pattern of trade. Their ports of Bombay and Calcutta, handling large European vessels, completely overshadowed the small Gujarati havens. Their tariffs, designed to establish monopolies for the East India Company, made some established routes no longer viable. When their pressure on the Jaipur court resulted in a sharp reduction of duties it was no longer cheaper to go through Shekhawati. In the second and third decades of the 19th century, it became clear that the future of commerce did not lie across Rajasthan.

This change should have brought ruin to the merchants of Shekhawati. In a sense it did; but they were not so easily beaten. Many of the menfolk migrated eastwards to ports on the Ganges. This river was the artery of a new colonial trade; Calcutta, its heart. In pursuit of business they moved downstream and settled afresh in the city, capital of the rising Empire. There they flourished. News of their success reached home. More men joined them. By the close of the 19th century, their economic power in Calcutta was unrivalled. Many men from Shekhawati were making enormous fortunes.

And what of the murals ? Merchants had occasionally patronized the painters as far back as the late 17th century, but profits from desert trade were limited, supporting only two or three wealthy traders in each town. After 1820, however, as the emigrants tightened their grip on the greater part of the subcontinent's commerce, the contraints were almost over. Many men from each desert town were pouring money homewards. From that time onwards they utterly eclipsed the Rajputs.

It was these emigrant merchants who financed painted Shekhawati, for their status remained there, in the homeland. The fortunes they made were partly turned to conspicuous building. Each man competed with his neighbour and the edifices grew larger and more ambitious as the century progressed. Whether it was a mansion or a memorial, a temple or a well, every building was covered with paintings. When famine struck they poured back more money. Their relief projects took the form of yet more palatial buildings decorated with yet more paintings.

Each building was an expression not merely of affluence but also of confidence in a new era of stable central government. The merchants felt secure to display their triumph for all to see. At first the pictures were limited to panels between the stone brackets which supported the projection of an upper storey over the lower facade. Soon they spread to any surface worthy of becoming a feature. Outer walls, inner courtyards, sitting rooms, bedrooms – all received the painter's attention.

In a way, the merchants created the painters. They came not only from the itinerant teams whose ancestors had painted for the Rajput barons of the previous century. The demand was too great for them alone. In every little township rich men were building and each wanted murals. Many architect/masons, many masons versed in mural technique, shifted into the region from Jaipur and its environs. Any local mason with skill as a draughtsman was encouraged to develop his talent. Each was straying into a new discipline, unimpeded by the restrictions imposed on the trained painter. Looking around him he saw everywhere inspiration for the pictures he would paint.

These mason/painters were to set Shekhawati apart. Their style had come firstly from the Mughal court, but it reached them via the murals and miniatures of Jaipur And there were other influences around, not merely from the neighbouring courts of Rajasthan.

What is so special about the murals of Shekhawati ? For the most part they are the glorious result of a cultural collision between East and West. A vision of the world portrayed by European artists had a profound effect on Indian painters during the 19th century. Court painters had been aware of the alien idiom two centuries earlier, had even dallied with it. But it took the combination of enormous wealth, readily accessible lithographs and very receptive painters to divert the vernacular style.

Shekhawati's pictures cover a transformation from an 18th century and early 19th century, when deities, princes and beasts were depicted in lively two-dimensional paintings, to an early 20th century, when the artists, armed with some of the West's techniques, found nothing and no one too trivial to display. They strove gamely for a third dimension through use of shadow and a foreign system of perspective. At worst they copied slavishly. At best they produced a lively fusion – their own unique school of art. This is seen at its most successful on the outer and inner walls of turn-of-the-century mansions.

This, then, is one of the most unusual art collections in the world. From it, each year, some of the pictures are erased. There are buildings described here that will have disappeared within a decade. How many will survive another century ?

Much depends on the expatriate Marwari merchant community. They have the funds and the power to stem the destruction. They have the incentive too. These are their buildings !

Top:
Churu: The south wall of a *haveli* owned by the Joshi family at the northern edge of the town. A railway picture shows Bikaner station on one side and faraway Jodhpur on the other. (c1930).

Bottom:
Fatehpur: Its footings pulverised by salts crystallisi in the fabric, this *haveli* has duly collapsed to reveal its paintings. Several buildings succumb to this fate each yea

Top:
Sardarshahr (opposite (1)):
Above the street on a *haveli*
wall is this ship in a harbour
filled with sailing vessels.
The artist has probably
copied the writing along the
hull from his imported tin of
paint. Pity he held it the
wrong way up! (c1910).

Bottom:
Sujangarh: On the wall of a
house belonging to the Sethia
family the British appear to
lose their sangfroid when
confronted by a cobra.
(c1920).

Shekhawati - The Painted Region

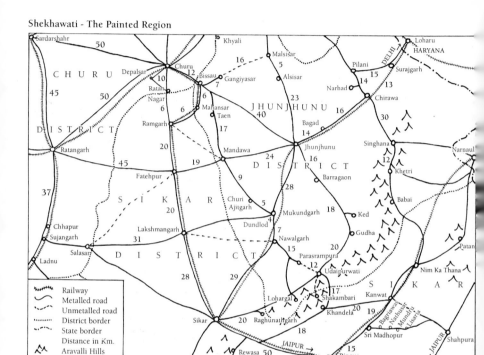

Railway
Metalled road
Unmetalled road
District border
State border
Distance in Km.
Aravalli Hills

The Painted Region

To the people of India, the name Rajasthan conjures visions of desert, Maharajas, colourful clothing against a buff landscape, fortresses, camels and heroism. They are no less familiar with the image of the Marwari business community which came out of that desert.

Of the states of modern India, Rajasthan is second only to Madhya Pradesh in area. It lies to the west, where the country is at its broadest. Gujarat, to the south, separates it from the Arabian Sea. Fertile Haryana and Punjab hold back its deserts from the foothills of the Himalayas. To the east lies Madhya Pradesh, the heart of India; to the west, Pakistan.

For centuries Rajasthan was divided into principalities, large and small, each vying with its neighbours for power. The most successful rulers, all Hindus, and all but one of the Rajput caste, extended their borders to enclose fair-sized kingdoms. Smaller states continued to exist, either owing allegiance to one or other of the Maharajas, the great kings, or maintaining a fierce independence. Conflict along and within these borders was commonplace. Only in the face of some common enemy was any semblance of unity forged. It was invariably short-lived!

Shekhawati is a convenient name to describe the three modern districts of Rajasthan rich in murals. As an administrative unit before Independence it covered the western part of Sikar district and all of Jhunjhunu. To the Shekhawat Rajput barons it extends eastwards across the Aravalli Hills. In either case, it was the north-west extent of the Maharaja of Jaipur's domain. Churu lay across the frontier in the principality of Bikaner, but the mural phenomenon recognized no such divisions. Of the 10 towns important enough to warrant street maps in this guide, nine fall in true Shekhawati. Churu alone does not.

The first written reference to Shekhawati seems to have been in the early 17th century. The name derives from Rao Shekha, a baron of the Kachhawaha clan of — Rajputs related to the rulers of Amber and Jaipur. During the 15th century, Shekha conquered, and briefly held, a considerable territory in this part of Rajasthan. That retained by his heirs, the Shekhawats, was known as Shekhawati. For many years it lay almost entirely to the east of the Aravallis, but in the early 18th century, the descendants of Shekha extended their holdings both north and west, beyond the hills. It was this new region that was to become the administrative *nizamat* of Shekhawati under the government of Jaipur State. It was also to contain perhaps 90 per cent of the painted buildings in the three districts of Churu, Jhunjhunu and Sikar.

Those three districts cover an area of about 30,500 sq.km. Comparatively fertile and well-watered on the eastern fringes, to the west the land becomes arid, a classic desert of rolling, drifting dunes interspersed with poor millet fields and sparse grazing for sheep and goats. The jagged line of the Aravallis is largely responsible for this contrast. Crossing the east of the region, their peaks rising to above 3,000 feet, they bar the rain-bearing clouds of the monsoon as they move north westwards.

Within living memory, these hills were densely covered with trees and shrubs. The jungle sheltered a variety of large mammals which the local barons conserved for hunting. The villagers were prevented from clearing the vegetation. After Independence, the rulers acceded to the new Republic of India. Feudal prohibitions were ignored and the villagers, in their search for firewood, made forays into this once-hallowed forest – at first timidly, then with zest. Today the hills stand bare and rocky. The wildlife has gone.

The Aravallis also formed a barrier between Shekhawati and Jaipur, the Maharaja's capital. During the 18th Century, several small forts were built along their crest, helping to reinforce the division. Three passes, at Singhana, Udaipurwati and near Sikar, enabled troops

Jhunjhunu: View over part of
the old town towards the
Badalgarh (11), a fort built at
the close of the 17th century.
On the left is the Bissau
Mahal (10) where Shyam
Singh murdered his cousin
and his son in 1808. In the
background rises the hill,
Kana Pahar.

and merchants to cut through.

The plains to the west of the hills, despite their aridity, support numerous villages. The people depend on a single annual crop of millet or pulses. The success of that crop relies on the monsoon. Three good rainfalls between mid-July and September are enough to yield a reasonable harvest. The surplus is stored in little mud granaries raised on legs and roofed with thatch. The mud architecture of Shekhawati is itself worthy of examination.

Livestock plays a large part in the life of the people. Many households possess their own cow, which supplies the family with milk. The farmers use camels for ploughing and pulling carts along the sandy tracks. It is not long since the camel was the primary form of transport throughout the region. Flocks of goats and sheep in the charge of village boys go out each morning to graze on the scanty desert vegetation. The goat is the main source of meat; sheep provide wool, a major commodity in the area.

The People

The population of Shekhawati is divided between two major religions, Muslim and Hindu; the latter are further subdivided according to the complex caste system. The Muslims form a minority throughout the area, varying between 10 and 30 per cent of the population, although in towns such as Fatehpur and Jhunjhunu their role is important.

Caste remains crucial to the lives of the people. In Shekhawati every marriage is arranged along caste lines, within the larger caste grouping and outside the individual's sub-caste. Divide the Hindus into four separate, endogamous castes and one has the skeleton on which the society is constructed:

BRAHMIN: The priestly and learned caste. Since this group traditionally accords prestige to learning and piety, Brahmins tend to take up the priesthood or aspire to academic success and such jobs as teaching. They were always privileged, acceptors not givers. Donations to the priestly caste brought merit to the giver; violence against one of their number was a heinous offence. Traditionally they are strictly vegetarian. As with all groups there is a great variation in material wealth. Some are very poor, struggling to till a bit of land or slaving as servants, some rich.

RAJPUT: Rajputs are by tradition the rulers and fighters. They chose courage and martial skill as their highest goal. In the history of Rajasthan their standards of bravery and honour have become legendary, embracing the womenfolk no less than the men. When the odds in battle became impossible they would set out to die fighting clad in saffron, leaving their women to burn themselves to death rather than fall into the hands of the enemy.

Rajputs are divided into a number of sub-castes and innumerable clans. The Kchhwaha sub-caste dominated in Jaipur State, the Maharaja being a Kachhawaha as were most of his barons, including the Shekhawats. The Rathors ruled over Jodhpur and Bikaner, the Thakur of Churu being amongst them.

The Rajputs may eat meat (not including beef or, in the case of the Shekhawats, pork) and have a penchant for intoxicants. The men take pride in their growth of facial hair. They range from erstwhile Maharajas to the smallest cultivators. Their sons are likely to develop a yen for a military career, but in the urban environment caste differences are softened and Rajputs, as members of other castes, may be found in a large variety of occupations.

VAISHYA: Most important are the Banias. Said to have originated from the Jat agriculturists who till so much of North India, the Banias are merchants, heirs to canny farmers who bought up and distributed their neighbours' grain. In Shekhawati one group, the Aggarwals, dominate. They are strictly vegetarian by tradition. The caste aspiration is, quite simply, to acquire money and gold. Their life is the least physically active of any group, much of it being spent seated cross-legged, buying, selling, lending and haggling – yet they were to be the greatest conquerors to rise out of this region. Also among the Vaishyas come the Jat farmers and various craftsmen, including the potters who so often painted.

SHUDRA: This embraces all the rest of a diverse Hindu world; those who serve the upper castes, such as the leatherworker, the scavenger and the sweeper. These folks were – and for many remain – untouchable, liable to pollute their seniors in the system. Each subdivision jealously holds its position in the structure, thus each helps to maintain it.

Beyond this classification come those entirely out of the Hindu fold, the untouchable Mlechha – Muslims, Christians and the tribal communities who dwell in the forests and the hills.

Muslims played an important part in the construction and painting of local buildings. But it was the Hindu community that dominated the mural era. They were the rulers. They were the rich merchants who were the greatest patrons. They became the majority of the painters. It was their religious themes that inspired very many of the pictures.

The Towns

Most of the larger settlements in Shekhawati were raised to town status during the 18th century. Many reflect the influence of Jaipur city, which was laid out on a strict grid plan in the late 1720s. Each is centered on a bazaar of small shops – most of them run by Banias – and a *sabji* mandi , vegetable market, where produce is sold in part by the cultivators themselves.

The sharpest social division in the town is between Hindu and Muslim. The Muslim part of town is characterised by mosques with their minarets, often new buildings that have come up with the flow of Gulf money. The call to prayer echoes through the streets, aided by loudspeakers. These are used by both faiths – merely to antagonize each other, one sometimes feels. The meat market is in the Muslim quarter.

The rest of the town is no less divided. The richest section is that dominated by the great mansions of the successful Banias. Brahmins tend to collect in their own part of town. Carpenters, masons, weavers each have their own *mohalla* , quarter. On the very margin live the lowest communities in the system, such as the leatherworkers and the scavengers.

The divisions of the town still hold in the older sectors. When the building boom of the 19th century brought more masons into the region, they settled in the appropriate part of town, where they often had relatives. Today, if a carpenter excels and becomes rich, he does not move into a smarter *mohalla* . He merely builds himself an impressive house in his own quarter. With many centuries of division, each caste developed its separate mythology, form of dress and even taste in food. Such are the divisions that it is not difficult, with some practice, to guess a man's caste from his facial structure.

Until recently the costume of both men and women helped to identify their religious and caste grouping. Today, the young men, if they can afford it, affect western-style clothes, whilst many women have abandoned the loose skirt, the *ghaghra,* in favour of the ubiquitous sari. Muslim women tend to wear loose pantaloons and a long loose shirt falling below the knee. Sometimes they cover this with the all-enveloping *burkha.*

Both religions cling to their own calendar, which is punctuated by fasts and holidays. The Hindus are particularly influenced by the day and month. Certain days are auspicious for travel in certain directions, others are not. For most castes, marriages are only performed during set seasons, and wives have to return to their parents at set times. On some days women cannot eat until evening when they have sighted the moon, nor may they handle food

Top:
Near a desert village north of Churu women make their way towards the well.

Bottom:
No Brahmin can consider himself as such until he has gone through a confirmation ceremony. Arvind and Ravindra Sharma of Churu perform the rituals prior to Arvind's marriage.

Top:
Bissau: Young men putting on
their make-up for the annual
Ramlila performance. Taking
place in the bazaar on the nine
evenings leading up to the
autumn festival of Dassehra,
this pageant is based on the
adventures of Rama.

Bottom:
Mandawa: Holi being
celebrated in the streets. Men,
many of them intoxicated with
liquor or *bhang*, beat drums
and dance or cover each other
with coloured powder. I was
no less colourful that day!

during their menstrual periods.

Festivals abound, some celebrated throughout India, some confined to Rajasthan or just to one temple in one village. Amongst the most widely-celebrated, three are specially important:

Holi: Falling in March at the spring equinox, this festival is a time for spring madness. A whole fortnight before there is a build-up of night-time dancing and drumming in the streets. Both are confined to the menfolk, the deficiency made up by a number of men who appear in the guise of girls. The drum, *daph*, resembles a large tambourine without its metal attachments. The dancers, many of them in fancy dress, move round in a circle and the drummers beat their *daphs* as they dance, also using them to accentuate their movements. This dancing is particularly good in Churu. On the final night, each quarter has its own fire. The following morning men and boys patrol the streets showering everyone with coloured powder. The women only play Holi within their households and those of their neighbours. In some towns, such as Mandawa, there is a bright procession on this last day. The new year in the Vikram Samvat calendar, according to which the year 2000 AD coincides with 2057 VS, starts soon after Holi.

Dassehra: This commemorates the day when Rama set out against Ravana, the wicked King of Lanka who had abducted Sita, his wife. For nine consecutive nights there are performances of the Hindu epic, the *Ramayana*. In Shekhawati the best of these is in the little town of Bissau, where the story is acted out in instalments by local young men in masks. There is no dialogue. If you know the tale you can follow it as well as the next man. On the final night an effigy of Ravana is burned and some Rajputs still sacrifice goats. At this time there are also two days of wrestling at Gangiyasar, near Bissau.

Diwali: This festival is largely in honour of the goddess of wealth, Lakshmi, and marks the start of a new financial year. Prior to Diwali there is a fever of spring-cleaning. In this process, white and coloured limewashes play a part, often being applied over faded or damaged murals. The last night is said to be the darkest of the year, but every house is decorated with candles or little oil lamps. The richer folk use strings of electric light bulbs, but the resulting overload on the system often leads to power failure! For Banias this festival is very important. They pray to the Goddess and dedicate their new account books.

Holi is the festival most commonly shown in the murals, but two others, peculiar to Rajasthan, also appear. Gangaur, shortly after Holi, is a time when girls pray for a good husband, whilst married women call blessings upon the head of the one with whom they are lumbered. There is a procession in which women carry effigies of the god, Iser, and his consort Gauri to their marriage, after which they are immersed in a well. Teej falls in August, during the monsoon. Women wear red and put up swings on trees, spending part of the day playing on them.

Each year these festivals lose a little of their significance. I have been long enough in the region to note their gradual decline. Holi, the most rowdy and human of all, becomes more controlled. The village fairs shrink, but vary partly with the success of the rains.

On all sides of each town stretches a dry and dusty landscape governed by extremes of temperature. In May and June the mercury sometimes passes 48 C. In the early hours of a January day it may sink below freezing point. Summer winds bring sandstorms, sometimes so dense as to turn day to night. With luck, mid-July will bring the monsoon, reducing the summer heat and nourishing the annual millet crop.

From this land, where the elements are severe, where famine is no stranger, where the desert rules, arose the men who called in the painters.

The History

Not far west of the centre of North India as it was before the Partition of 1947, Shekhawati was liable to feel the effects of any disturbance in that part of the subcontinent. To a certain degree it was protected from covetous hands by the very poverty and inhospitality of its landscape. Two groups of foreign invaders, the Mughals and the British, provided the environment which gave rise to painted Shekhawati. Neither directly held the region.

The Macrocosm — North India:

The 17th Century — Zenith of Mughal Power

In the early 16th century, Babur, a minor Muslim prince of Uzbekistan, deprived of his lands, set out with a small army of followers. A military genius with a sharp enquiring mind, his personality attracted loyalty. Having taken part of what is now Afghanistan, he followed the example of many before him by casting his eyes towards the great plains of India. By 1526 he had defeated Ibrahim Lodi, the ruler of Delhi. During the four years of life that remained to him, he consolidated his power over North India.

If Babur was the first of the Great Mughals, to his grandson, Akbar, must go the credit for creating the true Mughal Empire. Inheriting the throne at the age of 13, he ruled for half a century, during which time he extended his frontiers, brought stability within them and established a strong administration. His Islam was so tempered with free-thinking that some Muslims viewed him as a heretic. His tolerance and respect for other faiths endeared him to his Hindu subjects. On his death in 1605 he left a land transformed by his rule.

The throne passed to his son, who took the name Jahangir. He reigned until 1627. On his death, his son, Shah Jahan, the builder of the Taj Mahal, became Emperor. All three rulers were patrons of the arts and attracted intellectuals and craftsmen to their courts. Akbar himself was largely responsible for the import of the Persian painters from whose work would evolve the Mughal school of miniature painting which gave rise to the later Rajasthani styles.

Shah Jahan shifted his capital from Agra to Delhi, founding a new city and building the great Red Fort to house his court. As he grew older, rivalry developed between his heirs. He himself favoured his eldest son, the liberal Dara Shikoh, but it was the second, the orthodox Muslim, Aurangzeb, who imprisoned his father to seize power in 1658. He then defeated and killed his brothers.

Aurangzeb reigned for 48 years. He was a frugal man, a great administrator, an able general, but in his religion he was unyielding. There was one true faith – Islam. Hindus, though the vast majority of his subjects, were to feel the weight of his disapproval.

The 18th Century — Decline and Turmoil:

Aurangzeb lived until 1707, in power till the last. His son, Bahadur Shah, who succeeded him, survived only five years. Beyond him lay the path to ruin. In the next eight years, six men briefly came and bloodily went from the Delhi throne before Mohammed Shah finally held it. The dynasty never recovered its glory, gradually slipping into irrelevance as its constituent parts broke away. By the close of the century they could joke of the current ruler "From Delhi to Palam is the realm of Shah Alam". Palam, a village on the edge of the city, is now famous for its airport. Shah Alam, cruelly blinded, was one of the last "emperors"

The Mughal system of law and order, sustained to a degree by its own momentum, gradually crumbled. Viceroys and rulers, out of courtesy, continued to recognize the Emperor, but ignored his edicts. Gradually new forces rose, hoping to fill the vacuum, or at least to gather some booty from the wreck. Soon there were only two real contestants. The Marathas aspired, but the British succeeded.

Beside the famous Taj Mahal Hotel in Bombay stands an equestrian statue of Shivaji, the hero of the Maharashtrian people. Despite his low caste origins, he rose during the second half of the 17th century to confront Aurangzeb as his most formidable enemy. The Emperor was still fighting Shivaji's Maratha descendants when he died.

The Marathas became very powerful, seized Central India, even took Delhi and held a later Emperor. They even recovered from a terrible defeat at the hands of the Afghans and maintained their hold on Central India. In the lands beyond their direct jurisdiction they used a simple method to extract tribute. When their army arrived at the gates of a town the ruler and inhabitants would be offered a straight choice – submit to paying *chouth*, one quarter of their wealth, or face plunder and ruin. It didn't take long for them to become hated and feared.

If only the Marathas had remained united.... If the descendants of Shivaji had not fallen under the sway of their Brahmin ministers.... If they had offered security as they expanded rather than appearing in the guise of transient robbers.... But they failed in all those historic 'ifs'

The 19th Century – British Rule

The British arrived in India as traders, representing the East India Company, which had obtained its charter in 1599. With concessions from the Mughal court they set up trading posts. In the late 17th century they founded three new ports, destined to become great seaboard cities – Madras, Bombay and Calcutta.

It has been suggested that they owed their Indian Empire to their rivalry with the French. In competition in Southern India, each supported opposite sides in every local rivalry. The British tended to back the winners. In 1757, with the Battle of Plassey, they became the major power in Bengal. Once they obtained power over it, that region, once the richest in the Mughal Empire, was systematically plundered by unscrupulous administrators and merchants.

The late 18th and early 19th centuries saw the expansion and consolidation of British power. If, for the rulers they overcame, that expansion brought humiliation at the hands of alien infidels, it equally gave stability and the rule of law to the common folk. It is certain that the administration set up by the British and consolidated through the 19th century was unrivalled in the history of the subcontinent.

Taxes on the peasants were reduced. Marauders no longer came at will to loot their crops and burn their villages. But there were those that suffered. The British Industrial Revolution shaped the colonial economy. The textile mills of Manchester produced better fabric more cheaply. That brought ruin and starvation to the spinners and weavers whose products had once been so popular in the West. It also brought fabulous fortunes to the Shekhawati Banias.

Under the new Empire, business boomed. A new pattern of trade developed. Innovations in transport smoothed its circulation. The indigenous economy suffered. The British gained. The Golden Bird, as they say in modern India, was plucked. But in the process, an environment was created which, as a side-effect, produced the bulk of the painted walls in Shekhawati.

The 20th Century – The Road to Freedom:

Stability and prosperity during the 19th century gave rise to an urban middle class. The introduction of British forms of education gave that class access to liberal and democratic concepts. It took little effort to realize that these were not applied in India. Thus rose the Congress, in search of self- government, to evict the Raj.

The Microcosm — Jaipur, Bikaner and Shekhawati:

The 17th Century:

North India entered the 17th century under the great Akbar. Although forced to submit to his rule, the Rajput princes of Rajasthan were unlikely to acquiesce to any overlord for long, least of all to a foreign Muslim. In their brushes with successive Emperors they proved their courage. Equally, they displayed their inability to unite, even against such a formidable adversary.

Rajasthan was divided between five large, and several smaller, kingdoms. The five were Amber, Bikaner, Jaisalmer, Jodhpur (or Marwar) and Udaipur (or Mewar). The first two shared the region which was destined to become so rich in murals.

Amber was the most affluent and powerful of these states. It was also nearest to two Mughal capitals – Agra, then from the middle of the century, Delhi. Of all the Rajput rulers, successive rajas of Amber maintained the best relations with the Emperor and some rose to high rank in the court. Akbar married the sister of the father of Raja Man Singh and the Raja became one of his most trusted courtiers and generals. His memorial, built at Amber in 1620, contains murals which are the oldest dateable ancestors to those of Shekhawati.

The Shekhawati of the 17th century comprised estates lying mainly to the east of that spine of the Aravalli Hills which now cuts through Sikar District and forms an eastern border to Jhunjhunu. But the Rajputs had already made inroads through the Udaipurwati and Sikar Gaps. The Shekhawat *thakurs*, barons, were in alliance with, rather than subservient to the Amber throne.

Two towns were minor centres of power. Khandela had been granted by Akbar to the Shekhawat, Raisalji, along with the title 'Raja'. Udaipurwati, part of his estate, was inherited by his son, Bhojraj. From Bhojraj descended Sardul Singh, who was to acquire Jhunjhunu. From his brother, Tirmul, descended the rulers of Sikar.

At this period, almost the entire area which was to constitute the Shekhawati *nizamat* of Jaipur State, now the district of Jhunjhunu and the western part of Sikar, was in the hands of Muslim *nawabs*. These men had established themselves during the mid 15th century with the support of the Delhi sultans. The two most powerful were the *nawabs* of Fatehpur and of Jhunjhunu, both Kaimkhanis (descendants of one Kaim Khan), whose common ancestor, a Chauhan Rajput, had embraced Islam. Other Muslim barons held smaller estates at Narhad, Bagad, Sultana, Papurna and elsewhere.

To the west of these Muslim-held lands lay Bikaner State. Although large in area, it was agriculturally poor, much of the territory being true desert. A Raja, Ratan Singh, once told a British officer that he was known to his neighbours as "the king of burrs" – a reference to the dry scrub which covered so much of his land. The east of Bikaner State centred on the town of Churu, whose *thakur* was the seniormost baron in the kingdom. From time to time his distance from the court at Bikaner encouraged him to assert his independence.

The 18th Century – An Era of Strife:

At the beginning of the 18th century, the region of Sikar was in the hands of Daulat Singh Shekhawat, a descendant of Tirmulji. His son, Sheo Singh, inherited the estate in 1721 and it was he who built the town.

The tribe of "Bhojrajka" Shekhawats, descendants of Tirmul's brother, Bhojraj, held Udaipurwati and the lands to the west and north as far as Gudha and Parasrampura. Sardul

Singh, a member of this branch of the family, settled with his uncles in this last village. Later he moved to Jhunjhunu, where he succeeded in entering the Nawab's court. There he prospered. When the Nawab died in 1730 on his way to Delhi, Sardul Singh seized power in a bloodless coup. Thus the whole of modern Jhunjhunu District passed easily into the hands of the Shekhawats. The following year, Sardul Singh allied himself with Sheo Singh of Sikar. Together they evicted the Nawab of Fatehpur.

The Raja of Amber/Jaipur, Jai Singh II (1699–1744), had recently founded a new capital, Jaipur, from which the state was to take its name. A powerful ruler and a gifted man, he soon imposed his sovereignty over this expanded Shekhawati. Now Jaipur State bordered on Bikaner, and the Shekhawats, hitherto allies, became tributaries.

Jhunjhunu district is the richest in the painted region, thus the fate of Sardul Singh and his heirs is central. Tradition required Sardul Singh to divide his estate between his sons, five of whom survived him. The region became known as the Panchpana – the five estates. It did not stay in five divisions for long, since one of the brothers, Akhey Singh, died without issue. His share was redistributed amongst his brothers. In order of age, the five sons were: Zorawar Singh, who inherited Taen, Gangiyasar and Malsisar; Kishan Singh, who inherited the Khetri region and Alsisar; Akhey Singh, who died without an heir and whose land was redistributed; Nawal Singh, who founded Nawalgarh and Mandawa; Keshri Singh, who founded Bissau and Dundlod. The *thakurs* of every village in the region covered by the Panchpana are all descended from one or other of these men.

Several major invasions affected Shekhawati during the latter half of the 18th century. In 1767, the Jat Maharaja of Bharatpur, as an act of bravado, crossed the land east of the line of hills, only to suffer defeat at the hands of the Jaipur army in the Battle of Maonda. His infantry, led by two European mercenaries, Walter Reinhard (better known as 'Samru') and Rene Madec, succeeded in slaughtering the flower of Jaipur's nobility before retreating. Four contemporary murals depict this battle. In 1775 the Rao of Rewari invaded, but was soon repulsed. The Marathas intruded several times, most notably in 1792, when they plundered Udaipurwati and Singhana. In 1799 they accompanied George Thomas, an Irishman who cut out a short-lived kingdom for himself in neighbouring Haryana, on a raid which ended in the siege of Fatehpur.

The strife of the latter half of the century gave employment to large numbers of mercenary troops. Often they moved en masse towards some rising prince who seemed able to pay and fated to be successful. The Bharatpur army at Maonda contained a considerable force of Jat Sikhs from Punjab, as well as the small but important European element. As each prince failed so mercenaries were laid off, giving rise to bodies of armed men such as the Pindaris, Pathan freebooters, who lived by banditry. George Thomas, the "Irish raja", is said to have started his free-lance career in a Pindari band.

The efficacy of European infantry had long been recognized by Indian rulers. During the 1530s, the Sultan of Gujarat was prepared to offer the Portuguese a foothold in his domain in return for 500 infantry. In the 18th century, as the Empire dissolved into its constituent parts, the demand was high. There was a ready supply. Both the British and the French brought increasing numbers of troops to India. Their pay was low, their conditions poor and desertions frequent. The incentives offered by some of the princes were tempting. Reinhard had come to India with the French, deserted to the British and left them in turn for a series of nawabs and rajas. Even after French power collapsed in India, their officers played an important role, particularly in the Maratha & Sikh armies, until well into the 19th century.

Foreign freebooters duly reached Rajasthan and are recorded in the murals. Sometimes, one or two men are shown wearing hats and bearing muskets. The hat alone, with its little tuft on top, is enough to identify the foreigners amongst the turbanned natives. A Gangaur procession painted by a Jaipur man in Sikar (1) portrays several such figures. Each is labelled faranghi", an approximation to "European".

European mercenaries certainly came to the heart of the painted region in 1799, if not well before. George Thomas had several amongst his troops when he attacked Fatehpur, but so, it seems, did the force sent from Jaipur to confront him. This would have taken the quickest route to Fatehpur, passing through the hills at Udaipurwati. There, on a chhatri pillar, is a little piece of graffiti. It states simply: "William Harvey, Jeypore Service. 1799".

Only one of the Shekhawat barons, Shyam Singh of Bissau (1787–1833), managed to employ mercenaries. He had two such men, both said to have been French. One he sent northwards at the head of a small force to support Ranjit Singh, the Lion of Punjab. The other remains in Bissau (16), buried in an unmarked grave in a small Muslim cemetery.

The 19th Century: Disorder and Pacification:

By the early 19th century life was becoming increasingly difficult for the princes of Rajasthan. If the lack of central authority had meant that Delhi could no longer collect tribute, the Marathas had not been slow in filling the gap. They would pass through the states in force, taking what they could. Apart from attempts to fend them off, there were disputes between states which often led to bloodshed and further drained resources. Lack of funds weakened the authority of the rajas. That, in turn, encouraged the individual barons to ignore their decrees.

In 1808, Mountstuart Elphinstone, later to achieve fame as one of India's greatest administrators, led an embassy through Shekhawati and Churu on his way to Afghanistan. When he reached Bikaner, the raja, Surat Singh, tried to present him with the keys to the city. Hard pressed by enemies on two fronts, he saw accession to the British as the best solution to his problems. Elphinstone refused. The Raja managed to struggle on.

The Thakur of Churu, Sheo Singh, the most senior baron in Bikaner State, was acting with increasing independence. If he remained undisciplined, that sector of the kingdom might be lost. In 1813, Surat Singh marched eastwards. After a prolonged siege he took Churu. Sheo Singh swallowed a diamond, so they say, and died.

The Thakur's son tried to break away again in 1818. In that year, Bikaner and Jaipur both ratified treaties with the government in Calcutta, accepting British paramountcy. In turn, the British agreed to help the individual princes maintain the status quo within and beyond their frontiers. British troops joined those of the raja in suppressing the revolt in Churu. The Thakur was evicted and the town fell under the direct control of Bikaner.

Across the border in Jaipur there were similar problems. The Raja's treasury was low and his barons rebellious. The situation was not improved by poor administration under a regency which governed from 1818 for the child raja, Jai Singh III. He failed to achieve his majority because, when he began to show a degree of independence, his minister, Jhoonta Ram, promptly dosed him with poison.

In Shekhawati, the situation was predictable. The rajas of Sikar and Khetri had managed to keep their estates relatively intact, partly by dint of ignoring the custom of division of property and partly through a dearth of sons. Elsewhere, the land had been partitioned into many small holdings. Exactly a century after Sardul Singh evicted the Kaimkhani *nawabs* from Jhunjhunu, it was estimated that there were no fewer than 169 surviving male heirs to his

Parasrampura (2): A tiger hunt painted in natural pigments decorates part of the dome of Sardul Singh's *chhatri*. Probably a scene from his life – perhaps he is the man with the spear on the dark horse. The Shekhawat flag bearing a likeness of Hanuman flies on the elephant. As the infantry approach one man loads his musket. (1750).

Below:
The Aravalli Hills were a formidable barrier between the Maharaja's capital, Jaipur, and the barons of Shekhawati. The little town of Raghunathgarh lies at the foot of the hills, whilst above it stands a small fort.

Below, right:
Bissau (6): Europeans pass round a hookah in a garden full of roses and pomegranates. They decorate the vaulted ceiling of one of the rooms in the Govindram Girdarilal Sigtia Haveli. (c1890).

sons! Of these, 102 owed their descent to Zorawar Singh, the eldest.

In order to keep themselves in the style that they felt they deserved, these Shekhawats bled their peasantry dry and overtaxed the merchants who controlled the caravan trade. Still short of funds, many then turned to banditry, raiding into neighouring estates or across the border into Bikaner, even attacking caravans as they passed through the desert. The worst offenders were three groups of Shekhawats, the descendants firstly of Lad Khan, brother of Bhojraj, who were known as Ladkhanis; secondly heirs of Sardul Singh's brother, Salhedhi Singh, the Salhedhis; and thirdly the descendants of Zorawar Singh who, since they were so numerous, had suffered worst from the division of property.

During the first two decades of the century, the Thakur of Bissau acted as patron to the robbers operating from his part of Shekhawati. If he did not lead the raids, he was very much a party to them. It was the handiwork of a band of robbers from Bissau which first brought the problem to the attention of the British. It seemed that they had raided across the border into British-held territory, robbing and injuring men entitled to British protection. A force was prepared to make a counter attack on Bissau and punish Shyam Singh. The foray was called off when it was discovered that the attack had taken place in Jaipur territory. The goods were returned.

That was in 1812. Nearly 20 years were to pass before the British acted. During that time, complaints came thick and fast, both from neighbouring Bikaner and from merchants within and without Shekhawati. The British passed on such complaints to the court of Jaipur, but it was soon apparent that there was neither the strength nor the will to discipline the barons. The minister, Jhoontha Ram, had one close friend and ally in all his schemes. He was none other than Shyam Singh of Bissau!

With trade disrupted and unrest all along the Bikaner-Jaipur frontier, the British sent a Lt. Col. Abraham Lockett and a young Lt. Boileau with a force of about 500 to investigate the state of affairs.

Through the heat of April and May 1831 they travelled through Shekhawati and Churu. Both kept accounts of their journey. The report that Lockett submitted to Calcutta resulted in the raising of a small body of local cavalry, the "Shekhawuttee Brigade", under the command of an Anglo-Indian officer, Major Forster. This was funded by the rulers of Jaipur and Bikaner as well as by the local barons.

The Shekhawati Brigade was stationed at Jhunjhunu, where Forster built a new sector to the town, which still bears the name Forsterganj. From 1835 to 1843, this force was actively employed, responding to all complaints of robbery. The worst offenders amongst the barons were captured and their forts destroyed.

British intervention largely curbed the disorder on the frontier. But it did not restore prosperity to the caravan trade, which had been damaged as much by the new pattern of trade as by the bandits. Shekhawati was returned to the control of the Maharaja of Jaipur and an era of peace and stability followed, uninterrupted by the Mutiny of 1857, when some of the barons even sent troops to support the British. That peace has lasted to the present day, and it enabled the wealthy Banias to construct their great painted buildings.

The Patrons

The three modern districts of Churu, Jhunjhunu and Sikar are not agriculturally rich. Apart from copper, mined in the hills near Khetri, there are no major mineral resources to compensate for the poverty of the land. The fields may be better watered, thus richer, to the east of the line of hills, but the overall impression remains one of semi-desert. In any case, the concentration of murals is to the west of the hills, the more desiccated area.

Who, then, had sufficient capital to construct the extravagant buildings that characterize the local towns, thereby becoming the patrons of the painters? From where did the wealth derive in a land so unpromising?

The Rajputs

Shekhawati was a world of feudal barons frequently in conflict with their neighbours. In spite of the barren soil, most of the larger villages and towns are dominated by a fort or a fortified house. At first, the rulers monopolized the major building projects and it was they who summoned the painters. If merchants had sufficient money to compete they did well to conceal the fact.

During the 17th century, some of the Muslim nawabs employed men to decorate the interiors of their buildings. This work was not exacting, since Islam restricted the murals to floral and abstract designs. The few figurative paintings that survive from that period were financed by Hindu Banias or Rajputs.

When the Rajputs overthrew the Kaimkhani nawabs in the 1730s, they found themselves wealthy. Each of the four surviving sons of Sardul Singh promoted at least one of the villages they inherited to town status, building a fort, a temple and a town wall to protect their holdings. Each had a fort or palace in Jhunjhunu, their shared capital, and to each is raised a memorial *chhatri* on the eastern edge of the town. Most of these buildings still stand. Some are painted.

As long as they could afford it, their descendants tried to follow this example. Almost all the towns of Shekhawati were founded by one or other of these men during the 18th century. Several had memorials raised to them in Jhunjhunu along with the other family *chhatris*, but only the Bissau baron, Shyam Singh, added to the forts there.

Although the Rajputs financed only a small proportion of the local murals, they can justly claim responsibility for some of the finest work. Their era of patronage continued into the 19th century, but then they were overshadowed.

What were they like, these Rajput barons? Elphinstone, in his account of the journey to Afghanistan, describes meeting the Raja of Khetri, Abhey Singh, senior-most descendant of the four brothers:

"On 22nd October (1808) we reached Singauna, a handsome town, built of stone, on the skirt of a hill of purplish rock, about six hundred feet high. I was here met by Raja Ubhee Singh, the principal chief of the Shekhawut tribe. He was a little man with large eyes inflamed by the use of opium. He wore his beard turned up on each side towards his ears, which gave him a wild and fierce appearance. His dress was plain, and his speech and manners, like those of all his countrymen, rude and unpolished. He was, however, very civil, and made many professions of respect and attachment to the British. I saw him several times, and he was always drunk either with opium or with brandy. This was the case of all the Shekhawuttee Sirdars, who are seldom in a condition to appear until the effect of their last debauch is removed by a new dose; consequently it is only in the interval between sobriety and absolute stupefaction that they are fit for business."

The Shekhawat Rajputs were famous for their skill as horsemen. They formed the backbone of the Jaipur cavalry. When the British raised the Shekhawati Brigade, they drew on the tribes with the worst record for banditry for their recruits. Saledhis made up a third of the force, other Shekhawats a further third, Ladkhanis a sixth. The remainder was drawn from the Bidawat clan of Rathor Rajputs, from across the border in Bikaner. They, too, had developed a taste for brigandry.

When they founded their towns, the wiser barons encouraged merchants to settle within them. They kept their tariffs low to attract the lucrative caravan-borne transit trade across their borders. Their demands on their tenants were not such as to discourage cultivation or reduce the peasants to penury. Such *thakurs* were, unfortunately, in a minority.

The unwise taxed both merchants and farmers to the last degree. If this did not satisfy their needs, they formed robber associations. As the estates diminished in size with each passing generation, there was more incentive to follow the second course. The early years of the 19th century saw the administration of the whole region at its lowest ebb.

The decade of the 1830s produced conditions which led to the success of the second group of patrons, the merchants, who were to set Shekhawati apart from the rest of India for its mural wealth. By the time the Shekhawati Brigade was disbanded, the days of the robber raids were virtually over. Merchants slept more easily in their beds, but the overland trade never really recovered.

The Marwari Merchants

Nothing in the history of India compares with the successful migration of the Shekhawati merchants during the 19th century. It was a bloodless conquest, the echoes of which reverberate through the country to this day, for it resulted in perhaps the greatest concentration of wealth in the subcontinent. Those merchants were to finance the vast bulk of the painted buildings. They were to prove patrons par excellence.

From the beginning the community was mobile. The very names of some of their four sub-castes indicate an origin beyond the borders of Shekhawati. In each case, their representatives in the region formed only a small part of the whole.

From the north, from Haryana, came the Aggarwals and Saraogis. The former are by far the most numerous and important of local Banias. They take their name from Agre Sen, King of Agroha, the homeland they deserted. He is still revered by the community and a day is set aside in his memory. By religion, the Aggarwals are orthodox Vaishnavite Hindus, worshippers of Vishnu in his various incarnations. Here they differ from the Saraogis, who are followers of Jainism. In other respects, so close do the two groups consider themselves, that intermarriage is not uncommon.

The Aggarwals and Saraogis claim to have fled southward in the face of Muslim invasions. It is probable that many were also attracted into Rajasthan by the prospects it offered. Many remained to flourish in Haryana. Suresh, from whose village I had started my long cycle trip, was an Aggarwal. So were many other of the shopkeepers in that bazaar.

From the south-west, in the vicinity of Jodhpur, came two other sub-castes, the Oswals and the Maheshwaris. In Shekhawati, the former group are more plentiful. They, too, are Jains, deriving their name from an ancient holy town of their faith, Osian, some 65 km north of Jodhpur city, a focus of trade in earlier times. As it faded, no doubt the Oswals went in search of new pastures. They claim to be descended from Rajputs who converted to Jainism.

The Maheshwaris are said to come from the same general area and also claim Rajput descent. Their name is drawn from Mahesh, one of the titles of Shiva, to whom they are dedicated. In Shekhawati, though their numbers are few, they can boast one of the greatest of India's business families, the Birlas. They form a more important part of the Bania community in the west of Rajasthan, in Bikaner city and in Jaisalmer.

The Caravan Trade

For centuries, the desert of Shekhawati proved a formidable barrier to man and his endeavours. Overland travellers had to follow long diversions to skirt its arid wastes. A breakthrough came with the development of technology which led to the sinking of deep wells. This seems to have been around the close of the first millenium of the Christian era. Soon a chain of reliable water sources carried routes directly across the desert.

Caravans began to transport merchandise along these new routes, between the rich lands around the Indus in the west and those of Central India in the east; between Punjab and the Ganges Basin in the north and prosperous Gujarat with its ports to the south. No doubt merchants moved in to exploit a rapid boom in trade through the region. The local principalities must have felt the benefit of this transformation.

Until well into the present century, all merchandise through Rajasthan was carried by camel caravans and trains of bullocks. Where the tracks were sufficiently solid, bullock carts could be used. The camel cart is a post-Independence development. Camels were the prime element in transport and trade. When and how they arrived in India is uncertain, but there is some indication that they were an import. One episode in the story of the god-hero, Pabuji, particularly popular in the region, narrates how he first brought the camel to Rajasthan. This is depicted in some of the murals.

The cherished vision of desert caravans conjures beasts burdened with the Wonders of the Orient. The majority of the goods they carried was far less romantic. Rice, wheat, sugar, salt, opium, raw cotton and wool and the cloths derived from them were staple items. There were more interesting commodities, too, but they formed a small proportion of the total burden. A letter survives from a London business office to Mirzamal Poddar of Churu, one of the great merchants of his time. Dated 25th January 1833, it lists among the goods he handled cotton, silk, hemp, Kashmir shawls (a major item), coffee, sugar, elephants' teeth, tortoise shell, tin, spices, cinnamon, pepper, cassia-lignea, nutmeg, ginger, camphor, sena, cardamom, asafoetida, gums arabic and olibanum. Most of these would have passed through his Rajasthani network.

Churu was a very important trading town until the last decade of the 18th century. At the turn of that century, the concentration of traffic through neighbouring Shekhawati was due to two factors. The first was increasing disorder as a result of the decline of central authority. The second, the unrealistic tariffs levied by the rulers of Bikaner and Jaipur to raise more revenue.

Disorder and decline brings profit

The great port of the Mughal Empire was Surat, in Gujarat, lying to the north of modern Bombay. A constant stream of caravans crossed the country between Surat and the major Mughal centres of Agra, Ajmer and above all Delhi. To the port came Portuguese, Dutch, British and French traders eager to gain concessions from the Great Mughal. The road from the Mughal capital to Surat was one of the great highways of the Empire throughout the 17th century and into the early 18th. After that, the steady decline of imperial power brought a marked change. The Marathas encroached northwards, taking control of much of central India. They besieged Surat and, passing on, regularly threatened the flow of trade between the port and Delhi.

In response to the eclipse of Surat, small ports lying west along the coast increased their business. Some even seem to owe their foundation to this shift in trade. Just across the Gulf of Cambay from Surat, the ruler of Shihore founded Bhavnagar near the site of an older port. His motive was partly to have a seaboard capital allowing him an escape route from the dreaded Marathas, but the town did carry some of the merchandise diverted from Surat. Further along the coast, Porbandar, Nawanagar (now Jamnagar) and Portuguese-ruled Diu all profited from the changed circumstances. Further west, in the maritime principality of Kutch, Mandvi flourished and the ruler thought fit to found a new port, Lakhpat, which an earthquake in the early 19th century was to leave high and dry.

The advantage of these smaller harbours was that they were linked by more secure routes across Rajasthan, to the Ganges Basin, Delhi and Punjab. The Marathas and marauding gangs of Pindaris, the Pathan freebooters, rarely raided so far west.

By the late 18th century, two major entrepots were benefiting from this overland trade. In the south was Pali, in Jodhpur State, and in the north Bhiwani, in Haryana. The routes between these two towns crossed the region of Churu and Shekhawati. There is mention in early 19th century accounts of Shekhawati merchants moving into the two centres to gain added control of trade. Francklin, in his biography of George Thomas, written in 1803, describes Pali thus: "The town of Pawly is the greatest mart in this part of Rajpootana. Merchants exchange here commodities of Europe, Persia and Deccan for those of Kashmir, Punjab and Hindoostan. This trade is carried on camels and bullocks."

Seventy years later, a Captain Burton reporting to the Calcutta government, mentions the routes across Bikaner State: "The principal commercial lines followed are: from Delhi, via Bhiwani in Hissar (the greatest eastern mart for Rajputana) to Rajgarh in Bikaner, whence two lines proceed, one to Bikaner via Reni (Taranagar), the other via Churu, Ratangarh and Sujangarh to Phalodi, Nagor, Jodhpur and Pali in Marwar (Jodhpur State)."

Referring to the second of these routes as the most important, he goes on to mention the merchandise: "By it are conveyed from British territory sugar in various shapes, English piece goods, Benares silks, brocades, cloths, Delhi turbans, gold and silver lace, groceries, grain (particularly rice from Delhi), glassware, metals, precious and other, gold and silver thread, shoes, preserves, pickles and sherbets."

If a westward shift of the trade route between Delhi and the Coast was to their advantage, it hardly accounts for the concentration of merchants, and eventually murals, in Shekhawati. Other factors were involved. Foremost amongst these was the policy of Rajasthan's ruling princes.

By the late 18th and early 19th century, shortage of funds compelled the rulers to force as much revenue as possible out of the trade across their frontiers. They increased duties until the rates were exorbitant, seemingly unaware that this might defeat their own ends. Francklin's biography of George Thomas refers to this, describing how, by 1803, the "rapacity of the ruling prince" of Bikaner had destroyed commerce across his borders by heavy duties and "vexatious imposts". He claimed that this was to the advantage of Jaipur, but it was not that treasury that stood to gain, since its demands were no less.

Together, Jaipur and Bikaner spanned northern Rajasthan, but for a channel between them, a narrow passage where neither prince controlled tariffs. In Shekhawati, each individual baron set his own rates, and they were low. Here was the bottleneck that drew the merchants. The trade itself was not instrumental in funding the construction of many painted buildings. This was no time for ostentatious display. It was not wise to draw the baron's attention to one's affluence.

It is hard to be sure how long this concentration of trade persisted through Shekhawati. It is not difficult to pinpoint its end. In May 1822, a British official posted at Jaipur wrote to the Resident at Delhi telling him that because of the high duties there, traders prefered a long diversion through Shekhawati. He specifically names Lakshmangarh as a beneficiary. Three years later the Resident at Jaipur was writing to his counterpart in Delhi, saying that he had persuaded the court to cut their duties by 75 per cent under the assurance that they would actually gain from the move. He, too, points out that trade from the Ganges ports was avoiding Jaipur and heading through Bhiwani and Shekhawati on its way to Ajmer and Pali. The contacts the Shekhawati merchants made with the Ganges ports would prove important later.

With the reduction in tariffs, Shekhawati must have suffered an abrupt slump in trade. It can be no coincidence that the great migration starts from precisely the same time, resulting in the fortunes that gave rise to a painted Shekhawati!

From the 1820s onwards, caravan trade across the region was to represent an ever-decreasing proportion of the local Banias' source of wealth. Reduced to a more moderate flow after the inflated traffic of those earlier years, it continued throughout the 19th century. Opinions as to whether it was better to pass through Churu or Shekhawati varied along with fluctuations in the rates of duty well into the century. At times the merchants would prefer to cross Churu, where they were only taxed once on entering Bikaner State. At others, they chose Shekhawati, despite being faced with taxes at the border of each little estate, because the total bill would be lower.

There is a record of some of the duties. In 1843, the British persuaded the Bikaner Government also to reduce its rates so that each camel-load was charged 8 annas (half a rupee) instead of eight rupees. A cartload was to be charged one rupee whilst loads carried by bullock, pony or mule would be liable to pay 2 per cent of their value.

The wealthy Banias were already powerful. They would tolerate only a certain amount of extortion by their Rajput rulers. A classic example of their firmness led to the foundation of Ramgarh and the decline of Churu. The Aggarwal family known as Poddar were the major merchants in Churu at the close of the 18th century, dealing largely in woollen products. The Thakur of Churu, Sheo Singh, seeing a chance to solve his financial difficulties, sharply raised his duties on wool. The Poddars protested, but to no avail. In 1791, with the co-operation of the Raja of Sikar, they shifted across the border to Jaipur State, into his territory. There they founded the town of Ramgarh, known even today as 'Sethon ka Ramgarh' (The Ramgarh of the Wealthy Merchants) to differentiate it from the many other Ramgarhs in the country.

In 1835, Boileau visited the town, and describes it thus: "... Ramgurh, a frontier town of a very flourishing appearance, neatly fortified and filled with the mansions of wealthy bankers, whose fleeces have as yet suffered little from the generally unsparing shears of the Shekhawats. The Sikar authorities seemed to have found that levying heavy fines upon the merchants of Ramgurh, would cause them speedily to vacate that place, and thus kill the goose which laid the only golden eggs in their country."

So the raja seems to have kept his promise of support to the Poddars. Boileau went on to visit Churu and describes it as: ".... once flourishing city, but trade long lost, fortifications broken down, bazaars nearly deserted. The merchants have made themselves scarce in

Ramgurh and elsewhere."

Ramgarh was not the only example of a town founded by merchants as the result of a dispute with the local baron. The Devra family of Bissau fell out with the *thakur*, Hammir Singh. They tried to outdo Ramgarh by building their town, Ratannagar, right on the border between Jaipur and Bikaner States. But this was in 1860, when the era for such moves was past. The place never really took off, and now it has something of the appearance of a ghost town.

When the British sent Colonel Lockett to study the conditions in Shekhawati, their complaint was that the brigandry of a section of the Rajputs had dislocated trade. That was not the whole story. The year was 1831, not a decade since the lowering of Jaipur tariffs had reduced the attractiveness of the Shekhawati route. There was yet another element. The East India Company was increasing protectionist measures in favour of its own monopolies. Col. James Tod, in his classic history of Rajasthan, written in the 1820s, was highly critical of this policy and blamed the duties imposed on salt and opium in particular for damaging the desert trade. Lockett found no shortage of merchants ready to complain of the depredations of the Rajputs, but it is hardly surprising that even when the looting was curbed the trade did not fully recover.

The Migration

On the positive side, however, the rise of British power brought an unprecedented era of tranquillity and order. The Calcutta government had shown itself willing and able to control the more drastic actions of the princely rulers. The Company actively encouraged *seths*, wealthy merchants, to extend their business into those areas which fell directly under its control. It offered them guarantees that any property in the home state would be protected during their absence. The merchants, faced with a slump at home, took up the opportunity.

A new pattern of trade had developed. The British ports of Calcutta and Bombay, catering for large European vessels, had eclipsed the smaller ones. Calcutta, the capital of British India until 1911, handled not only the bulk of overseas trade, but also a busy flow of traffic up and down the Ganges. Raw materials from the vast Ganges Basin and beyond were borne downstream. The boats returned upriver with the products of Britain's Industrial Revolution, especially cheap cloth. The market was the whole of the North Indian plain.

The Shekhawati Banias soon established branches at the river ports, especially Farrukhabad and Mirzapur. The first steamship had arrived in India in 1819. Very soon these vessels were the most important carriers of merchandise on the river. Mirzapur, downstream from the confluence of the Jamuna and the Ganges, became the highest point for steam navigation, and it went through a boom in which cotton and indigo trading played a major role.

The merchants did very well out of these developments, but it was obvious that the capital offered greater opportunities. From 1820 onwards, there was a steady migration of these men into Calcutta. There they made their greatest conquest.

In competition with the local Bengali merchants, the new arrivals had the advantage of a wide network of offices spread throughout the Ganges Basin and its hinterland. Despite the 1,500 kilometres which separated them from their homeland, they were to become the main brokers for British traders. As they rose in the business community of the city, the Rajasthani merchants acquired a new name. The natives called them Marwaris, from the name given to their language and to inhabitants of the central Rajasthani state of Jodhpur or Marwar.

By the close of the 19th century, the Marwaris reigned supreme in Calcutta. In Bombay, and later in Karachi, they faced stiff opposition from the local mercantile class, Gujaratis and Parsis in the former, Sindhis in the latter, each group famous for its business acumen. But they managed to leave their mark on both cities and even did well as far south as Madras. Beyond Calcutta, some of the new arrivals began to move up the Brahmaputra into Assam. There they played an important part among the colonizers from the plains of North India. They dealt in cotton, jute, tea, rice and opium for export. In return they distributed cargoes of manufactured goods, particularly "Turkey Red" dyed cotton cloth from Manchester and the Vale of Leven.

It was characteristic of the community that they aided their fellows. Many they employed as clerks and accountants, no doubt feeling more secure with men of common origin and language, men over whom they had a considerable hold. An established merchant would set up a *basa*, a hostel for new arrivals. He could draw on this reservoir to increase his staff.

Initially, the Shekhawati Bania was a pioneer in a strange land, setting up a lonely establishment far from the life he knew. He would have been married long before leaving home, probably as a small child. His parents' choice of bride took account of caste, economic and astrological factors, rather more than sensual ones. His wife and children would remain at home in his father's household. The journey between Rajasthan and Calcutta was long and arduous. They would not see each other for many months, even years.

In the mid 1850s, the railway reached India. The network spread rapidly across the subcontinent, revolutionizing travel, shrinking the huge country. Soon the paddle-steamers that plied the Ganges were made redundant. Although it did not reach Shekhawati until the beginning of the present century, each extension of the line reduced the difficulty of travel for the homeward bound Marwari. The emigrant tried to return for one of the major festivals, preferably Diwali, sacred to Lakshmi, the Goddess of Wealth, the beginning of the new financial year.

In the early 20th century, some of the Marwaris began to invest capital in manufacturing industry. Gradually, India was constructing an industrial base in the face of colonial trade, which created a tough climate for that fragile plant. Near the major cities, there appeared textile factories, jute mills, saw mills, rice mills. They were often the product of Marwari finance. Profits soared. As the century advanced, their commitment now complete, the men began to shift their whole families out of Rajasthan to join them in their adopted city.

The Marwari seth of the turn of the century was generally an orthodox Hindu or Jain. Strictly vegetarian and simply dressed, in his adopted home he lived an austere life. In contrast, he would incur vast expenditure in the desert homeland for family rituals, marriages and deaths. In 1879, at the age of eight, Puranmal Singhania of Fatehpur married the daughter of Jainarayana Poddar of Ramgarh. There were 2,000 people in his marriage procession to Ramgarh, five elephants and a total of 800 horses, bullock-drawn vehicles and camels. The cost was Rs.125,000. Such extravagance was not unusual. The homeland remained the repository of the Bania's status. The many magnificent buildings in Shekhawati are, and were intended to be, a physical reminder of the huge fortunes that were made far away.

By the 1920s, the trade boom was coming to an end. The movement eastwards from the three districts continued, but the great Marwari families whose names as industrialists were to become familiar across and beyond the subcontinent were already established. The greatest among them all is the Birla clan of Pilani. Their ascent began when Shiv Narayan Birla set out by camel for Ahmedabad in 1857, a journey of 20 days, on his way to Bombay. There he laid the foundations of his family's vast fortune. Today it is one of the most important industrial groups in the country.

There are others whose names are widely familiar for their wealth or for the products of their industries. Goenka, Dalmia, Bajaj, Kedia, Khaitan, Poddar, Ruia, Jhunjhunuwala, Singhania – all owe their origin to that little tract of land lying to the west of the Aravalli Hills. There are many more such families.

Many of the clan names date from the 19th century, chosen to differentiate one merchant from another of a similar subcaste. Some originate from the name of a village or town. The Poddars who moved from Ganeri village into Lakshmangarh and Fatehpur became Ganeriwala. The Choudharys from Ked became Kedia. The Singhanias came from Singhana and it is hardly necessary to explain the origins of Jhunjhunuwalas or Fatehpurias.

Others derived their names from a famous ancestor, in the same manner as the Rajput descendants of Bhojraj became Bhojrajka. The Mandawa family known as Dhandhania (they came from the village of Dhandhan), has a branch called Bhagchandka, heirs of one Bhagchand.

Although very successful, the Marwaris did not achieve their position as the greatest group of Indian industrialists until after Independence. As the British sold up their factories and companies, the Rajasthani Banias were in the forefront of the buyers. They made their new acquisitions flourish. It has been claimed that the community now controls over 50 per cent of India's industrial wealth – no mean proportion. Their hold on the nation's press is correspondingly powerful.

There were many Bania families who never moved out of Shekhawati. They remain there still as little shopkeepers in some dusty bazaar. They haggle with their customers, run speculation 'books' on the chance of rain or the result of an election, lend money to farmers before the sowing season, taking their family jewellery as security. They are the poor relatives.

The migrants, in accepting their fate, have embarked on a process which will end inevitably in their total estrangement from the homeland. The older generation still puts pressure on children and grandchildren to return "home" for such ceremonies as the first haircut of a son. They attend festivals, above all the annual fair at the Rani Sati Temple in Jhunjhunu. They visit the holy places that relate to their family mythology – Khatu, Salasar, Jeen Mata, Lohargal. These patriarchs may come back also to inaugurate or visit some family gift to the town – a college, school, clinic or hospital. In spite of their long absence, their power in the town is unimpaired. Their wealth assures them of that.

But, for the new generation that is growing up, urban men accustomed to the luxuries of city life, there is no nostalgia. The old town is merely a poor, dirty, godforsaken place. The romantic attitude to the rural idyll which characterizes the people of the conurbations of the West is, as yet, alien to the urban Third World. They have too recently escaped from its hardships. In India, the facilities in small towns are poor, travel and communications unreliable, food is limited in quality and variety and most luxuries are quite unavailable. From time to time, the elements still rage.

If the Marwari of a century ago was an orthodox, simple-living vegetarian hemmed in by taboos, his descendant in the 1990s is more often than not westernised in his education and aspirations. Like many of his fellows, he may smoke, drink and eat meat – though society requires that he conceal these frailties from his elders. So far he is not in search of roots, for he has yet to lose them. Some young Marwaris in Calcutta or Delhi have never been to the homeland. Some are uncertain as to their town of origin. The family still holds property there, but it is of no value. Its share in a crumbling painted haveli has, with each generation, become smaller. The joint-owners could never agree what should be done with it. The elderly may return there to pass their last days.

These then, were the second, far more important, group of patrons. Throughout their emigration and their rise to affluence, they considered themselves as sons of Shekhawati, men of Bikaner or Jaipur States. It was here that their social position mattered. The austerity of their personal lives was not coupled with any reduction in their ego. Each step in the ascent was registered by the construction of some sort of building in the hometown. Each structure vied with others put up by rival families and, as a final touch, the walls were painted.

Right:
During Mughal and British rule Rajput princes retained control of large tracts of the country, but they owed allegiance to the central government. A group of princes pose in a painting by Balu Ram in Sneh Ram Ladia Haveli Mandawa (20) dating from 1940.

Below:
Pilani. Between the brackets of a small *haveli* a merchant does his accounts, his pen stuck behind his ear. On the left of the picture is his ink-well and on the right his pen box. (c1915).

Below, right:
Not all the Banias emigrated to the cities. Many remained to run local shops and businesses. Here a group of Churu men are shown at a ceremony prior to a marriage. The compact turbans are typical of their caste.

PUT CHIEF S'ASSEMBLY.

The Buildings

The great burst of extravagant building began in the 1830s and continued into the early years of the 20th century. It left the towns and many of the villages of Shekhawati transformed. There had been fine architecture before. The Shekhawat Rajputs had built; so had the Kaimkhani *nawabs* before them. Long before either, in the 10th century, under an earlier Chauhan Rajput rule, the beautifully-carved temple of Harashnath had been constructed on a hill-top near Sikar. Handsome buildings were nothing new, but never in the history of the region could anything rival those of the 19th century for sheer quantity of quality.

Such is the nature of Shekhawati that building materials could not easily be transported over any great distance. There were few passable stretches of road, and these existed only when they were not enveloped by moving sands. In the days before the steam engine brought the country its most radical revolution in communications, transport was mainly by camel and bullock. There was no first class building stone except in the west of Churu district. There, a fine red sandstone is quarried, too remote from the expanding towns to be of much importance during the boom. The carved stone elements – standard brackets, pillars and decorative panels – such as are seen in all the more substantial local buildings, were worked near quarries along the foot of the Aravalli Hills, particularly at Raghunathgarh.

For the walls, three materials were used, depending on local availability. These were brick, stone fragments and greyish lumps of hardpan known as *dhandhala*. Away from the hills, brick was commonly used in the south and south-east of Shekhawati. Near them, in such towns as Jhunjhunu, Khetri, Singhana and Udaipur, flat fragments of stone predominate. Over the central and northern part of the region, however, *dhandhala* was the main building material. Many of the best painted towns fall in this *dhandhala* belt, where a lime-rich hardpan has formed for centuries just below the surface of the soil. It is dug from shallow pits as ragged, shapeless lumps. Previously, some of the material was so good that it was shaped into passable ashlar or even paving, but this has long been dug out. It is remarkable what the local masons could do with such unpromising material, used alone or in combination with brick. *Dhandhala* also provided a major source for impure lime with which to prepare mortar. The best quality lime, essential in fine plaster work, was derived by burning the blue-grey marble which is dug at Kirod and Bhasawa, near Nawalgarh.

Timber is a rare commodity in a desert landscape. Although in Shekhawati trees are quite plentiful, the local species are neither tall nor massive enough to be much use, even if their timber were of better quality. There is one exception, a tree known locally as "rohira", which bears large red or yellow blossoms in the spring. That alone has been important in the havelis as a source for much of the fine carved woodwork. The lack of plentiful timber for beams resulted in most of the rooms being fairly small and vaulted.

Forts And Palaces

May 13th 1831, Fatehpur. "I visited the Rao Raja this morning in the fort. The hour was very early (5 o'clock) but the streets throughout which we passed were notwithstanding crowded with people, and the fort equally so. All his troops were drawn up to receive us, and a salute fired on our entering the inner gate of the Fort, from several guns in the courtyard. The stables of his Khas Russalas (cavalry) are directly attached to the Mehul (palace) in which the Seekur chief resides, so that if suddenly attacked, he can fight or fly in a moment. This I observed to be the case in several other Towns I had visited, during my tour through Shekhawutee, and among a community of freebooters, who must always be on the alert, the arrangement seems not unnecessary. They must be prepared at all times, for the state of the society is such, that they never can consider themselves altogether secure from attack. A Palace to be sure, with dirty stables attached to it, and horses picketed throughout the whole square leading to it, had at first a singular appearance."

Lockett's description of a Shekhawati fort during the volatile early decades of the 19th century is beautifully illustrated by a mural painted some 10 years later in a small fort at Nawalgarh (8).

The first priority of a Rajput thakur on setting up his headquarters in a town or village was to build a stronghold for the protection of himself and his holding. This always dominates any eminence, however slight, the better to command its surroundings. Where there is a nearby hill, the fort might well cap it, as it does at Khetri and Lakshmangarh. More frequently it stands near the main bazaar in the centre of the walled town. Thus it remains at Nawalgarh, where both fort and walls survive, or at Mandawa and Bissau, where the walls have gone.

The stronghold was strictly functional, with thick walls, difficult to scale, and perhaps a ditch at its foot. The majority were built during the 18th century, when much of the country was insecure. At that time, the plan would be square or rectangular, a bastion at each corner to cover the body of the wall during assault. Later, around 1790, there was a move towards a series of rounded buttresses, offering no flat surfaces to much-improved artillery.

There would be a single entrance through one or more archways, each sealed by massive wooden gates reinforced with iron. Amongst the refinements, long spikes project from the outer surface of each leaf at the level of an elephant's forehead – a disincentive to the beasts trying to smash through the gate. Within the walls, much of the open space was used to tether horses and camels. The Shekhawats were famous for their cavalry.

The majority of the forts in Jhunjhunu and Sikar district date from the period of consolidation which followed the Shekhawat takeover of Jhunjhunu and Fatehpur estates. Each was built by a separate baron not only to protect his holdings but also to reflect his social position. On the Bikaner side of the frontier, some of the more important towns were directly held by the Maharaja, their garrisons manned by his officers. In Shekhawati, each fort was the possession and home of the local *thakur*. Not surprisingly, he expended more effort on decorating his residential quarters.

In the smaller forts of the Shekhawats and those that crown the Aravalli Hills, the residential section would be simple, for these only housed a garrison. Elsewhere, there would be some style. The best apartments, at Mandawa and Mahansar, could claim fine murals, but only Jhunjhunu, Khetri and Sikar boasted palaces. In every case the residence expanded with the family, so that generally it exhibits a mixture of styles.

When *thakur* s rebelled unsuccessfully against their overlords, they were likely to have their fortifications razed. This was the fate of several forts during the 19th century. When Maharaja Surat Singh of Bikaner suppressed the Churu Thakur in 1813, he pulled down the walls of the town and damaged the fort, which must then have had a considerable residential portion. He bestowed the same fate on nearby Depalsar, carrying off the fort gates to present to the temple of Karni Mata, the patroness of his family, at Deshnoke.

In Shekhawati, during the 1830s, the British, in the name of the ruler of Jaipur, made a veritable shopping list of forts ripe for possible destruction. Each was classified according to the cost of its demolition in time and money. The smaller places, such as Taen and Gangiyasar

The fort at Khyali as it was in 1831. It was destroyed in 1837 by the Shekhawati Brigade. (From a drawing by Lieut. A. H. E. Boileau).

would involve a six-day outing, 12 barrels of gunpowder and an expenditure of Rs. 500. For large forts, such as Deogarh near Sikar, they allowed a month, 50 barrels of powder and Rs. 2,260. Many of the forts listed survived, usually due to the co-operation of their owners. The Shyamgarh at Jhunjhunu was one of the first to go, being levelled in 1834. Later, two of the four bastions of Taen were demolished, Balaran was slighted and of the stronghold at Khyali only a tiny section of wall – a gesture – remains, along with an earlier drawing by Boileau. Some escaped the wrath of the Shekhawati Brigade by mere chance. The fort of Shyam Singh at Bissau was a prime target and there are several tales as to how the *thakur* preserved it. In fact, Shyam Singh died in 1833, two years before the Brigade became active, and his heir proved more amenable.

Today, very few of the forts are inhabited by the family that built them. The Rajputs, too, deserted the homeland, in their case in favour of the state capital, Jaipur. There, each major baron built a pied-a-terre, named after his thikana, estate – Nawalgarh House, Mandawa House, Bissau House. Many of the forts have been sold, often to Banias, many abandoned, especially those posed on some once-strategic hill-top and now deprived of all significance.

Fort building did not end with the Shekhawati Brigade. The aspiration to fortification, so much bound to the Rajput tradition, long survived. The stronghold of Thailasar, in Churu district, came up in 1948!

The Temple Or Mandir

Hindu places of worship in Shekhawati vary in size from some tiny shrine standing in a side street to the massive, ever-expanding Rani Sati Temple in Jhunjhunu, the heart of Marwari pilgrimage. Many of those built prior to 1920 are rich in murals.

During the 18th century, the most important builders were Rajput barons. As each founded a town, he put up a temple to his preferred deity. This was usually some aspect of Krishna – perhaps Gopinath, Gopal or Raghunath. The Shekhawats associate themselves particularly with Hanuman, Rama's faithful monkey ally. He is depicted on the clan flag. In his name, however, shrines rather than temples were dedicated.

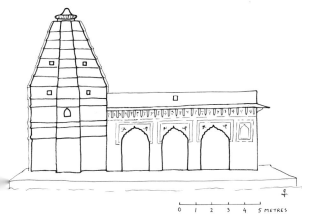

Temple: The design popular in Shekhawati during 17th & 18th century.

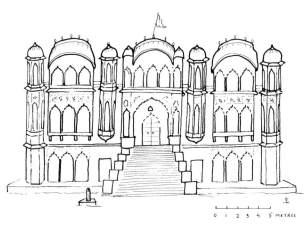

Temple: The design popular in Shekhawati during 19th century.

The 18th century temple usually followed a simple pattern, resembling the layout of a Christian chapel. The body of the building would be rectangular or, in more ambitious examples, cruciform. The entrance was at the east end, opposite the shrine containing the deity. At either side of the building there was often a secondary doorway.

The temple usually stood in a small courtyard, which was enclosed by a single storey of building. This would include the priest's dwelling. The shrine itself would be surmounted by a sikhara or spire, often rather squat. A well was always within easy reach of the place. Frequently it was sunk just beside the outer wall of the priest's rooms, so that he could draw water without leaving his compound.

The ceiling of the building was vaulted, curved sides supporting a flat area in the centre. This vault was sometimes richly painted. In the cruciform temples, the central ceiling would be domed, with a small, vaulted three-arched chamber as a porch on each of three sides.

Examples of the simple rectangular style are common. Those richly painted include that of Gopinath in Sikar (7), again of Gopinath in Parasrampura (2) and, less painted, Kalyan in Jhunjhunu and Gopinath in Nawalgarh (2). Four beautiful examples stand in a series of tiny villages near Sri Madhopur in Sikar district. Sri Bihari in Bagriawas, Chaturbhuj in Nathusar and Gopinath in Lisaria. And the fourth? That is the temple of Shyamji at Mundru. It was certainly one of the sequence constructed and painted around 1710. The other three contain interesting early murals – but what of Mundru? No one knows, since drifting sand has buried all but the top of its tower!

Of the larger, cruciform, painted temples, two are outstanding, both financed by wealthy merchants. That of Sri Bihari in Jhunjhunu (12) is architecturally the finest, but the temple of Gopinath in Sri Madhopur, east of the Aravalli ridge, comes an honourable second.

During the 19th century, temple building became increasingly the monopoly of wealthy Banias. There was a change in preference towards an architectural style both larger and lighter. As with most innovations in Shekhawati, the example came from Jaipur. There temples are often raised well above street-level and constructed around a courtyard. Steps run up from the street to the door which gives through a *tibari*, a three-arched chamber, on to the courtyard. On all four sides are *tibaris*, that opposite the entrance forming the porch to the shrine, which in Shekhawati is often painted.

The courtyard is enclosed within a single tier of rooms. The flat roof projects slightly on all sides and is supported by carved stone brackets. These often frame painted panels which, protected from direct sunlight, may be the best preserved paintings.

If the temple is raised on a basement, this contains shops and storerooms, each giving directly on to the street. The roof is surrounded by decorative canopies and domes, breaking the horizontal line with flamboyant shapes. The roof projects over the external walls, too, and is again sustained by brackets. The *sikhara* is usually absent.

The priest, generally a married man, lives in the rooms off the courtyard nearest the door. He survives on donations, often enhanced by an allowance from the family who built the temple. Both man and god tend to sleep in the middle of the day. The temples are then closed.

Such handsome 19th century temples are commonplace in Shekhawti. Each *seth*, (wealthy merchant) would do his best to leave at least one in his memory. The larger towns may boast several, differing in size and deity. Churu is particularly well-endowed (6,7,16 and others). Perhaps the most imposing of all is that known as the Barra Mandir, Big Temple, in Mahansar (2).

In the early 20th century, temple architecture continued to follow this pattern but, as time progressed, there was a return to something more akin to the 18th century design. Modern examples resemble the old plan, with a *sikhara* over the shrine.

Although religious themes tend to dominate, as they do elsewhere, the murals in temples can be very variable – folk tales, soldiers, trains and even British officials may join Vishnu's incarnations!

The Havelis

The *haveli* was to the Bania what the fort was to the Rajput – his home, his status, his headquarters and his defence. The origin of the word denotes an enclosed area. This is very much the feeling that it gives, with its blind outer walls and everything turned inward on to the central courtyard. Only the upper facade looks out, and then through shutters generally closed.

The great era of the Shekhawati *haveli* was the middle and late 19th century. Many of the finest examples enclose two courts, broadly differentiated into an inner courtyard for the womenfolk and an outer forecourt for the men. Where there was only a single court, an enclosed compound, perhaps combined with a wing extended from the facade, would serve as forecourt.

The street entrance of a *haveli* with two courts is sealed by massive, iron-reinforced gates.

A. Facade of a haveli: Large double doors, each pierced by a smaller doorway, lead into the forecourt. Projecting rooms are supported by stone brackets.

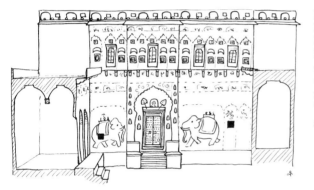

B. Forecourt of haveli: On the left the double-vault of the *baithak* supported by a large beam. Above the door two *torans* left from the marriages of daughters and the ubiquitous figure of Ganesh. The room above the entrance is generally the master bedroom.

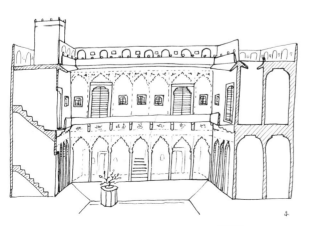

C. Courtyard of haveli: On the left steps emerge on roof through a little structure, *peokala*. A plant of sacred *tulsi* is tended in the courtyard. Upper right, a roofless room, *chandani*.

These were, and are, generally locked. A small door in one of the leaves serves the occupants for their daily comings and goings. Since the mansion was often raised on a basement, a ramp may lead up to the gateway. It was particularly for guests, or womenfolk arriving concealed in their *rath*, (bullock-drawn carriage) that the great double gates would be dragged open. A smaller gate gave into the *naal*, a narrow compound along the side of the *haveli*, leading to a garage for the *rath*.

Within the gateway arch, rooms on either side would constitute the quarters of a *chowkhidar* or watchman. To him fell the responsibility for opening, closing and defending the gate. In a large, wealthy household, there would be several of these guards, and they were armed.

The forecourt was accessible to all visitors. Here the *baithak*, the main reception room, is situated. The word derives from the verb *baithna*, to sit. This would also serve as the merchant's office. The *baithak* would be the largest and best room in the house, often with two adjoining vaulted ceilings supported by a fine wooden beam running between them. This beam may be beautifully carved or decorated with paintings.

In the *baithak*, the overall impression is one of whiteness. Furniture is notable in its absence. The floor would be covered by a thin mattress over which a white sheet was spread. Here the people sit, reclining against white bolsters. The plaster of the walls and floor is often of a highly-burnished white, the product of many hours of polishing with agate. Such plaster is locally known as *shimla*.

At either side of the main chamber, raised high above floor level, there are often low rooms. These are accessible from the women's section without passing through the *baithak*. They give onto it through little arches high in the walls, in front of which screens could be draped. From this vantage point, women of the household could attend functions, seeing but unseen.

It is quite usual to find two *baithaks* facing each other across the forecourt. The building would be inhabited by an extended family and one set of men might be doing business on one side of the courtyard, whilst another was entertaining a few friends on the other.

At one end of the forecourt, usually opposite the gate, is the entrance to the inner sanctum. Steps may lead up to the door, which is set back in a cusped archway. The murals sheltered in this arch are often the best in the house.

The door frame might be made of stone (as at Lakshmangarh, Nawalgarh and Jhunjhunu) or of finely carved wood (as at Churu, Ramgarh, Mandawa and Bissau), according to availability. Always carved into the lintel, or set in a little niche above the door (often both), is the figure of Ganesh. The elephant-headed god of wisdom, son of Shiva, Ganesh presides over the entrance as the deity invoked first at any Hindu ceremony.

Above the door there are almost always some *torans*. These are flat objects, some 30 cm square, set on a wooden shaft. They are made of wood and metal and invariably have a parrot design worked on them. Each *toran* represents the marriage of a girl from the house and the parrot is a messenger of love. When the bridegroom arrives at the door, a show is made of fighting him off. He touches the lintel with a leafy branch and, his conquest made, the *toran* is fixed above the door permanently. Some, bright and triangular, are left from recent weddings. Others, ancient and battered, tell of couples long gone. Over the entrance of the fort at Gangiyasar there are no less than 40 *torans*. But then the family of Zorawar Singh, the baron's ancestor, was always prolific. That was its downfall.

The door passes into a vaulted, domed or wooden-ceilinged porch. Ahead stands a blank wall, protecting the privacy of the womenfolk. This is pierced by a little window, serving as the peep hole in an urban door might. In the past there was strict purdah in the courtyard. The daughters-in-law needed due warning of the approach of any visiting male or other male relative so that they could veil themselves. The visitor announced himself by jangling the chain which locked the door, or one of the rungs attached to it. An older woman would check his identity through the spy-hole and decide whether or not he might enter. Only women, members of the family, or very close friends could proceed beyond this point. The way led round one or both sides of the blind wall.

All the housework of the haveli takes place within the courtyard. Previously, it became almost the whole world for the newly-arrived daughter-in-law. She could rarely pass out through the door into the forecourt or beyond. The daughters of the household were freer – their imprisonment was yet to come.

The circumference of the courtyard is paved, whilst the centre is bare soil, largely sand. This sand, a pile of which is kept at one side, is used as an abrasive to clean the cooking and eating utensils. In a raised pot grows the sacred basil, *tulsi*, carefully tended by the family.

Since the household often consisted of a large joint family, there would be two, or even four, kitchens. Those most frequently used have left their mark on the paintings as patches of soot in each corner.

The three-arched *tibaris* on the ground floor may themselves act as bedrooms. They give in turn onto rooms that are used either for sleeping or storage. There are also two *parindas*, each a narrow room with a small barred window through the outer wall. In the best buildings the door of this room is of beautifully carved wood, pierced with geometric designs. The function of the *parinda* is to store earthern pots of water in a through draught so that it is kept cool.

No room was specifically designed to serve as a bathroom. If required, one of the corner kitchens could serve the purpose. Both women and men would often bathe in the open, especially in winter when they could enjoy the warmth of the sun. It is not customary to bathe naked, even in the privacy of the bathroom, so the men could wash in the forecourt, the women in the courtyard, without offending propriety. For lavatories, the women used some sheltered area of the compound. This might well be part of the *naal*, which often ran along the side of a haveli. The sweepers would come each morning to clear up. They still do – but they seem to carry the night soil less and less distance from its source. Men generally prefer to walk a little outside the village or town, morning and evening, each carrying his little pot of water. This replaces paper for many of the people of the world, who find the western custom inefficient and unclean.

In the centre of three sides of the courtyard, a door opens on to the stairs. These lead up to the walkway which surrounds the courtyard, linking the second floor rooms. This projects over the paving below and is supported by series of carved stone brackets. The rooms are mostly bedrooms. The stairs continue on to the flat roof, the stairwell protected by a little structure called a *pedkala*, with steps leading up on to its roof so that people can sit there in the cool evening breeze. The stairwell is called the *jinna*. The painters made a visual pun on this in one 1930s *haveli*, placing a portrait of the Muslim League leader over the door on to the stairs. His name? Mohammad Ali Jinnah ! On the roof itself there are often several small structures known as *choubara*, a name indicating that they are open on four sides (they are usually not). These are used either as spare bedrooms or, more usually, for storage. In the heat of summer, most of the family sleep on the roof and the *choubara* can be a convenient place to store *charpoys*, or bed frames, and bedding.

As with the residential section of the fort, the haveli often began with only a small section initially constructed. The building expanded with the affluence and size of the family. Some never grew beyond half the ground floor of the courtyard, now sealed by a wall. Others enclosed the court with a single storey. There were those havelis which, starting from small beginnings, ended as large mansions with two courts. Only the change in style of the architecture and the murals betrays that they were built in sections. The great, wealthy *seths* launched directly into a massive double courtyard project. Certainly such buildings as the Surana Hawa Mahal in Churu (3) were not constructed in stages.

The *haveli's* form continually evolved. The earliest foreign visitor to leave an account was Mountstuart Elphinstone. He came to Churu in the autumn of 1808 and mentions that all its houses were terraced. The only two *havelis* which were certainly there when he came are indeed joined to their neighbours. This could have provided a greater sense of security in unsettled times. His description does not preclude there being one or two of the larger, separate havelis which were to become so familiar. There certainly were, if not in Churu, in Ramgarh, Jhunjhunu, Fatehpur and Nawalgarh, but they were very few.

The oldest *havelis* to have survived were built at the end of the 18th century. It is rare for such buildings to be dated, but one, in a state of ruin, has an inscription on its porch ceiling giving the year 1780 for its construction. The age of other ancient mansions must remain partly conjecture.

In the development of the Shekhawati *haveli* between the late 18th century and the 1930s, five main trends manifest themselves:

1) A steady progress from the defensive towards the palatial.
2) The increasing enclosure of the upper storey, both in the courtyard and on the facade.
3) The assimilation of western features and forms into the design.
4) The disappearance of flat wooden ceilings in favour of vaults in porches and upper rooms.
5) The development of figurative murals and their extension over the external walls.

1) From defensive to palatial: Since I first came into Shekhawati, a number of the oldest, generally ruined, mansions have been demolished. The few that remain still illustrate the fortified appearance of many such buildings. On three sides, the blank outer wall would be finished in coarse plaster, probably the same mix as the mortar, crudely applied. The upper facade and the area around the door would be more decorative but even they were sometimes coarsely finished. On the roof, *choubaras* at each corner might give the building a fort-like air.

As the 19th century progressed, the emphasis lay increasingly on the decorative appearance of the exterior. The number of windows increased and occasionally included some, albeit barred, on the lower storey. The visible walls were finished with a view to their appearance, if not with murals or burnished white plaster, at least in the finest mix of buff plaster, known as *loi*. Stucco decoration became popular, often accentuating architectural forms, as with the arch above a window, or duplicating them, as with false pillars. By the 1930s, all idea of defence had gone and many havelis displayed colonnades of slender stone pillars on the ground as well as the upper floors.

2) The increased enclosure of the upper storey: A feature of the earlier haveli facade was some sort of structure above the door which broke the roof line and stressed the entrance. Often this was an arch similar to those which later decorated temples. Sometimes the gateway section was higher than the roof at either side. Either way, there was a tendency for at least three open-arched windows on the upper facade above the door, giving on to a little balcony. In some cases, these windows, supported by carved stone pillars, ran the length of the upper

facade. Such open arches were common until the middle of the 19th century. Then a preference grew for rectangular windows closed by decorative wood and metal shutters. As the number of windows increased they became a feature on all sides of the upper storey, sometimes alternating in size to increase the effect. By the close of the century, the open arches of the facade were a thing of the past.

In the oldest mansions, the upper storey of the interior is characterised by its openness. Second-floor rooms were set back from the courtyard, giving space for a walled terrace on all sides. This was divided in half by stairs, open to the sky, which ran up to the roof. That design disappeared early in the 19th century and few examples survive, one being the oldest Harlalka Haveli, some 100 m west of the bus stand in Mandawa.

As these terraces disappeared, they were replaced by the *chandani*, a tiny court adjacent to a bedroom and open to the sky. In summer the masonry absorbs and holds the terrible heat. At night an enclosed room becomes an oven as the walls emit the day's stored heat. The little patch of sky above the *chandani* made a great difference to the temperature. One could sleep there in relative comfort. As the century progressed, however, *chandanis* became fewer. Now they are a rarity. Those who want to be cool at night have to take their bedding onto the roof. This is screened on all sides by a wall perforated by rectangular "windows" to allow increased flow of air.

3) The assimilation of western features: The 19th century had traversed several decades before European features began to appear in the architecture of Shekhawati. An early example of what was to become a major trend is seen on the roof of the Bakhtawar Mahal in Khetri (2). Lockett refers to this structure in 1831: "On the top of the second storey we found a bungalow built after the English fashion". It is a small pavilion, entered between rounded pillars and copied from some colonial bungalow in Delhi or Calcutta. Some time was to elapse before European styles really took hold.

Towards the end of the century, such elements as rounded arches replacing the traditional cusped form, wrought and cast iron railings, round pillars in the place of the "palm-trunk", all indicated foreign influence. Stucco decoration included fruit and floral motifs straight from Victorian Britain. As the 20th century developed, the traditional *haveli* had been nearly lost under a mass of new ideas. *Malji ka Kamra* in Churu (1) could pass almost unnoticed in a small Sicilian town as a triumph of local "wedding cake" architecture!

4) The disappearance of wooden ceilings: Presumably, supply and demand played a part in this trend. The porch of most older *havelis* would generally have a flat wooden ceiling and, in the oldest examples, it is on this woodwork that there is sometimes an inscription giving the date of the building. Some of the upper rooms also had wooden ceilings, which might be decorated with polished pieces of metal to give something of the effect of mirrorwork. Although carved woodwork increased in both quantity and intricacy of design, these ceilings gradually disappeared around the middle of the 19th century.

5) The development and extension of murals on the outer walls: Some of the earliest surviving havelis have fine plaster work only on their facades where there are often traces of some painted design, perhaps floral patterns, on either side of the door arch. There might be the occasional poor figurative panel – perhaps Ganesh above the door – but little attention seems to have been expended on decorating the outer walls. If there was painting it would be within the rooms, probably dominated by non-figurative designs. The earliest dated haveli with good painted panels between its brackets is one built by the Parekh family in 1820 and set back from the north side of Churu bazaar. The panels were surely the work of a trained

Shani Temple, Ramgarh (12): Rich in mirrorwork and painting this little temple makes up for its size by its decoration. At the point of the arch, Surya, the sun god, is depicted. Ganesh presides over the lintel. Beyond the courtyard, between pillars coated with mirrors, is the shrine of Shaniji, the Saturn god. (c1840).

Top:
Churu (3): An impressive double *haveli* built by the Jain family of Surana. It is said to have 1111 windows! Locally it is known as the Hawa Mahal (Wind Palace) on account of those windows. (c1875).

Bottom:
Fatehpur (7): The facade of Nand Lal Devra Haveli. The gateway on the left gives on to the forecourt with its fine *baithak*. That on the right leads into the *naal*, a narrow compound along the side of the building where the *rath* (carriage) would be kept. (c1880).

artist, not a local mason.

It is not until the late 1830s that external walls begin to boast good figurative work. When it appears, it is sophisticated, indicating again that the painters were experienced men moving into the area. Once murals did come, however, they soon extended themselves across the whole of the outer wall. It was well into the 20th century before the demand slackened.

There were other trends too. Some were local, such as the use of red sandstone as a feature in fine *havelis* of the earlier period in Churu and Ramgarh. Everywhere, in the later years, there was an urge for greater height. Some havelis reach five or six storeys. And the quality of woodwork declined markedly. The 20th century mansions may be huge, but their doors and shutters are often poorly made.

It is easy to sustain the argument that had there been accessible supplies of good buildings stone, such as the red stone from Bidasar, the whole painted Shekhawati phenomenon would never have taken place. To the west and south of the region, where there is such stone, the rich merchants preferred carved havelis with beautiful pierced windows. There are painted exteriors in Bikaner, but they are half-hearted.

One of the few carved stone *haveli* s in Shekhawati stands in Fatehpur (4). It dates from early in the 19th century. To the west such buildings become the norm until finally, at Jaisalmer, the carved stone *haveli* achieves its full magnificence. They could have used lime and paint – but they chose stone.

The age of the Shekhawati *haveli* is well passed. Most of the owners are settled far away. Divided inheritance has given each of them very little interest in the fate of the family mansion, yet veto powers on its future. Some have been locked, crumbling, for decades. A very few are excellently maintained by a small staff who are responsible for the place in the owners' absence. The majority are occupied by tenants who have no interest in spending money on the upkeep of the place. Unless the Bania community itself forms a trust to protect their heritage, nothing will be done. The money is there, but the desire may well come too late!

The Chhatri

"At Purusrampoora is a handsome white domed building, the chutree or mausoleum of Sardool Singh, commonly called Sadajee, the founder of Shekhawutee power..." Thus Boileau mentions his passing visit to Parasrampura (1) in 1835. If he saw the beautiful murals within that dome, he was not sufficiently impressed to mention them!

The word "*chhatri*" literally translates as "umbrella". In India, this object has a significance far beyond its function, being associated with both royalty and deity. Gods and kings appear in state or procession beneath the shelter of a fine umbrella. In architecture it denotes a dome, the basic element of so many Hindu memorials. Shekhawati is dotted with them, each set up on the cremation site of someone distinguished or wealthy enough to warrant the expense.

A *chhatri* may be isolated or it may be one of many in a cremation ground. It may be a very simple structure, a little dome on four rough pillars standing on a low plinth. It may be a large ornate pile, its basement containing several rooms and a Shiva temple, the dome sustained by as many as 32 pillars with decorative domes and arches surrounding it along the edge of the roof of that basement. The size of the monument reflects the wealth and importance of the man who erected it. Oddly, it is often known by his name rather than that of the man to whom it was raised.

The origin of the memorial dome seems to lie in the Islamic tomb. As a Hindu monument,

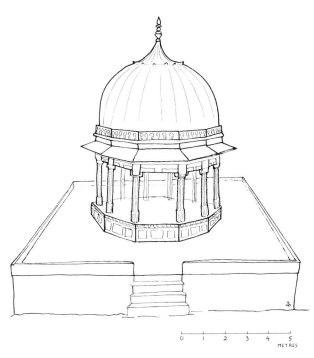

18th century *chhatri* raised on a low basement.

0 1 2 3 4 5
METRES

therefore, it is fairly new. In Shekhawati, few survive pre-dating the 17th century, and the oldest bear no inscriptions. In the region of Udaipurwati, already in Rajput hands in the 17th century, some were erected over local *thakurs*. One of the earliest with a dated inscription stands at the village of Ked and was raised in memory of a Bania in 1695, but extensively restored 70 years later. The man it commemorates is said to have been the ancestor of many merchants who bear the name Kedia.

After the takeover of Fatehpur and Jhunjhunu, Rajput *chhatris* become relatively widespread. One of the oldest is in Jhunjhunu (1), built to Bahadur Singh, the son of Sardul Singh who predeceased him. Another stands at a lonely desert site south of Parasrampura, near the hamlet of Tonk Chilari. Sardul Singh must have built both in the 1730s. The second has a history. It stands in memory of Prem Singh, who saved Sardul Singh from assassination. A relative of the Fatehpur Nawab, seeking revenge, came to him disguised as a fakir, a religious mendicant. Prem Singh shielded him with his body and died in his place. Its interior was painted by some practised artist, who seems to have inspired the man who painted Sardul Singh's *chhatri* in 1750.

Sardul Singh's *chhatri*, which Boileau describes above, is one of the finest painted memorials erected in the region during the 18th century. Raised on a low platform, it consists of a large dome resting on twelve pillars. The inner surface is alive with figurative painting in natural colours (Parasrampura (1)).

The Rajputs dominated *chhatri* building during the rest of the century, the time of their prime. Fine examples are plentiful. At Jhunjhunu (1) are the *chhatris* of six sons of Sardul Singh, as well as others of his descendants. At Sikar (1), those of Devi Singh and his family stand outside the walls of the town. In Churu (8), only one of the Rajput *chhatris* remains. The others have been destroyed since Independence. Many of the towns that became capitals of

57

small estates have their own groups of memorials.

The 19th century was the era of great Bania *chhatris*. Theirs were to be the most ambitious of all, some almost becoming temples to the departed seth. None can rival those of Ramgarh (1) & (2), and of them, that bearing the name of Ram Gopal Poddar (2) is the finest both for its architecture and its murals. The town was built as a merchant centre and its monuments testify to the success of the enterprise. Others are to be seen near most of the Shekhawati towns, particularly at Mandawa (12) & (13), Churu (9) and near (19), Fatehpur (18), (23) & (24), and the solitary one at Mahansar (5).

In drawing up a chronology for the murals, *chhatris* and temples proved extremely important since both frequently have dated inscriptions. This is usually on a small pillar, *kirtistambh*, at the entrance of the building, although in earlier memorials it may be incised into an ochre panel within the dome. There the name of the man it commemorated is written, also that of the builder, the amount he spent on construction, the date, and often the name of the mason.

A large *chhatri* acquired an important social function. It was usually set in its own compound at the edge of a town but was open to anyone who wished to come. It provided shade in a cooling breeze. Men would gather there to talk, smoke or play games such as *chaupad*, a kind of draughts requiring a cross-shaped board. The outline of this board can sometimes be seen incised in the floor under the dome. Often there was a well nearby, providing water to anyone choosing to stay in the basement of the building. The local youth might select the compound as their gymnasium. There they would do their workouts and engage in wrestling bouts. To them, too, the well came in useful.

Today many of the *chhatris* have been taken over as schools. Never austere, they have been transformed into the haunt of children, echoing with their chatter and laughter! What better memorial?

The Well Or *Kuan*

The Shekhawati *kuan*, the well, is rarely the simple structure that survives in the West only in folklore. Here, in the desert, water is at a premium and its value fully appreciated. During our survey, the oldest dated building we discovered was a well in Chirawa (11). Its carved *kirtistambh* bears a date equivalent to 1190. At nearby Narhad, once an important town, now half-abandoned, stands the oldest building attributable to the business caste. Again it is a well, a small structure with an unusual style of *chhatri* at each corner of its platform. It is dated at 1508. Wells are buildings to take seriously and they have been maintained and cherished through the centuries.

At its most simple, the well-head is marked by two or four tall pillars. These were usually painted, but in their exposed position years of sun and rain have reduced the decoration to mere changes in the shade of the plaster. Between the pillars, wooden pulley wheels are set. On these run the ropes which raise and lower pots or goatskins. Somewhere close by will be a shrine to Hanuman, Rama's monkey ally.

The finest well-shafts are surrounded by a raised platform of masonry in which small reservoirs and channels are sunk. On one or two sides a ramp descends, excavated deep into the earth, its length corresponding to the depth of the water-table. This makes the task of raising water less onerous. The men who operate such wells are drawn from the Mali caste (small-holders). One lowers a skin, held open by a metal hoop around its rim, into the shaft. The rope is attached to the yoke of some beast of burden – perhaps a pair of bullocks. The second man, seated on the yoke, drives the beasts down the ramp, hauling the skin full of

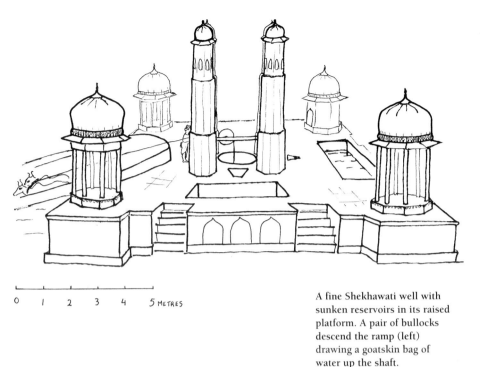

0 | 1 | 2 | 3 | 4 | 5 METRES

A fine Shekhawati well with sunken reservoirs in its raised platform. A pair of bullocks descend the ramp (left) drawing a goatskin bag of water up the shaft.

water up the shaft. As it reaches the top the first – often with a call upon the name of god which echoes satisfyingly down the shaft – catches up the skin and spills it into the first of a system of channels. These carry the water into the small reservoirs – the delight of children in the hotter months – then beyond, to feed an irrigation network. The land around is green with vegetables. Smaller wells also have ramps, but it is usually women, not animals, that haul the water.

Apart from the pillars, murals may decorate the *chhatris* on the platform and even the interior of the shaft. Only once have I seen well pillars which had retained much of their original brightness. They were those of a well in Churu (17). The red and blue paintwork had been shaded all its days by the high wall of a *dharamshala*, a caravansarai, and had thus survived. But nothing protected it from the Diwali "spring-clean" of 1981. It succumbed to the whitewash brush!

Wells are numerous. Each major caste division required its own water supply to avoid the risk of polluting, or being polluted by, its neighbours. The majority of fine wells were the result of Bania finance. Sometimes they merely refurbished a much older shaft sunk, perhaps, by Rajputs, nawabs or even long-forgotten merchants. Examples are plentiful: the late 17th century Bhikaala Kuan in Jhunjhunu (14), the Seksaria Well at Churu (19) and the Harlalka Well at Mandawa (14) (both still in use morning and evening), the Kanoria Well at Nawalgarh (21), *Chauhan ka Kuan*, built by one of the wives of a nawab in Fatehpur (6). Chirawa can boast not only the oldest (11), but also two of the best painted wells (6) and (10).

With the increasing spread of tapped water and tube wells, the days of the old-fashioned well are numbered. Many are now used for pumping up water into the main supply. Some, now dry or no longer necessary, slowly crumble into dust. The land may be valuable and the well is expendable. Where are the wells of Europe now?

The *Bowri*

In some of the towns of Shekhawati, a ruler or a merchant financed the sinking of a *bowri*, a step well, a major feat of engineering. This is a vast, masonry-lined chasm reaching down to below the water-table – no mean depth in this region. From one end steps lead down to the water's edge. At the opposite end is a normal well shaft. Such a *bowri* was a very popular feature in these desert towns. Most have become dry as the water-table sinks, to become rubbish dumps and public latrines. The worst is that in the centre of Fatehpur, now neglected after 375 years service to the town. Best maintained is that at Sikar (3). The Mertani Bowri, one of three at Jhunjhunu (21), has recently been cleaned and poorly restored.

The Dharamshala Or Caravan Sarai

The *dharamshala* provides the cheapest accommodation for travellers in Shekhawati. The quality varies enormously. Some are almost derelict, last resorts with bare, dirty cells and an elderly attendant who spends his life smoking marijuana in the gateway. He receives a pittance from the Bania family who, having endowed it, may not have visited the place for years. Some are smart establishments with large, well-lit rooms, ceiling fans, even attached bathrooms, their prices hardly undercutting the local hotel.

The primary function of a dharamshala today is to house marriage - parties - baraats - during the appointed seasons. For most castes there are strictly-defined periods in the year during which weddings may take place.

When a *baraat* arrives at a bride's village, it is the responsibility of her family to house and feed it. Today this is generally only for some 24 hours, but it may be more. Since a *baraat* often numbers a hundred or more men and boys, it is impossible for most households to accommodate it. So they rent the *dharamshala* and there members of the family, or professional caterers, will wait on them until they leave. These days the *baraat* provides the building with its only raison d'etre and it may be locked when the season is over.

In the days before metalled roads or railways, the days of long trains of camels laden with merchandise, the *dharamshala* had another, more important, duty: it was the staging post for such caravans. As such it was of direct importance to the merchants. It was no doubt this that encouraged a prosperous Bania to add a *dharamshala* to the list of buildings he put up. The place generally bears that man's name.

It was built on the edge of the town, on one of the main routes, but as the place has expanded it is now well inside the busy centre. There is an imposing arched gateway, sufficiently high to allow heavily-laden camels to pass with ease. This leads into a large courtyard, surrounded by a one, or rarely two-storied building. This contains cell-like rooms and large *tibaris*, the open chambers entered by three arches. The central feature of the courtyard is its tree, planted to provide shade for the oxen and camels. Cherished since then, it has grown old and spread wide. The era of the beasts for which it was intended has long past, but men crouch happily in its shade, smoking, chatting or dozing out the heat of the day.

As with the haveli, when the great gates were closed, access to the courtyard was through a small door in one of its leaves. There would be a well nearby and some small patch of compound would serve as a lavatory.

Few *dharamshalas* have to rely on such basic amenities today. There will be electricity, running water, lavatories and even rooms in which to bathe.

As a rule, if a *dharamshala* has murals, they are poor. The gateway may be well painted,

A *dharamshala* or *sarai*: Shop doors are set in the facade. A large gateway gives onto the courtyard. Here a tree was always planted to provide shade.

but the walls surrounding the courtyard usually bear only the most hurried work. This, of all the local buildings, is the one with which I have become most familiar over the years.

Examples are plentiful, situated near most of the old town gates or the sites where they once stood. Because their paintings are rarely good, I have included few in the guide. In Churu there is that built by Bhagwan Das Bagla (17), one of a group of buildings in Nawalgarh (5), but perhaps the finest is that built by the Sureka family in Ramgarh (15).

The *Johara*

Of all the constructions which the *seths* financed, a *johara*, when filled with monsoon rain, is surely the most beautiful. It is simply a square, masonry-lined pit descending in steps. Usually some 40 m across, it was dug at the lowest point where the topography forms something of a saucer. But the *johara* is often transformed by the addition of elegant domes at each corner and arched canopies along each side, both supported by slender stone pillars, all duplicated by their reflections below. One descends steps through decorative arches at the centre of each side down to the water's edge. Morning and evening the women come down from nearby houses to fill their pots. As day fades, goat-herds homeward bound with their flocks run down to the water, and beast will kneel by boy to drink.

When there is a heavy shower, water flows into the tank through small channels that pierce the surrounding wall. During a decent monsoon it is surprising how rapidly it fills. Frogs and shrimps appear as if from nowhere to inhabit the depths. When it is full, the water may be three or four metres deep in the centre. As the monsoon season is forgotten, the water gradually shrinks away, briefly replenished by a winter shower. When summer comes round again there is usually little water left.

Many of the greatest construction projects in Shekhawati were undertaken partly as famine relief. The closing years of the 19th century, when famine destroyed many people in Rajasthan, saw the building of some beautiful *joharas*. Most date from the terrible Chaupan Akaal – the Famine of Fifty-Six (1956 VS or 1899 AD). They remain as suitable memorials to those who did not survive to use them.

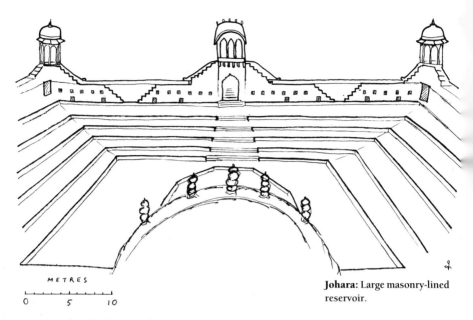

METRES
0   5   10

Johara: Large masonry-lined reservoir.

Examples of *joharas* built during the Chaupan Akaal include that of Ram Gopal Ganeriwala, outside Fatehpur (19) and one north of Malsisar (2) built jointly by a merchant and the Thakur. But surely the most beautiful is Sethani ka Johara (the Tank of the Wealthy Lady) west of Churu (18). Rarely dry, it was my favourite asylum during the five years I lived in Churu.

Some tanks may have paintings on their walls above water level. More often it is the plaster within the decorative domes which bears pictures. They are rarely very good. The outer surfaces of domes, canopies and arches were all once painted. Now only traces of colour still remain on the stucco decoration. When they were new, the effect must have been very striking.

The Shop

Painted shops are an attractive feature of the main street in a few of the towns of Shekhawati. The bazaar of Ramgarh has by far the best collection. Such shops are two, sometimes three storeys high, the upper floors being used either for storage or for a workshop, perhaps a tailor's establishment.

The ground floor is rectangular in plan, narrow at the facade. Above it, set back, there is usually a *tibari*. From either end of this a slender wing projects forward to the front of the building, so that a terrace is enclosed on three sides but open on the facade. The third storey, if any, consists of another, smaller *tibari*. The facade and the three sides of the terrace are often painted. Less frequently, there are pictures within the shop or on the vaulted ceiling of the second-floor tibari. Although no town can compete with Ramgarh, most bazaars have some painted shops. They are particularly prone to Diwali improvements and each year several are painted over or radically altered.

The Gaoshala

The construction and endowment of a *gaoshala* is peculiarly Hindu gesture of piety. This is nothing less than a hospice for super-annuated, incapacitated or merely neglected cows.

The cow is held sacred by Hindus. In the household it becomes a loved member of the family, freed into the streets to forage during the day but returning each evening to be fed and cared for. Its accidental killing can cause great tension and grief; its slaying, riots.

The *gaoshala* is an enclosed compound with sheltered stalls and stored fodder for the animals, which are free to wander as they please. Although there will be a paid staff, there are usually regular volunteers who come each day to help.

There are few, if any, paintings but for some large, rough pictures of cows on the outer walls. Sometimes the entrance arch is decorated, as at Churu (1 km north of 9).

The endowment of the *seth* who initially built the place is supplemented by donations from the local community and there is usually an annual fair to raise more funds.

Modern Constructions Of The Seths

As the 20th century progressed, the rich merchant – become – industrialist, now settled far away, became more practical. He continued to fund projects in the town he had left, but through a charitable trust dedicated to such schemes. These have greatly benefited the desert communities, resulting in colleges, schools, clinics, hospitals, as well as the clock tower that stands in the bazaar of most local towns.

The doyen of the Marwari community was undoubtedly the late G.D.Birla, whose family remain one of the wealthiest of all clans in India. He hailed from the little village of Pilani, in Jhunjhunu district. Fifty years ago Pilani would have numbered amongst the many unknown, dusty settlements that scatter the great expanse of the Indian plains. Today the name is familiar throughout India. Here, the Birlas founded the Birla Institute of Technical Sciences. Known as BITS, it is perhaps the best institution of its kind in the country. Its medium of instruction being English, it attracts students from all over India as well as a number from overseas.

Traditional ideas of beauty are no longer reflected in these new buildings. They have a duty to perform and are designed with that in mind. As a final touch, their walls are painted – with that cream-yellow wash so popular with the Indian Public Works Department. Our Rajasthani village merchants have become urbanized, sensible – and the murals have gone.

The Painters And Decorators

 T he stars of the show were the painters. Who were they and from where did they come? In an era when literacy was rare, few works were signed, and in the absence of records or contemporary accounts, much must be left to conjecture. Surviving evidence suggests that the painters may conveniently be divided into two groups:

1) Itinerant teams of craftsmen coming into the region from the south-east, from the direction of Jaipur.

2) Local men, mostly masons by caste, who acquired and developed the skill to meet a rapidly growing demand for painted buildings during the 19th century.

The Itinerants

Akbar, the brilliant Mughal emperor, expanded his domain and ruled over much of the subcontinent in a reign which lasted from 1556 to 1605. Not confining himself to martial conquest, he proved an excellent royal patron, allowing his interests to wander in many directions. It was probably his personal intervention which encouraged artists from Persia to settle at the court in Agra and Fatehpur Sikri. . There they founded an atelier from which evolved the distinctive Mughal school of miniature painting. This was profoundly to influence developments in painting throughout the Empire. Most famous amongst the descendants of that school were those which grew up in Rajasthan and in the foothills of the western Himalayas.

If Rajasthani miniature painting was transformed by contact with Mughal court art, the impact on mural painting was no less. Perhaps the oldest survivor of a new trend is seen within the *chhatri* of Raja Man Singh at Amber, the old capital of Dhundar or Jaipur State. This is dated 1620 and contains early figurative ancestors to the murals of Shekhawati.

Raja Man Singh was a prominent general in Akbar's army and spent much of his life at the Imperial court. Both he and his entourage would have been familiar with the new fashion in painting. It is likely that his family chose to decorate his *chhatri* in the most modern manner. Probably they summoned men to paint the interior of the dome in imitation of the new style and, satisfied, asked them also to decorate the Mughal Gate at Bairat, some 70 km north-east of Amber. There is also "Makhdoom Shah ka Rauza" in the Hadipura mohalla of Amber, painted in about 1625. Little remains of earlier Mughal-influenced wall-painting in Rajasthan.

Did the painters, having completed these two contracts, remain in Amber or did they return whence they came? Were they, perhaps, local men who had expressly set out to master the new idiom? One thing is certain; of all the Rajasthani courts, Amber/Jaipur maintained the most cordial relations with the Mughal overlords. It was therefore best placed to import styles and craftsmen.

Little 17th century figurative mural work has survived in Rajasthan. Good fortune alone has preserved Man Singh's *chhatri*, Makhdoom Shah's Rauza and the Mughal Gate. No doubt other paintings disappeared when buildings were destroyed or refurbished.

The 18th century was to attract a flood of craftsmen to Jaipur. The city was founded in 1727 by Raja Jai Singh II (1700-1743), another monarch generous in his patronage. As the Mughal capital – by then Delhi – weakened its hold on the Empire during the struggle for succession which followed the death of Bahadur Shah in 1712, the position of artists and craftsmen became difficult, their services less in demand. The construction of Jai Singh's new city required all manner of artisans. There was work to be done and money to pay for it.

Skilled plasterers and muralists must have joined the migration to benefit from this project. Almost from its inception, Jaipur seems to have been recognized as the capital of Indian wall-painting. When the Maratha Peshwa, Baji Rao I, completed his new palace, the Shaniwarawada, in Pune in the 1730s, it is said that he summoned a Jaipur painter, to decorate its interior.

But it was the 19th century which was to prove the great epoch of mural painting in North-west India. Much was arguably the work of Jaipur craftsmen. There are few specific references, few signed works. The fine paintings in the Tambekarwada in Baroda, which date from the 1840s, are attributed to Jaipur, as are many of the murals that embellish the palaces of Rajasthan. T.H.Hendlay, writing in 1883, states that "The finest specimen the writer has seen of a painted interior is the Phul Mahal or Flower Palace at Jodhpore, the fifteen years work of a Jeypore artist."

The scarcity of inscriptions which specify the name or origin of the painter makes it difficult to attribute the best of the 18th century murals in Shekhawati. Tradition invariably describes the artists as being either local or from Jaipur. Five inscriptions of the period on buildings in the heartland of painted Shekhawati all name craftsmen from the east – the Jaipur – side of the Aravalli Ridge. Three came from the vicinity of Khandela, in Sikar district, but the only two specifically named as painters both came from the Jaipur direction. The *chhatri* of Badridas Saha in Nawalgarh (south-east of Podder Gate) was painted by Kiran Khati of Sanganeer, 10 km south of Jaipur, in 1770, and that of Devi Singh in Sikar (1) by Lala Ram Chitera of Jaipur in the 1790s. No inscriptions indicate any other direction of origin for the craftsmen. Backed by local tradition, it seems safe to assume that most of the sophisticated painters came from the south-east, especially from the environs of Jaipur.

Of the two 18th century painters named, only Kiran Khati betrays his caste. He came from the carpenter community, which gave rise to many painters in other parts of Rajasthan. The suffix "Chitera" added to Lala Ram's name merely describes him as a painter. Perhaps he, too, was a carpenter.

The 19th century is not generous either with inscriptions containing information on painters. Although masons are not infrequently named, there is rarely any specific mention of the artist. By the turn of the century, presumably as literacy became more widespread, an increasing number of local men dated and signed their work. Tradition maintains that the finest interior paintings of this period were still executed by Jaipur men. A solitary inscription supports this – nothing opposes it. The inscription is on one of the best of all those interiors, that of the Chini Mahal in Sikar (5). It states that Birdichand Chitera of Jaipur was the artist and dates the work as 1864.

Perhaps the accuracy of a map-view of Jaipur city covering much of the interior of a dome in the fort at Nawalgarh (1) indicates the origin of its painters. It would be convenient if that were so since it is probable that the same team painted two other fine contemporary interiors, that of the *math* – home of an ascetic – of Prem Giriji in Malsisar (3) and that of the *Sone ki Dukan* (Golden Shop) in Mahansar (4). All three were painted around 1850.

Local masons themselves often talk of 20th century interior work in their own town as being by Jaipuris. Some of this was painted in their own lifetimes. A room of the Kedarmal Ladia Haveli in Mandawa (15), painted around 1910, and the interior of the Shantinath Temple in Churu, painted in the 1930s, are both attributed to Jaipur men.

Negative evidence is also important. Throughout the two centuries that enclose the best Shekhawati murals, there seems to be no written or oral evidence that artists came into the area from any direction save the south-east. No doubt there were occasional vagrants from Bikaner or Jodhpur, but they played no major role.

This dominance of Jaipur was not merely due to its role as the seat of the Maharaja who ruled over Shekhawati, but that undoubtedly played a part. From time to time the local barons had to attend at court. In the city many of them enlisted *seth* s to launch or revive the commercial life of their towns. They must also have selected craftsmen there. The Banias, in their turn, even if they had no ties of origin with the city, would visit it as the nearest commercial centre of any size and also to discuss their problems with the administration. It is probable that they, too, enlisted masons and painters in Jaipur for their many construction projects.

As for Churu and its surroundings, despite the fact that it fell under the jurisdiction of Bikaner, it turned towards Shekhawati for architectural and artistic inspiration. There is no marked difference between the painted *havelis* of Churu and Ratangarh, the two richest towns in Churu district, and those across the border in true Shekhawati. In contrast, where murals appear on the outer walls of *havelis* in Bikaner city, they are quite different, the frames usually enclosing floral rather than figurative work.

Bikaner had its own community of excellent masons, both Muslim and Hindu. Some of the former, the Ustas, claim descent from Mughal Delhi. They say that they were summoned to the city during the 18th century to work on the fort and its palaces. Today some of them are employed in the maintenace of delicate stone *jalis*, or pierced stone windows, and murals. They certainly had the skill to contribute towards a painted Shekhawati. One indication that even here the artistic sway of Jaipur was strong is seen in the fort at Nagaur. Although the town lies closer to Jodhpur and Bikaner, its murals seem to have been influenced by work at Amber in the 18th, and that in Shekhawati in the mid 19th, century.

Some Jaipur craftsmen, attracted by the opportunities that Shekhawati offered, chose to settle there. Kesardev Srikrishnaram Ghoghalia, whose family were painters, claims that his clan moved to Lakshmangarh from Niwaee, near Jaipur, when the town was founded in 1805. A couple of early 20th century painted havelis in the town bear the names of his ancestors as the artists. Such immigrants must have had a powerful influence over local men.

The Local Men

It is likely that designs decorating a group of 17th century *maths*, abodes of holy men, in Fatehpur, one dated as early as 1631, are contemporary with the buildings. It is probable, too, that they were painted by local Muslim masons. If this is so, then they were already familiar with the technique of Rajasthani fresco. The work is largely confined to geometric arabesques, flowers and vases, and the little figurative painting is poor.

If the best 18th and early 19th century work was painted by Jaipur men from the mid 19th century, numerically at least, local masons became the main muralists. Some, like Kesardevji's ancestors, may have been immigrants from Jaipur, but others rose from the resident community.

It is not until the close of the 19th century that there is much solid evidence as to the identity of the painters. Only then did the custom of signing and dating work become popular. Many of the painters gave their town of origin and their caste suffix. The Hindus often describe themselves as Kumhar by caste, potters; the Muslims as Chejara, specifically a mason caste in a casteless religion. Both backgrounds gave good preparation to painters. The young potter learns to handle a brush in order to decorate his work, whilst fine plasterwork forms an intricate part of a mason's training.

The Kumhar caste gives rise to the Hindu masons. There is no division between men following the two different trades. One brother may turn pots, the other build houses. The builders who showed a latent talent for draughtsmanship were encouraged to develop that skill by the enormous demand for painted buildings during the late 19th century. Many Hindu masons have adopted the suffix Chejara in place of Kumhar, and the old painters generally describe themselves thus.

It is not hard to trace the old mason/painters and their descendants. Like every other caste, the masons inhabit their own mohalla , sector of the town, huddled about their own temple or mosque. The Hindus will live beside and among the potters. They belong to the Vaishya caste – the third division of the Hindu community, said to have been created from the thighs of Lord Vishnu.

The sector inhabited by the potters is usually at the edge of the town. Characteristically, some of its compound walls are made from large damaged pots cemented together and covered with a mixture of mud and cow-dung. Since many of these pots are almost complete, the effect is rather strange, giving the wall a weird, bulbous appearance.

Signed work is scarce in those towns where the mason community is largely Muslim, such as Ramgarh, Fatehpur and Bissau. It is far more common where Hindus dominated, as at Nawalgarh and Mandawa. Certainly, Muslim Chejaras played an important role both as mason/architects and as painters. On my first visit to Ramgarh in 1975, I talked to a very old *seth* who remembered well the extensive mural work in process. He was quite clear on the point. "We rich Hindus paid for the work", he told me, "but it was the Muslims that did it."

In the case of Ramgarh, the most extensively painted town in Shekhawati, he was right. There the mason community remains almost entirely Muslim, its origin said to have been Fatehpur some 20 km to the south. People in the town still attribute to Fatehpur men several of the painted monuments in their town, amongst them the Ram Gopal Poddar Chhatri (1), the most ambitious such memorial in the region. The name of a Muslim, Chejara Ali, appears on several of the finest mid 19th century *chhatris* in the town. He never specifies his place of origin, nor whether he painted as well as built.

The mason alley, be it Muslim or Hindu, is notable for its piles of bricks, stacks of stone and rough lumps of *dhandhala* along with other building materials. The sounds that pervade it are those of steel on stone, whilst conversation is of walls, doorways, steps, paint .... and money. Into such a world the mason is born. Within its confines the child grows, the youth marries and the man dies. It is home. The neighbours form the tribe that claims his loyalty beyond the immediate ties of family.

The Chejaras who took part in the final stages of the building boom at the beginning of the century are mostly dead. When I first came into the area, there were a handful of very old men. I met and questioned some of them. They varied as much as any group of individuals as sources of information. Sometimes ego sharply pushed fact aside as a man exaggerated his role or that of his relatives; as he remembered that which he had forgotten or, more probably, never knew. Then one came across a wise old man, with a clear mind and precise answers. Not all of them painted, but most had experience of helping in one capacity or another and had thus become familiar with the basic techniques involved.

When I visit such an old man I may find him seated in a small, ill-lit room, or perhaps in the winter sunshine of the compound, surrounded by plump, naked descendants who tease a puppy in the dust. He passes his life, it seems, on his *charpoy* , his mind focussed god-knows-where. He may be a Muslim, his long wavy beard a symbol of orthodoxy when confronted so closely by his own mortality. In that case, the walls of the room will be decorated with bright postcards from Arabia and gaudy prints of mosques, the Kaaba at Mecca or prayers in Arabic calligraphy. If he is Hindu, in the place of these will be a multiplicity of gods. Lord Krishna will be there, Shiva, with the Ganges flowing down from his hair, and Lakshmi, standing on her lotus, dispensing the wealth of which she is patron. The two men have a very different concept of a future beyond the death that so soon confronts them.

The old man looks up. After greetings have been exchanged, water and tea offered and the reason for this unusual visit explained, he narrates his experience of the painting era.

Most of the masons I have questioned were between 65 and 80 years old and would have been first involved with painting projects between 1910 and 1930. They started young, these boys. They still do! School was not on their path. It was not a question of deprivation. It was something they never aspired to, never desired. The study of their caste discipline was a full-time education in itself. Each embarked on it as soon as he could walk. He was accustomed to see the men of his *gali* , alley, at work all around him. As a toddler he might sometimes be taken to the site where his father was currently employed. The tools, the methods, the tricks, the vocabulary were his own special heritage. He was possessive about them. These he had in common with the extended family that was his caste – in common, too, with the masons of the other religion. They set him slightly apart from other boys of his age. They were, in their turn, acquiring their own caste mythology.

The old man will tell you how he started work at the age of five or ten. Age means little in India, where birthdays are rarely celebrated – the average villager could not tell his day, or even year, of birth. It is sufficient to know that he was a young boy, feeling very much a man, when he went out to a building site to work for the first time. He started on the light jobs, fetching and carrying for his father, graduating from making a nuisance of himself to making himself useful. As building went on around him, he grew accustomed to the system, picking up the language and philosophy of his metier.

His first direct involvement with the painting process was almost always in the onerous task of grinding *sandala* or *kara* , a smooth paste over which the slaked lime which formed the final plaster layer would be applied. The old men differ on many points, but on this they agree: grinding *sandala* was a tedious task, left to women and boys.

It was not until he reached his teens that he was allowed to take any real part in painting. How did he learn to draw in the meantime? Most boys did not. Of those that did, some say that they had a guru, an older man whose work they admired and whose advice they sought. He might give them technical hints, sketches to copy, shapes or patterns to repeat, might criticize. Others claim that their skill was largely self-taught; that no one really had the time or inclination to teach. Such men describe how, as boys, they would draw with a stick in the dust, or with charcoal, or ink on paper, copying life or, more often, a picture on a favourite wall. Dissatisfied with their efforts they would erase them, try again, erase, until the result was pleasing. Whether or not he had a guru, each boy usually admired the work of one or two individuals in his community.

Each has many stories of the skill of various painters. The late Jhabarmal Chejara of Mandawa told me of one artist from Lakshmangarh who could paint two pictures of Krishna simultaneously, side by side, one with his left hand the other with his right. When complete, there was not an inch of difference between them. Another old man in Rajgarh talked of one Kalu Khan of Jhunjhunu who was famous for his realism. Clearly not a modest fellow, Kalu Khan claimed the only talent he lacked was that of giving life to his pictures. Apparently, he

op:
neh Ram Ladia Haveli,
Mandawa (20): Balu Ram, a
popular artist in this town,
painted the interior of this
aithak in 1940. Although he
must have used a print as the
inspiration for this picture it
retains his individual touch.

Bottom:
Jivrajka Haveli, Nawalgarh
(26): The artist has portrayed
an unusual scene on the
ceiling of this porch.
Hanuman is driving a carriage
which resembles a temple.
The passengers are Krishna,
characteristically blue and
wearing his peacock feather

headdress, his wife Rukmini
and Rama's brother,
Lakshmana. (c1900).

was often referred to as the "pigeon man", since his signature was a life-like pigeon somewhere on his walls. Surely that must have been his work I saw in a *chhatri* in the village of Niman. Walking into one of its secondary domes, I looked up to glimpse a pair of pigeons crouching on a ledge about to fly. I ducked – but there was no flurry of wings, nor ever will be. Kalu Khan, as he admitted, had his limitations!

Some painters acquired a reputation for speed. One of the Kothari family of Churu told me of Nasruddin of Jhunjhunu who, in the early part of the century, did some work on their *haveli*. He could complete 60 panels a day. When I asked to see some of his work, it turned out all had been whitewashed over, which might reflect on the quality of those 60 panels!

The boy graduated slowly. From grinding *sandala* he might, as he grew stronger, find himself carrying loads of plaster or stone up and down ladders to supply the older men. This, too, was work that he shared with the womenfolk.

If he did get to wield a brush he would start off with ground designs, painting in those familiar repetitive patterns. By the time he was 17 or 18, the competent painter would be proficient at his trade. If he were exceptionally gifted would he get to draw the outlines of the pictures. Only a small minority of masons progressed very far along the road to becoming specialized painters.

Most of the painters I met recalled their peak as coming when they were in their twenties. They would list havelis, temples or mosques where they had worked at that age as their best achievements. This seems only to reflect one thing: it was in the 1920s and '30s, when they were still young, that the demand for all these buildings, and thus the paintings that embellish them, dried up. The heroes that they described were often in their forties or fifties when they reached their peak in the eyes of their admirers. The generation I met as old men had less and less opportunity to paint as they reached maturity.

As the demand faded, so did the incentive for the youth to master the art. For those that did, the chance to practice it diminished. Taste altered, too, turning towards the kind of mural that is still very occasionally painted today. It represents the latest stage in a rapid 20th century evolution in style – garishly painted poster art.

Often the old mason will have one or two panels of his own work painted in tempera on his walls. These usually owe more to Constable than to his own tradition, showing dark woods, European cottages, lawns, rivers, a lake with swans. The choice seems completely one of opposites. Nothing could contrast more with the landscape outside his house – the dust, the dunes, the much-lopped trees, the aridity. These pictures relate directly to a school of popular art which has spread across the Middle East and South Asia. Examples are ubiquitous, decorating lorries, buses and hoardings. Elsewhere it has been politicized, riding on a wave of popular emotion, as in Bangladesh when the country achieved freedom. The cycle-rickshaws in Dacca, I remember, bore gory illustratons of the civil war on their side and back panels.

Not all the local painters were masons by caste. Sometimes men crossed the divisions to take up work not associated with their own group. Several painted walls are signed by men of the Mali caste, a group more frequently associated with gardening and the operating of wells. In Bissau I met one such man, Narung Mali. He estimated his age at around 75 and, he said, was the fourth generation of painters in his family. He seemed to have no idea and even less interest as to how his family moved into the craft. Such men were uncommon and would have worked, as he did, with a team of masons. He told me that they had been summoned to repaint the courtyard of Malji Kothari's Haveli in Churu (2), in preparation for the marriage of the *seth's* son in 1933.

Two of the men who stand out amongst the local painters of the 20th century are Binja of Mukundgarh at the turn of the century and, in the 1930s and 40s, Balu Ram of Mandawa. Many old men talk of Balu Ram as the best painter of their time. He was a Kumhar who specialized as a mason but soon showed an aptitude for drawing. He was born around the turn of the century and died when he was in his fifties, so that when I first came to Shekhawati several of his contemporaries remained to talk of him. These men would name certain buildings on which he had worked. Once seen, his style is not difficult to recognize. He not only signed his work (sometimes even in English) but gave himself the suffix "Chitrakar", which designated him as a painter rather than a mason, a title rare on these walls. He was often called upon to paint local worthies, copying them from photographs. Such pictures are dull, in muted colours, the subject seated in a chair placed at a slight angle to the observer. He also painted freer copies, landscapes, views of places he had seen in western illustrations. He seems to have had a collection of pictures of Venice to draw upon.

At the eastern end of Mandawa bazaar there stands an ornate gate, erected by a local *seth* and known after him as Sonthliya Gate. The structure houses several rooms and in one of these are some of Balu Ram's pictures. High on the wall are portraits – the Thakur and his son and local *seths*. Just above floor level are landscapes. There is something of Douanier Rousseau in a scene of a canal with, to one side, dense green jungle. Peering from its midst, not immediately obvious, is a little lion. He has signed his work and dated it 1938.

The late 19th and early 20th centuries must have been a period of considerable prosperity for the masons. Today the boom is long past and the community, having grown during the good times, finds that the towns are no longer expanding fast enough to support it. In the face of unemployment, its sons increasingly turn away from their homeland, towards the cities, or the great, golden world of the Gulf.

Masons do well in the Gulf, raising the edifice of yet another boom, founded this time on oil. There is a demand for men capable of working in the terrible heat that is summer in that region; men who will be content with the meanest share of the oil wealth. Luckily for the Gulf states such labour is not far off, queuing and bribing for the chance of such work. The life may be tough, but so is the young mason and the money he can earn is beyond his wildest dreams. He knows little of the difference in the cost of living – but he soon learns.

Most of the masons who move to the Gulf are Muslims. Arabia holds more attraction for them than for the Hindus. Mecca is not far off and they share a common faith with the native population. Hindus are aware of religious hostility, and the prospect of moving to a land where the people think of them as idolatrous *kafirs*, infidels, is hardly encouraging.

Responsibility for the rest of the family is a point of honour with these men, and they are proud of the extent to which their relatives depend on them. The majority of those settled in the Gulf put themselves through all sorts of privations in order to remit a large percentage of their earnings home. Their relatives will exaggerate how much their son/brother/cousin sends back. Their period in the Gulf may be rounded off by what seems a crowning irrationality. Flying back into Delhi, to an airport situated close to a station on the main line to Shekhawati, they may choose to take a taxi 300 km home! Status has played a large part in their remittance home. They have given their family and friends an illusion of affluence. By spending what is, in their village, an immense sum on arriving in their dusty little *gali*, scattering dogs and goats, in the luxury of a yellow and black Delhi taxi, they are completing the illusion which they have tried to create. The glory is not theirs alone; it spreads over all those close to them.

Few would grudge the extravagance .... except their rivals!

One of the interesting results of this migration has been that some of the money sent back by Muslim Chejaras is turned to the construction and repair of mosques. When completed, these will be painted, turquoise dominating the colours. The few who really flourish in the Gulf build themselves large mansions, painted in bright blocks of colour. In this last stage of painting in Shekhawati, masons have become not only the artists, but also the patrons.

Opposite page:
Rewasa: A rare picture showing the muralists actually at work. In the centre the buffalo drags a heavy stone wheel round in a *gharat*, grinding mortar. On the right a boy grinds the final plaster, whilst others carry it up to men on the scaffolding who apply it. The man on the left seems to be putting on, or burnishing, an arc of red. (c1900).

Making And Painting The Walls

The walls of Shekhawati were made of stone fragments, brick or irregular lumps of hardpan known as *dhandhala bhata* , whichever was most easily available. *Dhandhala* was particularly important in some of the best painted towns including Bissau, Churu, Mandawa and Ramgarh. Visiting Ramgarh in 1841, Major Thoresby was told that rich deposits in the neighbourhood had been an important factor in choosing that site for the town. Apparently in other respects the place was not very favourable.

Dhandhala is not only used as a rough building stone; burnt, it provides a coarse lime. The local mortar consists of a mixture of this and crushed brick or burnt *khor*, the clay from which that brick is made, in a proportion of about one part to three. It was ground in a *gharat*, such as can still be seen on building sites. This consists of a trench, some 40 cm deep and wide, dug to form a circle about 7 m in diameter. In the centre of this circle a pivot is fixed in the ground to which a pole is attached. At the trench this pole becomes the axle of a massive stone wheel.

Blindfolded, a buffalo or camel plods continuously round, dragging this wheel through the trench and crushing the mortar which it contains.

When the basic wall is completed, it will be plastered. The first, coarser layer is about 1 cm thick and is known either as *lipai* or *chuna* . A finer version of the mortar, this is applied while the wall is still damp, beaten on to improve adhesion and to lessen the risk of cracking. The surface is slashed and perforated to enhance the bond with the subsequent layer, then left to dry for a week to a fortnight. If the wall is at the back or side of the building, not destined to be a feature, this will be the final coat.

On the facade, or any wall surface which is easily visible from the street, another plaster will generally be added. This is *loi* . The mixture is the same, but it is ground into a fine paste. This is done either using a hand-mill of the sort employed for making flour or, more usually, by grinding it with a flat stone over a plane stone surface, a tedious job allotted to boys and women. Most of the old men who had any part in painting mention it as their debut into the craft.

Before *loi* can be applied, the dry *lipai* surface must be dowsed for an hour or more. The plaster is then trowelled on, working one level at a time down the wall, and smoothed over with a plasterer's float until it is about 2 mm thick. The joint between *loi* and *lipai* has generally proved the weakest. It is from here that murals may fall away from the wall. Masons blame this on insufficient dowsing of the *lipai* surface.

Up to this point, the method is fairly standard with few individual variations. Sometimes the fine *loi* was left as a finish in itself, and very attractive it appears when livened with some relief decoration imitating such architectural features as arches and pillars. Occasionally murals were painted on *loi* , usually only in white lime, but rarely even in colour. Probably many of the walls left with a *loi* finish were intended for painting but were never completed.

The plaster layers applied within rooms and memorials in readiness for the most intricate tempera were prepared in much the same way. Only their sheltered position accounts for the fact that they rarely fall away. Instead, they tend to suffer from percolating damp.

The great majority of Shekhawati murals were painted on large expanses of exposed outer wall. Given the pressure of demand during the building boom of the 19th century and the large areas to be painted, it is unlikely that any very elaborate technique was used.

The Final Layers

The finish of the wall in preparation for painting seems to have varied considerably according to the availability of material and the amount that the patron was prepared to spend. For the best work, the masons followed the same technique as was used to produce a white burnished plaster locally known as *shimla* or in Jaipur as *arayish* . This beautiful polished surface is an attractive feature of many Rajasthani palaces and mansions. The Mughals imported the technique from Gujarat to embellish their buldings. Today, it is rarely produced but in a report written in 1884 a government official mentions it:

"Chunam plaster is much used all over Rajputana, but the industry properly belongs to Jaipur, where it often resembles marble so closely that one is deceived. It is executed at a rate of five rupees per hundred superficial feet, i.e. an area of ten feet square."

The wall was thoroughly drenched and a layer of plaster variously known as *karo* or *sandala* was trowelled on then smoothed with a plasterer's float. This plaster would be about 1-2 mm thick and consisted of pure lime and finely-ground marble dust. The source of marble was the great chasm which has been quarried out at Makrana, some 65 km south of Sikar, whilst limestone came from Kirod, not far from Nawalgarh, and was transported raw to be burnt on site. Up to this point the lime used was slaked for a short period; a few days or a week was sufficient. For the last layers it was essential that this period be increased to a matter of months, sometimes even a year, and the water had to be frequently changed. The masons also mention the addition of curd before this lime was used.

When, after several days, the *karo* layer was dry, the last stage of work took place in a single day. The masons started by dowsing the surface they hoped to complete and working it over with abrasive stone to make it completely smooth. Then they painted on a thick, creamy mixture of lime and *jhiki*, the fine marble dust, the proportions being about four parts lime to one of *jhiki* . This material had to be finely ground, a task which fell again to the women and boys of the team.

The new plaster was allowed to set for several minutes so that the action of brushing on the next layers would not disturb it; then a final three coats were applied. These consisted of pure lime whitewash carefully sieved through cloth to avoid any lumps. Again the plaster was given a short time to set, then the men set to work with pieces of agate, referred to as *Narmada patthar* , Narmada stone, since it came from the banks of that river in Gujarat. The team only embarked upon an area that they could complete before the material set. Any plaster that dried before it was thoroughly burnished would have to be removed and replastered the following day. In order to protect themselves and the wall from the direct desert sun, the workers would improvise a tent from any old cloth available. Sometimes this cloth has left its imprint in the drying plaster.

This is only one of the techniques for preparing the wall which is described in Shekhawati. Many masons and householders stress that the dust of sea shells was used in the place of that of marble. One woman even showed me a store of such shells in her *haveli*, put away many years previously against any repair. With the closest sea more than 700 km away, the cost of such shells must have been high.

If this was the method used for the finest work there were other, cheaper ways of producing a similar, if less-enduring, result. Many of the masons mention neither marble nor shell-dust in their recipes except when talking of some special room such as the Golden Shop in Mahansar. Their techniques seem to have been less exacting. The only time I have seen the fresco method being used in the region was in Churu in 1980. The Kothari family were repainting the base of the outer walls of their *haveli* (Churu 2), which had suffered badly from the crystallization of salts carried up into the fabric by rising damp. Over a renewed *loi* surface the mason applied a thin layer of a fine grey paste consisting of finely-ground *dhandhala* and lime. After this had set, he brushed two layers of lime over the damp surface. The painter filled in the missing elements of the decoration along the foot of the wall whilst the lime was still damp. The whole surface was burnished with agate. Such a method would seem more practical when faced with the great expanses of external wall that have been painted in Shekhawati.

The Pigments

The powdered colours in use during the first half of the 19th century differed little from those of the centuries preceding. Most common were red, green and yellow ochres, lamp black and lime, the latter used not merely as white but also to lighten other colours. Within rooms and temples, a wider range of colours was used including indigo, natural ultramarine, vermilion, a lead-based pink which turned catastrophically black, verdigris and even gold and silver paints.

A major change in this palette was wrought by the arrival of artificial pigments produced by the thriving 19th century chemical industry of Germany. These made their first impact in the 1860s, when artificial ultramarine blue and chrome red reached the Indian market in bulk. Emerald green, an arsenic compound, also became popular about this time. One mason told me that the green was used to kill rats! Germany remained the main source of paints until the First World War cut off supplies. As each new colour appeared, it took its place on the walls of Shekhawati.

Setting Out And Painting The Pictures

Two methods of mural painting dominated in Shekhawati. For the fine work inside buildings a secco technique was used, the plaster having dried before painting was started. On parts of the outer walls and for the dado of rectangular designs within the rooms a local fresco technique replaced it, the pigment being applied onto wet plaster.

The Wet Method

The masons erected scaffolding against the wall and, having thoroughly wetted the

Top:
Everyone describes this task as a tedious one best left to women and boys. Here a mason's wife grinds the mixture of burnt clay and lime to make a buff plaster called 'loi'.

Bottom:
The mason has just repaired the crumbling footing of this haveli in Churu. Unusually, it is the Jain proprietor who has decided to try his hand at filling in the decoration !

surface, they started work from the top downwards, brushing on the final plasters. They would only apply as much plaster as they could paint in a single day and uneven joints can be seen between areas worked on consecutive days.

The drawings which were to guide the painters were incised into the soft surface with a stylus variously described as "made from an umbrella rib" or "the *naharna* used by barbers to clean their clients' nails". The first task was to divide the wall into sections framed by decorative designs derived either from the plant world or from such architectural features as arches and pillars. These seem complex at first glance but careful examination of the surface reveals how the men were able to execute them rapidly. Imprinted in the plaster are a series of large and small arcs made, compass-like, with a stylus on a string. There are also straight lines formed by plucking a taut string against the wall. This string was often dusted with charcoal or ochre, which has sometimes been trapped in the setting plaster, disfiguring the picture. These lines served as a grid on which familiar decorative designs could be drawn freehand. The number of motifs in common usage was very small.

Often the plaster for the designs framing a large panel and that which was to bear the picture itself were applied separately. The uneven joint between the two surfaces remains clear. Now the painter had to display his talent as a draughtsman. Some writers mention the use of stencils at this point. All masons deny it! They claim that their pictures were produced entirely from memory or with the help of drawings for reference. In this they are supported not only by the evidence preserved in surface of the wall but also by the following account by T.H.Hendley, writing in 1883 during the busiest era of mural painting in Rajasthan:

"With regards to wall-painting, the artist generally sketches from memory where the work is on a large scale, and from a carefully prepared design where more elaborate drawings are required. If figures are to be repeated, as in the case of ceilings, floors or facades, with geometrical patterns, the outlines are produced by fine charcoal powder rubbed through holes in a paper stencil plate."

I have once or twice come across repetitive figures and writing produced by just this method. The best example of such figurative work is seen within a *chhatri* dome (about 100 m east of Fatehpur 17) and is visible only because the work is unfinished. Camels and horses recur around the domed ceiling and the tell-tale dotted outlines are still clearly visible.

The late Jhabarmal Chejara, a mason from Mandawa, showed me some stencils. He called them *khako*, and all were of writing, the outlines of the letters pierced through brown paper. Each was some phrase in praise of god, such as "Jai Ram" or "Hare Krishna", which were often set out as a frieze on the later walls. Rarely, one element of the frieze is slightly awry, indicating carelessness on the part of the man holding the stencil!

An artist had to be exceptionally skilled to decide the layout of his pictures without any preliminary plan. Some speak of sketches on paper. Some say that drawings were made on the *karo* surface. I have never seen any trace of them, but that layer is rarely exposed. In an out-building in the compound surrounding the *chhatri* of Gulraj Singhania in Fatehpur (24), however, there are charcoal drawings of horses, elephants, and men on the *loi*-finished wall. The elephants match in size and appearance those which, painted, embellish the external wall of that compound.

Painters often painstakingly copied some new picture which had come their way, first dividing it up with a pencil grid, but most men seemed to have been transferring the ideas in their head to the wet wall. Their drawings usually show several corrections before the painter finally committed himself to colour. Often an extra layer of lime was brushed over the sketch to make it less obvious.

There were some tricks involved in producing figurative work rapidly. Compass arcs were a frequent support. They could be used to help produce the correct proportions, the required curve to the bottom of the *ghaghra*, the local full skirt, or as a guide to the shape of an elephant. On the north wall of a haveli in Mandawa (15), a horse has been constructed around two incised circles, one for the pelvic the other for the pectoral region. In some pictures it is even possible to detect lines linking the eyes of two figures so that in the finished work they would clearly be looking into at each other's eyes. In most cases the evidence is preserved in the setting lime!

As the pictures were drawn, other members of the team filled in the colours. The paints, which had been stored in powder form, were mixed with limewater derived from the slaking lime. For large areas, thick paint would be applied in several layers, constantly massaged into the damp surface with a smooth piece of agate or a tiny trowel. Often mentioned by the masons, agate was an important item in the painter's equipment. The edge of the colour would be trimmed with the stylus to ensure a clean outline. This tool was also used to incise designs through blocks of colour, a sort of scraperboard technique especially employed on the rectangles of colour that decorate the foot of an internal wall. Brushes were made from the hair of a goat or a young donkey; oddly, camel hair was never mentioned.

When using the fresco method, it is essential to keep the plaster from setting too rapidly. The addition of curds to the lime was intended to slow down the carbonation process. As the plaster set the pigment was wholly or partially trapped in the calcium carbonate surface. Tests on fresco work elsewhere in Rajasthan show that no other medium was used to hold the colour to the wall yet local masons frequently mention the addition of *saresh*, a gum made from camel bones, in Shekhawati work.

The finished surface would be burnished after it was dry using a cloth bag full of talcum powder. Details were added to the picture, using some form of gum with the pigment to make the paint adhere. Careful examination of a picture will show that the details stand proud of the general surface or have sometimes fallen away.

The small panels known as *gala* which are sheltered between the stone brackets supporting a projecting storey were applied when the lime was set, as was any decoration of stone surfaces. In the latter case, where either pillars or stone brackets were to be painted, a thin layer of lime and *jhiki* mix was applied then covered by three layers of limewash. Again *saresh* would be mixed in the paint.

The colour surface resulting from the fresco technique is characteristically glossy. Many masons say that this sheen was enhanced by rubbing over the finished painting with the flesh or oil of coconut.

The Dry Method

The traditional dry method used in Shekhawati was wholly dependent on a binding agent to secure the pigment firmly on to the drenched plaster surface. Almost always *saresh* is mentioned, less frequently a gum made from *akra* (Calotropis gigantica), a very widespread plant. Two other plants, locally known as *khinp* and *lassu* , are also said to provide a suitable gum.

The painters could take a more leisurely approach to tempera work since there was no race against setting plaster. The whole surface of the wall would be plastered, burnished and allowed to dry. Then the drawing would start. Again, stencils were not normally used and alterations can often be seen in the drawings. The fine, yet incomplete, paintings in the

Gopinath Temple at Parasrampura (2) illustrate this. The artist has roughly planned in charcoal then, laying out his pictures in ochre, has corrected his work until the position of a head or arm satisfied him. Interestingly, too, he did not set out all his pictures simultaneously. Having drawn a group of subjects he coloured them before embarking on the next section of vaulted ceiling.

The dry method was almost invariably used in decorating interior walls, rooms, temples, or the domed ceilings of *chhatris*. These pictures were more detailed than was practicable using the wet technique. Almost certainly the pictures were first planned on paper, then copied on to the wall, as Hendley describes.

Direct copying was certainly commonplace in the later stages of the painting phenomenon, and it is sometimes clear that the artist is not quite sure what he is copying. At other times he carefully imitates every detail. In a room of the *haveli* which stands at the west end of Alsisar bazaar, a painter has copied the picture label of a Manchester textile company. He has accurately reproduced not only the firm's name but even a blank space followed by "yds." where the salesman was intended to fill in the length of cloth in that bale!

The outlines for these paintings were drawn in ochre, ink or pencil, a straight-edge and compass being used to lay out the background designs. When the artist included a town in his picture the buildings would be set out on a grid of lines.

The drawings complete, the colours would be filled in. The painters applied each pigment in turn, filling in all the greens, for example, in the different outlines before moving to the next colour. During the late 19th and early 20th centuries a varnish made of shellac dissolved in spirit was often painted over the dry surface. This has discoloured and dribbled with the years, detracting from the pictures.

What little wall painting takes place today is often carried out with ready-made distempers on a dry wall. The results are not very successful. In 1976, I watched a man decorating a gate of Bharatpur Fort in preparation for a visit from Mrs.Gandhi. Nine years later those pictures were barely discernible.

Repainting

It was quite common to repaint haveli walls. In preparation for some special occasion, generally a marriage, the murals might be wholly or partly replaced or if the householder felt that the *haveli* was beginning to look shabby, he might well summon the painters.

A Bissau man, Narung Mali, told me that his team of painters had been called to Churu in 1933 to repaint a large part of the haveli of Malji Kothari (Churu 2) in preparation for the marriage of his son. They had obliterated the earlier pictures and superimposed their own designs. Judging by the present appearance of the forecourt, which must be their work, this was a poor exchange!

Some of the finest murals are not contemporary with the building they cover. Those on the exterior of the Gulab Rai Ladia Haveli in Mandawa (18) were painted around the turn of the century, some 30 years after the construction of the building. No doubt there were earlier pictures, but the team which painted several other *havelis* in the town (including 4, 16 and 17) impressed the owner, so he commissioned them too. Paintings in temples were occasionally renewed, those in *chhatris* almost never.

Today, no householder would waste money on restoring or replacing his murals. The fashion is over. His solution to their deterioration is a liberal dose of whitewash. How many square metres have succumbed to this fate since I arrived in the region in 1972 ?

The Paintings Themselves

Decoration of buildings with textural or painted designs must be almost as ancient as construction itself. There is little to indicate when the custom began or how it evolved, since the walls that form the decorated surface have a comparatively brief life span and are liable to renovation. In western India, perhaps the oldest ancestors to murals are the undated rock paintings showing men and beasts which are not uncommon in south Rajasthan and Madhya Pradesh.

The oldest surviving mural tradition in Rajasthan still decorates the mud architecture of the villages, although Shekhawati is not richly endowed with such work. A bare wall is enlivened by changes in texture or colour. White lime patterns accentuate the outlines of windows and doors. Flowers, animals, people or deities may be depicted as stylized, angular forms. A similar stylized figure has invaded most of the local Hindu homes. This shows a geometric representation of Lakshmi, Goddess of Fortune, and is painted in one of the rooms by the women of the household before each Diwali festival. Other such figures connected with Hindu ritual survive in the area, contrasting sharply with the figurative work which has made the local buildings so popular.

The sequence of the mural art which was to set Shekhawati apart remains partially intact back to the early 17th century. The earliest work, on the fair assumption that it is contemporary with the buildings it decorates, is in Fatehpur, on some *maths*, dwellings of pious ascetics, in the north of the town, just to the east of the Churu road. Inscriptions date some of these buildings to the 1630s. Most of the painting consists of geometric arabesques in red and green ochres, of vases and floral designs. What little figurative work there is remains angular and unsophisticated and shows men, women, elephants and horses. The local fresco technique and some of the motifs employed relate these paintings directly to those of the early decades of the 19th century, but the portrayal of the human form separates them.

Such decoration persists in Shekhawati and neighbouring areas well into the 18th century. A typical *chhatri* dome of the period has a projecting eave, *chhajja* around its outer surface. This is sustained by brackets in the spaces between which there are often geometric arabesques in ochre interspersed with the occasional elephant or flower. Apart from Fatehpur examples may be seen on the Choudhary Chhatri at Ked, the Rajput *chhatris* at Udaipurwati, a large *chhatri* beside the stream at Singhana or on the outer walls of the Kalyan Temple in Jhunjhunu.

Whilst working on the murals I divided them into two groups: the fine work which decorated the interiors of buildings and which seems to have been mostly the work of teams from Jaipur, and that decorating the outer walls, increasingly the product of local masons.

Fine Interiors

It is uncertain when Mughal-influenced figurative art first reached Shekhawati. Many of the buildings of that period must have disappeared. The earliest dated example is in the *chhatri* of Jogi Das Saha beside the *bowri* at Udaipurwati. This bears two dates, equivalent to A.D.1702 and 1704. Perhaps the name, Deba, in one of the inscriptions, is that of the mason or painter. Amongst the subjects is the emperor Aurangzeb, who died in 1707, overlooking an elephant fight. Udaipurwati was a likely point of entry for any new idea since it presided over the pass through the hills most often used by travellers from Jaipur to Fatehpur and Jhunjhunu. It had also become a popular meeting place for the local barons. A fascinating series of temples near Sri Madhopur, to the east, may be contemporary with this *chhatri* .

None is dated, but two pictures suggest that they were painted during the first years of the 18th century. One shows a Mughal ruler labelled as Narang Shah (another name for Aurangzeb 1758-1707), the other the Battle of Deoli (1697).

In both style and pigment – even in some of the subjects shown – these murals resemble the masterpieces at Parasrampura (1 & 2) which were painted around 1750. Perhaps the answer to their date lies in a fourth temple, certainly one of the series, in the village of Mundru. But a sand dune has buried the body of the building, leaving only its tower visible!

Those few early wall paintings showing Mughal influence did not open the flood gates to a torrent of such work. The heartland of Shekhawati, west of the hills, was still in the hands of Muslim rulers who disapproved of figurative painting. It is certain that the first decades of the 18th century produced more murals, but they have not survived. In the few temples from that period, abstract motifs overshadow poor figurative panels.

The next paintings that can be placed fairly reliably in the chronology are on a *chhatri* at Tonk Chileri, not far from Parasrampura. This was constructed by Sardul Singh who had expanded his territory so successfully at the expense of the Kaimkhani nawabs. It was this very success indeed which led to the memorial, for it marks the spot where one of his lieutenants saved him from an assassination attempt. One of the Kaimkhani clan came in the guise of a fakir and pleaded to meet the Thakur. When he was admitted he lunged at him with a knife. Prem Singh Karnawat threw himself between them and perished. Sardul Singh built the *chhatri* to his memory and it is almost certain that it was completed and painted during his final years. That dates it as circa 1740. Ochres dominate the pigments, but the paint that has been used to achieve the flesh colours of the faces has decayed to black.

Some 10 years later and a few miles to the north at Parasrampura, the Gopinath Temple and the *chhatri* of its builder, Sardul Singh, were both being painted. Although the pigments used were different, the painters, if not the same men, were strongly influenced by the earlier *chhatri* . A cursory examination will pick out several features which are too closely similar for coincidence.

As the 18th century progressed and passed into the 19th, good figurative wall paintings became more widespread within the local buildings. Generally they decorate the interiors of temples, *chhatris*, forts and palaces.

Fine murals, the work of sophisticated artists coming from the direction of Jaipur, continued to be a feature in the region well into the 20th century. During this period, the style evolved and new pigments, as they reached the Indian market, were integrated with, and finally replaced, the traditional colours. The best 18th century artists displayed a skilful use of line. Strong, two-dimensional figures are unimpeded by background save where it is crucial to the subject. Often a sequence of pictures, quite undivided by any border, illustrates episodes in some familiar story, perhaps the life of Krishna or Rama. In a memorial, events in the life of the man commemorated may be included, as in Sikar (1) and Parasrampura (1). As the 19th century progressed, the pictures become increasingly cluttered as the painters fell under the spell of western realism.

The earlier murals are largely in ochres, particularly red and green, black carbon and white lime. Where they would be well sheltered from the elements, scarcer or more delicate pigments were used – green copper chloride, blue indigo and natural ultramarine ground from lapis lazuli, red cinnabar and, rarely, gold. Lead-based pigments with a tendency to turn black were used throughout the two centuries for painting faces. The result can best be seen on the facade of Mandawa (15) and its neighbour.

Top:
Choudhary Haveli, Fatehpur
(5): Panels in one of the most
richly-painted havelis in
Shekhawati. Most of the
pictures illustrate folk tales,
but in the centre at the top
Krishna shelters the people
from a deluge, using the hill
of Govardhan as an umbrella.
(c1880).

Bottom:
Fatehpur. In the *baithak* of the
haveli of Durga Prasad Devra
near Dhobi ka Kuan is this
large copy of an English print
illustrating the Delhi Durbar o
1912. The house is generally
locked and the mirrors and
chandeliers swathed in scarlet
cloth for protection. (c1912).

they were intended to, and brought some home to decorate their walls, where a few remain, advertising long-defunct companies. The masons also acquired and copied them exactly. Once one is familar with some of the labels it is not unusual to be confronted by the identical picture on a *haveli* wall!

10) Decorative Designs

Nineteenth century architecture in Shekhawati exhibits a lightness which is the product of several elements in its construction. Canopies, cusped arches and domes supported by palm-trunk pillars all combined to break the straight lines of the building. They occur in three dimensions, topping a temple facade, surrounding the central dome of a *chhatri* , or as the ubiquitous cusped arches, sustained by delicate stone pillars which lead into the three-arched *tibari* . They also appear in relief as stucco canopies above windows, cusped arches slightly inset in the wall surface and as the pillars in relief that purport to bear them. Each plays its part in bringing life to the building. Elsewhere, they were painted to divide up the wall surface and to frame the picture panels. These architectural elements are not unique to Shekhawati. With little variation they are widespread across North India. They probably entered the region in force during the mid-18th century. Such buildings as the unfinished Khetri Mahal, no doubt the work of Jaipur men, must have profoundly influenced local masons. Shekhawati, in architecture as in painting, owed much to the new city.

There are other motifs which are painted or carved in stone. They are used repeatedly to divide up walls and frame pictures. Again, none is peculiar to Shekhawati, only a local variation on patterns familiar over much of the country. Five particularly can be seen on almost every painted building.

Apart from decoration drawn directly from the plant world, two other designs are important. The first is the rectilinear decoration commonly used along the foot of both inner and outer walls. This can consist of a series of concentric rectangles outlined in black running along the wall. More impressively, rectangles will be painted in solid blocks of colour using the highly-burnished local fresco technique. Each would be perhaps 65 cm by one metre, its axis horizontal and its size including two or three bordering frames. Some of these borders would be decorated by incising a floral pattern along their length, cutting through the colour to the white plaster beneath in the manner of scraperboard. Sometimes pictures will be cut through the central block of colour using the same technique. An example of this is to be seen in the eastern-most of the Kothari *havelis* in Churu (2).

A final family of motifs owes its origin to Arabia. The word "arabesque" usually implies swirls and twirls of decoration, but it also describes the wonderful geometric patterns that evolved in the Islamic world. In Shekhawati, such motifs are reproduced as the subjects of pictures and they are amongst the oldest surviving paintings. Examples dating from the 17th and early 18th centuries appear on many *chhatris* and temples of the time.

The arabesque is always associated with Islam. Is it coincidental that it is particularly common in towns such as Ramgarh, Fatehpur and Bissau where the percentage of Muslims amongst the mason caste is very high? Fine examples can be seen in Ramgarh (4, 12, 14, 18, 20) and in the forecourt of the Bavan Tibari Haveli in Fatehpur (16). In the latter case it is possible to see how the painters used the same technique to reproduce these geometric motifs as they used elsewhere for decorative work, first setting out a grid with taut string. The arabesque seems to have lost its popularity after the middle of the 19th century.

. label of a Manchester
ompany of cloth dyers shows
man suspended above a
erpent-filled hell. Such labels,
esigned in India and printed
n England, were attached to
ales of cloth to end up, as
hese, stuck on some temple
vall. This picture is seen
opied in murals on three

havelis in Mandawa (16, 18
and 21).

Nawalgarh (near 32): On the
front of Babulal
Dharnidharka's large haveli
(about 75 m south of (32))
are some carefully copied
pictures. Here Nehru is
shown out for a drive in a
smart car. (1937).

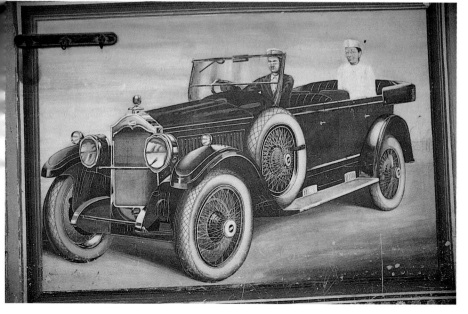

Painted exteriors

For all the high standard of the early paintings, they did not set Shekhawati greatly apart from the rest of the region. The sites were few and scattered, their interest largely academic. They had been financed by locally-produced wealth and that, in this arid tract of Rajasthan, was strictly limited. A transformation in the pattern of trade resulted in the period 1830-1930 becoming the century of the painted *haveli* .

Everything changed in the early 19th century. The first Bania migrants to the Ganges ports and down-river into Calcutta were soon repatriating wealth siphoned off from a source far richer than their homeland. As the power of the Rajput barons was curbed and banditry suppressed in the 1830s, the merchants gained confidence to display their affluence.

It is hard to be dogmatic about the nature of painted decoration on 18th century *havelis*. Those few that have survived are characteristically only lightly painted. The oldest dated example is a ruin in the centre of Churu which was built in 1780. Compared with the great mansions which were to come, it is very small, but probably fairly typical of a modest *haveli* of its time. The only trace of painting on its facade are floral designs either side of the entrance arch and a few faint lines in ochre emphasizing architectural features.

I have traced five accounts of visits to Shekhawati and Churu written by British officials between 1808 and 1841. Negative evidence is notoriously unreliable, but Elphinstone, who seems to have been an acute observer, never mentions murals as he crosses Shekhawati in 1808. Here he talks of Churu and describes its houses: "Though situated amongst naked sandhills, it has a very handsome appearance. The houses are all terraced and both they and the walls of the town are built of a kind of limestone of so pure a white that it gives an air of great neatness to everything composed of it. It is, however, soft and crumbles into a white powder mixed here and there with shells."

It seems unlikely that Elphinstone would have totally overlooked such extensive decoration as typified later *havelis*. He does make slips however and would be hard put to it to turn up a shell in the *dhandala* which he describes. He had probably been told of and had misunderstood, the process of integrating shell powder into fine plaster.

The first of these men to mention painted outer walls is Lockett. During the summer of 1831 he travelled right across Shekhawati from Singhana to Sikar, visiting Churu on his way. In describing "Mundawah" he says, "The buildings are in general handsome, and the upper stories of some of them painted in a very neat manner." When he describes murals in the palace at Khetri (2) he mentions their subjects. Could it be that these Mandawa paintings were neat, geometric arabesques rather than figurative work? It is interesting also that he specifies the upper storey, since today it is on the lower, sheltered to some degree from the weather, that the pictures are most obvious.

Even Thoresby fails to specify the exact nature of the paint-work. Visiting Ramgarh in early 1841 he describes the town as seeming to give reality to a vision from eastern romance. The *seths* handsome *havelis* are, he tells us, "...ornamented and painted in various devices outwardly". He, too, seems to suggest geometric designs rather than deities and people, but there were certainly figurative murals in the town by that time.

There are sometimes pictures in one or two rooms of these early *havelis*. Usually they show camels, elephants or a group of women musicians. The outer walls have invariably suffered badly over the years but do not seem to have been covered with paintings.

The oldest dated haveli with good figurative work on its outer walls appears to be that of the Parekh family, set back on the north side of Churu bazaar. The panels between the brackets on its facade are certainly the work of a trained hand, no doubt an architect/mason brought in from Jaipur. An inscription on the porch ceiling gives a date equivalent to 1820.

Once the fashion for painted outer walls caught on, it developed apace. By the close of the 19th century, most major buildings would be covered with pictures as a matter of course. After the first decade of the 20th century, decline set in, and 40 years later the age of the murals drew its last gasps.

In order to fit undated work into some sort of time-scale it was necessary to co-ordinate it with dated examples. Not only did pigments prove useful in dating pictures but also the intrusion of western influence in both style and subject. The evolution of local fashion, too, played a role. Prior to 1800, a large percentage of the women depicted wear a ghaghra , a skirt, with a horizontal striped pattern. After that date the pattern becomes rare. Men in murals painted around 1830 and 1840 often sport very fine mutton-chop whiskers. If such features are not very reliable they can be helpful in association with other evidence, such as a defaced inscription.

Best of all for developing a chronology are recognizable individuals who were briefly important – a king, an emperor, a baron. The Europeans first made their appearance as military men, their uniforms and weapons being affected by the local rulers for their troops. Their modes of transport, frequently depicted, proved very useful – paddle-steamers, sailing vessels, trains, cars, bicycles and, towards the end, even aeroplanes, all help to date a picture.

I had not been long in the region before I established a system of classification based on pigments. It went as follows:

1) Maroon
2) Red and blue
3) Multicoloured

These three divisions were related to external murals on *havelis*, temples and *chhatris* in particular. The painters of the fine interior murals quickly took up the pigments as they arrived, but the classification is not so reliable for their work. Ultramarine, for example, when used on an outer wall, invariably concerns the cheap factory product. In the shelter of a room or temple it may be crushed lapis lazuli, rare, but in use long before the compound was synthesized.

Maroon – 1820-65

Dark red ochre pigment is a feature of almost all the early fresco work. From the 17th well into the 19th century, most of the portrayal of human and animal forms on the outer walls and in some of the *chhatris* of Shekhawati can be described as "primitive". Unsophisticated and angular, such paintings seem to have been the work of local masons where the patron lacked either the wealth or the inclination to call in a skilled painter. Examples can be seen in the village of Gangiyasar, in a Shiva Temple at the Mataji Temple (2) which dates from around 1760 and also on the facade of two shops painted about a century later. Others may be seen in some of the small four-pillar *chhatris* at the edge of several towns.

In some places, figurative work of this "primitive" type contrasts sharply with sophisticated plant and arabesque designs immediately neighbouring it. These motifs have been produced geometrically by men unpractised in the freehand work that the figurative pictures require. Two good examples of such contrasting work are seen in the *chhatri* of Shyoji Ramji Poddar (1833) in Ramgarh (2) which stands in the locked compound, and the handsome Bavan Tibari Haveli (c 1840) in Fatehpur (16).

The ochres characterizing these "maroon" murals have usually been applied in thick layers, worked into the wet plaster surface in the manner of Rajasthani fresco. The result is extremely tenacious and in several places 17th century decoration can be seen unfaded on outer walls. The red pigments are coupled particularly with green and to a lesser extent yellow ochres and black carbon, which was particularly in vogue around 1860.

Figurative panels, especially those known as *galas*, placed between stone brackets on the outer walls, are always enclosed within a painted frame. On earlier buildings this was often a solid border of red or green ochre. As time progressed it became usual to lighten it with a small white flower and pair of leaves painted on, or incised through, the colour in each upper corner.

Under the heading "maroon", falls some of the most beautiful flowing draughtsmanship to be found on the outer walls of Shekhawati buildings. Painted mostly between 1820 and 1865, the pictures are two-dimensional. If there is any background it is simple – some arcs of radiating lines, perhaps, to represent grass, or an upward-curving line for a hill. Nothing distracts from the subject within the panel.

There is no certain indication as to who were the artists of the best maroon work, but there can be little doubt that some of them at least were skilled outsiders. If we accept that the painters of the interior of the Golden Shop in Mahansar (4) were skilled Jaipuris, what of the men who produced the fine contemporary work on the outer walls of that and other buildings in the town? The artist responsible for some of that work seems to have been the same as painted a well and *chhatri* in Mandawa (13 & 14). Did he also paint another *chhatri* in Mandawa (12) ? If so, is he the little figure carrying a spade and labelled as "Kalu Khan" who appears on one of its walls? What of Ali Chejara, whose name is written on two handsome double *chhatris* at Ramgarh (2), each with fine murals? Where did he come from and was he painter as well as mason?

It seems likely that some of the early maroon work was that of itinerant specialists. Who they were and where they came from will probably remain uncertain; but surely it was they who inspired the local masons.

Red and blue – 1860-1910

The bulk of the paintings surviving on the *havelis* of Shekhawati fall into this category. The transition was purely one of colour, brought about by the arrival of new pigments from abroad. With technical advances in the European chemical industry, especially in Germany, came dyes and pigments. Some of these were newly-developed colours, others, artificially synthesized pigments already familiar in their natural state.

Each innovation from the West would pass through the port-capital of Calcutta, often through the hands of merchants from Shekhawati. They were not slow to remark their potential. Thus new colours sometimes reached the local painters through the direct intercession of the merchants. The red and blue colour combination was not new. It had been used in the oldest ancestor of the murals, the *chhatri* of Man Singh at Amber, but a cheap, fast blue was not available to the early painters.

The change came around 1860 with the arrival in bulk of artificially manufactured ultramarine, a deep, satisfying light-fast blue. Ultramarine had been available for centuries, ground from lapis lazuli mined in Afghanistan, but it was expensive. The technique of synthesizing this pigment had been discovered simultaneously in France and Germany in 1828. It was soon mass-produced for use in the colouring of porcelain at Meissen.

In Shekhawati, the main source of blue had hitherto been indigo, a more restrained colour vulnerable to fading when exposed to light. It is only seen in the shelter of rooms. Indigo is listed as an important commodity in accounts of the local caravan trade during the 18th and early 19th centuries.

The new blue was generally coupled with a new red pigment. Previously cinnabar and ochre had been the principal reds used, but now red chrome joined them, again from the West. This had been developed in the first years of the 19th century. The red and blue became coupled as firmly as red and green ochres had been earlier.

By the time the red and blue combination invaded the walls of Shekhawati, both colours were being cheaply mass-produced, mostly in Germany, and were readily available to the painters. A German source for those 19th century paints is still widely recognized long after the trade has ceased. It probably explains why the word "Germany" appears in several pictures where artists have felt constrained to include some "English writing". The best example of this graces a painting of a ship in Sardarshahr (neighbouring 1). Ships need names, so along the length of the hull is painfully copied – surely from a paint tin – the words "Made in Germany". The painter gambled and lost, for the writing is upside down!

The painters had not used more sober earth colours out of choice, merely from necessity. When new, brighter pigments reached them, the natural colours were soon swept away and ultramarine replaced red ochre as the dominant pigment. The basic colour for the ground patterns in these pictures alternates between red and blue from panel to panel.

Even the blue on its own had a strong appeal. In 1864, Birdichand Chitera, a muralist from Jaipur, painted the Chini Mahal in Sikar (5) using ultramarine on a white lime ground to produce a porcelain effect – hence the name, which translates as "China Palace". This led to some *havelis*, particularly in Sikar, also being painted with this blue and white combination (12).

The red and blue era began around 1860 and some of the *chhatris* built in the 1860s in Ramgarh (2) exhibit both combinations on the same building. It continued into the first decade of the 20th century. The period sees more than just the invasion of foreign pigments. The ground designs become more complicated as the century moves towards its close. Areas which might once have been left as unbroken colour are now encroached by floral and leaf patterns. The pictures themselves indicate increasing signs of western influence in perspective and shading. Backgrounds become more cluttered. The choice of subjects, too, betray the intrusion of foreigners, as imported gadgets and European folk take up ever more wall space.

It is during the era of the red and blue combination that fine, confident two-dimensional drawing disappears. The artists looked at Victorian realism, then turning back to their own work saw it wanting.

Signed work became more common towards the turn of the century and tells us that most of the men working on the murals were local, generally masons. The late 19th century provided many vehicles by which western artistic ideas could reach the painters. Printing, both in black and white and colour, had reached a high standard. Newspapers, picture-labels, religious illustrations, pictures of royal occasions or European scenery were all easily available. The *seths* decorated their rooms with imported novelties, which often included large, framed lithographs (Mahansar 6).

Direct copying, probably always popular, was commonplace by the turn of the century. Several times I have stumbled across a Western print which has been the model for some familiar mural. Recently, in a friend's house in London, I noticed a coloured lithograph of the Delhi Durbar of 1912. It was identical to a large mural which decorates a *haveli* room in Fatehpur!

Multicoloured – 1900-1950

This heading covers most of the murals of 20th century Shekhawati as the craft declined and disappeared. A kaleidoscope of new, cheap colours were being produced in Germany and the masons were only too ready to add them to their palette. Some of the pigments were unfortunate. One particularly destructive colour was a yellow which clashes with every pigment that neighbours it and yet was clearly popular with the painters. Some of the new chemicals are said to have responded badly to the traditional fresco technique so that murals were increasingly painted in tempera on dry plaster. The fact that this method is less labour-intensive no doubt played its part.

The mason/painters whom I have met, painting in the decline of the mural boom, did most of their work on dry or damp plaster in tempera. There was an increasing tendency to sign work, but the artists rarely had much reason to boast. The standard of craftsmanship was steadily declining. Nothing compensated for the loss of the fine, clear line which had characterized the best maroon work. The murals show a tendency towards cluttered backgrounds and poorly grasped alien concepts of perspective and shading.

The ground patterns became simplified again during the 20th century and integrated changes in architectural form which had been adopted in the region. From Europe, via Calcutta and Bombay, rounded arches had arrived to replace the cusped ones. Fluted pillars displaced those based on the palm trunk; stucco foliage and blossoms, in a style more at home beside the Mediterranean than in the Indian desert, envelop their capitals.

The first rounded arches to appear in the paintings may have been inspired by cast iron work imported in sections and used to support some light, projecting roof over the terrace of a fort or *haveli* . Often Belgian glass lamps, popular with the *seths* for illuminating their *baithak* , would be shown, suspended from the apex of such an arch.

Even in this period of decline there were individual painters who produced interesting work. Binja of Mukundgarh, who always liked to include an erotic, has signed a number of walls in the vicinity of Nawalgarh. An anonymous man based in Chirawa developed his own characteristic soft view of the human face around 1920. There was also Balu Ram of Mandawa who was at his peak as late as 1940. He loved to copy, but often imposed his own personality on other people's prints.

Little was painted after the 1940s. The merchants had finally taken their families with them to their adopted city. The hometown had lost its original significance and, although they remained patrons, the *seths'* buildings were practical rather than pretty. The barons were stripped of their powers after Independence and those with any money moved to a pied-a-terre in Jaipur. Today, only the occasional mosque or temple requires the painters, and the decoration they produce varies little from that anywhere else in India.

The Subjects Of The Pictures

It is hard to be certain how much the patrons of the murals influenced their subject matter. The masons claim that they rarely suggested themes, merely asked for something better than the neighbours', mentioning certain buildings that particularly appealed to them. According to them, the *seths* ordered their paintings by area. Sometimes there is evidence of a preference. The *haveli* of a Jain family, for example, may include a few Jain saints on its walls. Elsewhere, the *seth* and his family may be depicted. The owners often insist that their ancestors played a major role in the choice of subject.

In all probability, the large majority of the illustrations were chosen by the painters, the same gods and heroes turning up repeatedly in very similar poses. In the case of temples it is likely that the priest and the patron would intervene.

Most of the figures represented definite characters, real or mythical, both to the man who put them there and to the contemporary onlooker. On occasion, the artist has been able to display the skill of literacy and label his subjects. Failing that, the identities of more obscure personages – local *seths* and *thakurs* or simply his own mates – have faded with him.

The subjects of the murals fall under ten headings:
1) Religious
2) Ragamala
3) Folk mythology
4) Historical events and personages
5) Everyday environment
6) Animals and plants
7) Erotica
8) Maps and places
9) The British and their contraptions
10) Decorative designs

Ganesh, God of wisdom, bowl of sweets in hand, his steed—a rat— tethered to his throne. He appears above the entrance of each Hindu building.

1) Religious themes

These are almost invariably orthodox Hindu in nature, although Jain and Sikh figures appear occasionally, and they are by far the commonest pictures. The mythology of Hinduism is extraordinarily complex, but a short summary may be helpful. Central to the religion is the concept of a trinity of interacting deities: Brahma, the Creator; Shiva, the Destroyer and Regenerator; and Vishnu, the Preserver. Each has a consort: for Brahma there is Saraswati, Goddess of Learning and Music; for Shiva, Parvati, who usually appears on the walls in the stern aspect of Durga; for Vishnu there is Lakshmi, Goddess of Fortune, to whom the Banias are particularly devoted.

Of this trinity, Vishnu is by far the most important in providing subjects. He has appeared in a number of incarnations – a basic 10 are generally recognized, but a further 12 or 14 are often added. Many would claim his incarnations to be as numerous as the stars. For the purposes of the Shekhawati painters, 24 seem to be accepted. Often all appear together in a series on the ceiling of a temple or the panels surrounding the interior of a *chhatri* dome, but two far surpass all the others in popularity. These, Rama and Krishna, must alone account for the majority of illustrations of all types.

Those shown in most of the collections of incarnations are, firstly the universally-recognized 10:

1) Matsya – the fish
2) Kurma – the tortoise
3) Varaha – the boar
4) Narsinha – the man-lion
5) Vamana – the dwarf
6) Parsurama – Rama with the axe
7) Rama – hero of the *Ramayana*
8) Krishna – the dark lover and teacher
9) Buddha – the Enlightened One
10) Kalki – the incarnation to come.

Nine of these are illustrated in the line drawings. Buddha is shown in the characteristic lotus pose. Added to these are a further 14:

1) Kapil Dev – a sage
2) Dattatraya – an ascetic
3) Yajna – a sacrifice
4) Rishabdev – a saintly king
5) Dhanwantari – a physician
6) Ved Vyasa – compiler of the Vedas
7) Prithu – a pious ruler
8) Hansa – a goose
9) Hayagriva – the horse-headed
10) Dhruva – a devotee
11) Gajendra Moksha – saviour of the Lord of Elephants
12) Badrinath – Lord of Badari
13) Jagannath – Lord of the Universe
14) Sankadik – four perfect youths

Rama and Krishna dominate totally. Rama is the hero of the most important Hindu epic, the *Ramayana*, read throughout India by the literate, and widely enacted as folk theatre, especially in the days preceding the autumn festival of Dassehra, which commemorates in part Rama's advance against his enemies. Exiled from the kingdom to which he was rightful

A. Matsya—The fish—slays a demon.

B. Kurma—the tortoise—acts as the fulcrum when Gods and demons churn the ocean.

C. Varaha—the boar—lifts the earth on his tusks whilst destroying a demon.

D. Narsinha—the man-lion—tears the evil Hiranyakasipu to shreds.

E. Vamana—the dwarf—receives water from the good king Bali

F. Parasurama—Rama—with an axe—destroys the thousand armed Rajput, Sahisterbahu.

G. Rama, with his brother, Lakshmana and his faithful ally, Hanuman.

H. Krishna plays his flute.

I. Kalki — the incarnation to come.
Nine incarnations of Vishnu taken from 19th century Shekhawati murals.

heir, he went into the jungle with Sita, his bride, and two of his brothers, Lakshmana and Shatrughna. Sita was abducted by Ravana, the ten-headed demon King of Lanka. Most of the epic describes Rama's attempts to rescue her aided by his faithful ally Hanuman, the monkey ruler, who leads an army of monkeys. Rama is usually shown as a blue figure bearing a bow, in the company of his brothers similarly armed, and Sita and Hanuman.

Krishna is also depicted in blue, usually as a child or a flirtatious youth. He was fostered by a family of cowherds, having escaped a massacre of innocents which his uncle Kansa, the evil king of Mathura, ordered. Raised near the town of Brindavan, he became popular amongst the local people, delivering them from various afflictions. He was constantly pursued by Kansa's allies in various guises. Each he destroyed, finally slaying Kansa himself. At other times he plays the flute and flirts with the *gopis*, milkmaids, with whom he passes much of his time. Most domes include a *rasamandala*, a dancing circle in which he miraculously reproduces himself so that each *gopi* finds him dancing next to her. Meanwhile, his beloved, Radha, awaits him patiently, the epitomy of dedicated womanhood.

In the Battle of Kurukshetra, which dominates the other great epic of Hinduism, the *Mahabharata*, he takes the side of the five worthy Pandava brothers to whom he is related. Krishna appears as the chariot driver to Arjuna, one of the brothers. Arjuna is assailed by doubt as to the morality of fighting against an army which contains some of his own kin as well as many wise and good men. Krishna justifies the battle in a celebrated discourse known as the *Bhagvad Gita* (The Song of the Lord).

In the murals he is generally portrayed as a youth, perhaps playing the flute, often teasing girls, sometimes in the chariot with Arjuna. Other pictures show him in the company of Radha or being married to Rukmini. Always he is characterized by a head- dress with a single projecting peacock feather. Krishna's life story frequently decorates temple or *chhatri* ceilings, interspersed with the adventures of Rama.

Shiva is shown as a long-haired ascetic seated on a tiger skin, a trident in his hand, a crescent moon above his brow and a snake around his wrist. The Ganges falls from heaven on to his head. Each of the gods has an animal which acts as his form of transport, his mount. For Shiva this is Nandi the bull, who kneels before him both in the pictures and at the entrance to his temples. Often he is shown with his family. His consort, Parvati, when shown alone, appears as the Goddess Durga, sword and trident in hand and riding a tiger. Often she is attended by two guardians, the black Bhairon and the white Bhairon, each with a trident, a trumpet and a dog. Of his two sons, Ganesh of the elephant head, God of Wisdom, is very important. He is invoked first amongst the gods at all religious ceremonies. Several differing accounts relate how he achieved such prominence. One I was told went as follows:

The gods were disputing who was the senior-most amongst them. To settle the point they agreed to hold a race around the world. At the signal, each mounted the creature that is his vehicle and set off. Now Ganesh rides a rat, so he should have been right out of the contest since, as my informant put it, "The was a very fatty man on a mouse". But instead of rushing off with the others he wrote the word "Rama" in the dust and, on his rat, rode round that. Since "Rama" is the name of god and thus contains the whole universe, he was declared the winner. He occurs on every painted Hindu building, always above the door and often twice, carved once into the middle of the lintel, the image coated with vermilion, and painted in the panel immediately above the apex of the door arch. The rat is also there, and his consorts, Riddhi and Siddhi, stand at either side, fanning him. He has a propensity for surviving attacks of whitewash which obliterate so many murals each year. Often his picture above the door is

A. Sassi and Punu
Sassi, a princess, is abandoned and raised among washermen. Punu, a prince, weds her in defiance of his parents. They kidnap him and Sassi dies in the desert searching her love.

B. Jagdev and Kankali Jagdev orders his wife to cut off his head and present it to the Goddess Kankali as a token of his devotion.

C. Laila and Majnu
This famous middle-eastern tale appears in the earliest murals. Majnu becomes crazed with love for Laila, but she is forced to marry another man. Here she visits Majnu in his guise as a fakir.

D. Dhola and Maru
Rajasthan's most popular tale. Married in infancy, they lived apart. When adult, Dhola came to fetch his wife. On their homeward journey they are attacked by Umra-Sumra and his gang. Maru, a good Rajput wife, fends them off.

E. Binjo and Sorath
Binjo plays the *veena* so beautifully that Sorath, his young aunt, falls in love with him. He returns her love and in the most popular scene she dances to his music.

F. Heer and Ranjha
A very popular Punjabi tale. Ranjha, who charms man and beast with his flute-playing, falls for Heer, daughter of a rich landowner. He becomes her father's cattleherd. After many tribulations they wed, but Heer's wicked uncle poisons her to prevent the match.

Below:
Mandawa: On the lower facade of a small Ladia *haveli* south of the Bhagchandka Haveli (7) are some fine ochre murals. Between the brackets are shown (left) Vishnu with his winged vehicle Garuda arriving to save Gajendra in the form of an elephant from an evil crocodile, and (right) Krishna holding up the Govardhan hill to shelter the people from a downpour sent by Indra. (c1840).

Above:
Sikar (8): This panel in the upper part of the courtyard of the Raghunath Temple appears to show some contemporary skirmish. In fact, it is a picture of the Battle of Kurukshetra, the climax of the *Mahabharata* epic. On the right Arjuna is shown in his chariot with Krishna at the reins as his driver and advisor. (c1840).

the only one left untouched.

Despite his position as Creator, Brahma is the least worshipped of the trinity. There are only a handful of temples dedicated to him in the whole country. In the paintings he appears occasionally, riding his goose and identified by his four heads. Most often he is to be seen as one of the deities in Rama's wedding procession but in Nawalgarh he and his consort, Saraswati, are often shown at either side of the entrance arch of a *haveli*. She rides a peacock or a goose and carries a stringed instrument, a *veena*, in her hand.

Scenes from the *Mahabharata* occur, but they are far less frequent than those from the *Ramayana*. Two of the most common, apart from Krishna with Arjuna, show the eldest of the Kaurava brothers attempting to strip the pious and beautiful Draupadi of her sari, which miraculously becomes endless, and Arjuna aiming at a fish target above him by looking at its reflection in a bowl of water. Another event where the Kaurava brothers (100 of them) hide up a tree and are shaken down by Bhima, the powerful Pandava, is popular, but it is a local addition to the epic.

There are many other religious themes which occur from time to time. Often one particular subject is popular in one particular town. In Fatehpur, pictures of Lakshmi, with or without Vishnu, painted on a deep blue ground, is a speciality. Another favourite there shows a man clinging to a *lingam*, the form in which Shiva is worshipped, as Yama, the god of death, approaches on his buffalo. In the picture, Shiva appears to intervene. Lakshmangarh has several favourites, including one of foster-mother Yashoda suckling the baby Krishna. In Bissau it is Arjuna and Krishna in their chariot confronted by an odd composite creature labelled as "Ajaibgulmari".

Some of the religious figures are less well-known. There is the teacher, Kabir, at his loom, or Dadu Dayal, one of his disciples, to whom the Poddar family seems to have been particularly devoted. Dadu Dayal was credited with protecting their cargoes. He is shown in several of the Ramgarh *chhatris* seated amongst his followers, a sailing ship manned by Europeans in the background. A merchant kneels at his feet. There are local god-heroes too, like Gugaji, who protects against snake-bite, Pabuji, who brought the camel to Rajasthan, and Ramdevji, who rides a horse bearing a spear.

2) Ragamala

"A garland of musical modes" roughly translates "*ragamala*". Indian art is unique in that it attempts to express the emotions of its musical modes, the *ragas* and *raginis*, in visual terms. Collections of such paintings are known as *ragamala* and occur from time to time amongst the murals. The system lists six *ragas* relating to six climatic seasons, each of which is connected to five *raginis*. To this total of 30 a further six are added, making 36 in all. The names given to the *raginis* are variable. Amongst labelled *ragamalas* in Shekhawati two of the most complete are that in the *chhatri* of Kishan Dutt Poddar in Ramgarh (2) and that in the fort at Mandawa (1). In many other places there are a handful of such pictures, with or without titles written beneath them.

3) Folk tales

In rural India, the folk hero and the historical figure are only narrowly divided. The country abounds with legends, but today their appeal has been much diminished by the rise of new figures more tangible than those of the old stories. The epoch of the film has swept away much folk drama and music. Now television is completing the destruction. Shekhawati's murals reflect another age, in which story-tellers played an important role; where travelling actors caused a major stir when they arrived in each small town. Now only the elderly pass on the tales to their fast-forgetting grandchildren. A century ago, who would not have been able to identify the Rajasthani folk heroes, Dhola and Maru, on the painted walls? Today there are few who can!

The stories are long and involved, tales of love, usually either across barriers of caste, in which case they end sadly, or in the face of more transient tribulations which the lovers win through, marry and live happily ever after. The artists usually pick out one scene to characterise the story.

Dhola-Maru is by far the most popular. Dhola is an historical figure, credited with the foundation of the Rajput kingdom of Amber/Jaipur. Both he and Maru were children of Rajput rulers and were married to each other as tiny infants. In such a situation both children would be raised in their respective family until puberty. Both forget the marriage, and Dhola's family is keen to suppress the story. The narrative tells of the adventures involved in their getting together again. The picture almost invariably chosen to illustrate the story shows the couple on a camel, fleeing from the robbers led by Umra-Sumra. As they close in, firing their muskets, Maru turns and lets fly a stream of arrows from her husband's bow. Other popular tales are Laila-Majnu (which appears in the 1620 *chhatri* of Man Singh in Amber and which is of Middle Eastern origin), Heer-Ranjha, Sassi-Punu, Binjo-Sorath and Sultan-Nehalde, each title being the names of the two lovers involved. More obscure stories sometimes appear, some of them telling of Rajput heroism, others of dedication through many rebirths. In places the tale of Jagdev and Kankali is depicted. To show his dedication to the goddess, Jagdev had his wife cut off his head and present it to her! Amongst the many stories that are identifiable, there are others which have been forgotten.

4) Historical Events and Personages

The historical events of more than two centuries provided rich material for the artists. The period extended from the last years of strong Mughal rule under the emperor, Aurangzeb, the turmoil of its 18th century decline, the rise of British power, its apogee and finally the freedom movement which evicted it.

The earliest dated portraits are those of Aurangzeb and the *seth* himself in the *chhatri* of Jogi Das Saha in Udaipur, painted in 1704. Judging by two subjects, the murals of the series of temples near Sri Madhopur may be equally early. That in Lisaria shows the Battle of Deoli fought between the Raja of Khandela and Mughal forces in 1697, whilst that in Nathusar shows a ruler labelled as Narang Shah, which is Aurangzeb. Aurangzeb died in 1707, so if the temples were painted in his lifetime we have as fairly accurate date.

A major historical event which appealed to several artists or, more probably, was ordered by their patrons, was the Battle of Maonda. This was fought in 1767 between the intruding army of Jawahir Singh of Bharatpur and the forces of Jaipur which were sent to chastise him. The two armies met at Maonda, in the east of modern Sikar district. Although Jaipur won, its losses were enormous. The battle is commemorated in murals within four *chhatris*. The most fascinating of these is in that raised at Ringus, probably over Bakshi Ram Sahai. Here many of the principal combatants are named, including Jawahir Singh, Har Sahai and Gur Sahai who, in the absence of the Raja, led the Jaipur force, and even the first European to be depicted. He is labelled as "Samru Faranghi" (Samru the Foreigner), the local name for the German mercenary Walter Reinhard. His direction of the Bharatpur infantry had much to do with the slaughter it wrought. The other three are that at Babai, erected to Lachhman Singh Rajawat who is depicted in the Ringus mural, one of three generations of his family slain that day, and that of Chand Singh, ruler of Sikar, built at the village of Ganeri and that of another Lachhman Singh near Teej Talab in Singhana.

Other episodes are shown which concern more local conflicts or unlabelled groups of Rajputs. Occasionally the characters may be recognized by their features. Thus, Sardul Singh, once seen with five sons in his *chhatri* at Parasrampura (1), with his bulging eyes, can be recognized with or without his sons in a temple nearby (2), in the *chhatri* at Tonk Chileri, and also in the temple of Sri Bihariji and one of the Shekhawat *chhatris*, both in Jhunjhunu (12 and 1).

Labelled historical paintings are always treasures, allowing one to identify figures hitherto familiar only through written accounts. Devi Singh's *chhatri* in Sikar (1), constructed in the late 1790s, contains no less than 80 panels, most of them labelled. Many show historical scenes including the ruler's meetings with other contemporary princes. There is also a view of the Gangaur procession in Jaipur, with several Europeans amongst the crowd.

The initial European interference in as far as it affected this part of India was the arrival of the mercenary during the second half of the 18th century. Such men had long been important in the infantry in an era of continual conflict and appear in several 18th century murals. Amongst these is a figure I long overlooked in the *Taknet chhatri* in Churu (8).

After Elphinstone's progress across the region in 1808 en route for Peshawar, the next major British intrusion was that of Lockett and Boileau with their entourage in 1831. Then, amongst others, came Major Alves in 1834, Forster who set up the headquarters of his Shekhawati Brigade in Jhunjhunu in 1835, and Thoresby who came partly to inspect it in 1841. Each arrived in considerable pomp. Not unnaturally they were taken as a good subject for the painters. Many mid-19th century murals show processions of British forces, most of which must refer to one or other of these parties.

Only Boileau warrants labelled portraits. There is an excellent one of him in the Raghunath Temple in Sikar (8). A full-face picture, it may well tell a story. Traditionally Indian portraits were always painted from the side, the profile. Boileau seems to have been keen to persuade local artists to adapt to full-face pictures and in one of his accounts mentions presenting a "camera lucida", which projected an image on to a screen, where it could be traced, with just this aim in view. It seems he had made a convert in Sikar. Another picture, on a haveli wall in Mahansar, shows him in conversation with a *qazi* .

Soon British power was established across the subcontinent. The forces of the Calcutta government, both Indian and British, became commonplace, often used as a horizontal frieze. Queen Victoria appears. So do her viceroys. Sometimes old murals are adjusted to accommodate, diplomatically, some imperial occasion. A few old panels on the side of a Saraogi *haveli* in Fatehpur (3) were obliterated to make way for loyal portraits of their majesties surrounded by a storm of Union Jacks. The impetus must have been the 1912 Delhi Durbar. The Marwari community, like any shrewd business group, usually keeps its politics very much in line with the climate of the day!

Some of the local dacoits, bandits, became folk heroes, earning a reputation for robbing the rich to serve the poor. One such pair were Dungarji and Jawahirji, who flourished during the second quarter of the 19th century. Dungar Singh was arrested by the British and held in Agra Jail. Jawahir Singh gathered his gang together, set out for Agra and freed him. These two occur occasionally in the paintings and there are several pictures of Dungar Singh's escape on *haveli* walls in Sardarshahr. More recent were Balji and Bhoorji, who were active until the 1930s, when they were shot near Bissau, just inside Jaipur State, by a Bikaner force which

मण्डावा विधान राभाक्षेत्र से

Mandawa: On the north side
of the main road leading west
away from the bus stand is
this fine little wall. Between
two sets of carved shutters
are the lovers Binjo and
Sorath. He plays his *veena* as
she dances.

pursued them across the frontier. They, too, sometimes appear on the walls.

Organized opposition to British rule produced the Mutiny of 1857, a display of feudal and religous indignation rather than a nationalist revolt. Although some of the local barons sent troops to aid the British, the Mutiny had little direct effect in Shekhawati. Two pictures showing sepoys being blown from the mouths of a cannon (one in the courtyard of the Gopinath Temple in Mukundgarh (2) and the other on the facade of the Thakurji Temple in Mandawa (11)) probably depict the retribution that followed the rebellion.

Imperial pictures are rare after the catastrophe of the First World War. Rajasthani troops were sent to serve, shedding their blood in Mesopotamia and on the Western Front. The Maharaja of Bikaner and his force particularly distinguished themselves. Pictures of that carnage are rare. One on a *haveli* in Sardarshahr shows mechanized warfare with lorry-loads of troops, guns and ships, whilst above them all stretches that so-alien, lowering, slate-grey sky.

In the 20th century, Congress leaders take up an increasing area of wall. Sometimes they are shown as portraits, sometimes in remarkable political tableaux. In the courtyard of a small *haveli* of the Devra family in Fatehpur, an improbable scene is portrayed. All the prominent leaders of the freedom movement stand with Mother India on a map of the subcontinent whilst George V benevolently hands them a document, which must represent Freedom. A small panel in Mandawa probably dating from the early 1940s, shows Mother India again, tricolor in hand, whilst beneath her a pathetic little Englishman, rucksack on back, is "quitting India". Gandhi and Nehru are the heroes of the final wall- paintings.

5) Everyday environment

Amongst the smaller panels, interspersed with religious and mythical themes, are illustrations of everyday life. These range from the courtly existence of the Maharaja's capital to the activities that surrounded the painter himself. These last include pictures of his caste-brothers firing pots and delivering them to market and also of the mason at his own work. Men are shown building walls, plastering them, and even applying paint with a trowel whilst a buffalo drags the heavy stone wheel around the *gharat* , grinding the mortar. Boys are busy grinding the fine plaster by hand whilst women carry up flat bowls of the stuff to the men who are applying it. Sometimes the *seth* oversees the work.

Most of the other folk in the town appear – the women at the well, that centre of their social life, the goldsmith, the carpenter, the swordsmith, the weaver, the dyer, the farmer at his plough, the water-carrier with his loaded goatskin, the *seth* or his *munim* , accountant, doing his sums, even the lowly sweeper, each at his allotted task.

There are domestic events, too, perhaps reflecting dramas in the artist's own household. These include paintings of childbirth in Mandawa (4 and 18) and frequent excerpts from the rituals pertaining to marriage. The *baraat* , the procession of the groom to the bride's house, is the most common. Others show the bride and the groom walking with their scarves tied together, or the return of the groom's party homeward, his bride concealed in the closed *dholi* , a sort of sedan chair.

The world that the mason inhabited was not one of unbroken labour. At regular intervals there were festivals. He included some of these on the walls. Perhaps an event in one of the great local families would involve much of the local community. Take the marriage procession of some rich *seth* 's son – that could be an immense occasion, an opportunity for the family to display the extent of its affluence. Such a *baraat* would make an excellent horizontal frieze later.

The most popular and all-disrupting festival then, as now, was the Spring celebration of

Holi. It is often depicted in Indian art and, not surprisingly, is included on the walls. Krishna may be shown; playing Holi with the gopis, all pelting each other with red powder. Sometimes they are shown in a dance called *gindar* , dancing in a circle, each clicking sticks with his neighbour. The *daph* appears, too, a type of drum which is characteristic of Holi in this part of the world. It consists of a deep hoop of wood some 60 cm in diameter, with parchment stretched across it, resembling nothing so much as a large tambourine.

Other festivities are recorded, of which the Rajasthani Gangaur is most common. This follows closely on Holi and is a women's day, when effigies of Gauri and her consort, Iser, are carried in procession by the womenfolk to be married at a temple and finally immersed in a tank or well. This procession, too, may be used as a long horizontal frieze, being particularly popular in Nawalgarh.

Another Rajasthani festival is Teej, which takes place during the monsoon. The women play on swings, which they hang from any suitable bough. If pictures of swinging women usually relate to this occasion, those of men flying kites refer to Makar Sankranti, a day of kite-flying in mid-January. Less widespread are illustrations of annual fairs in local villages and holy places. One such, at the holy spring of Lohargal, is sometimes shown.

6) Animals and plants

Domestic animals played a major role in the life of the local people. Many folk still living remember a time when almost all transport was by camel. The elephant was a symbol of power and wisdom on which the great travelled. As for the horse, Shekhawati was famous for its excellent cavalry troops. Naturally, all these animals occur repeatedly in the murals. Others owe their presence to a special significance, such as the religious role of the cow, or the reputation of the parrot as a messenger of love. Some are the prey of hunters – lions, tigers, deer, boar, and even hares are often shown in scenes of the chase. The tiger and the lion may well turn on their pursuers, and combat between man and beast is a common subject. The peacock, holy, ubiquitous and spectacular, is to be seen on every wall. The most familiar domestic bird to be shown is not the chicken, as one might expect, but the falcon perched on a hunter's wrist.

Some beasts appear by virtue of their oddity. The rhinoceros, which is shown in several late 19th century pictures in Ramgarh, makes its debut in a very early painting in the battered temple at Jagmalpura, near Sikar. A dated couplet places the picture in 1684. A giraffe suddenly features on several *havelis* in the mid-19th century and must be the same beast that the Maharaja of Jaipur purchased in 1849. The painters had certainly had an opportunity to see either it or its likeness!

Sometimes animals are used more for decoration than for their actual appearance. The fish, not common in Shekhawati, became a popular feature of designs in Ramgarh. It is shown on a number of mid-19th century buildings there, sometimes in composite circles and sometimes so oddly bird-like that it takes a mason to assure one that it is intended to be a fish! One particularly spectacular mammal, much loved by Indian painters, is the Blackbuck. The male has long spiralled horns and the black of its back and sides contrasts sharply with a white belly. It is possible to see it wild at a small sanctuary at Chhapur, in Churu district. It is common, particularly in the earlier murals. Appearing first in the 1620 *chhatri* at Amber, it must be included in almost all 18th century Shekhawati paintings. It is invariably present in certain Ragamala pictures.

Flowers and plants form the basis of much of the ground design on the walls. Sometimes, reproduced geometrically, they can become very effective subjects within the panels, the

Below:
Nawalgarh: High on a wall of a little house south of the Goenka Haveli (18) is this erotic gem. While one man is fully occupied with the donkey (identified in the writing as female) a man of the potter caste, like many of the painters, comes to spank him with his shoe. (c1900).

Above:
Mandawa (18): Erotic pictures are generally seen on the outer walls of houses, but neatly placed so that they are easily overlooked. This *haveli* was particularly rich in erotica, but some pictures have recently been obliterated. This couple, characteristically half-clothed, perform under the projecting eaves on the facade of Gulab Rai Ladia's *haveli* (c1890).

chhatri of Jali Ram Poddar in Churu (near 19) containing good examples.

7) Erotica

A rich aspect of life is the erotic. Neither painters nor patrons were averse to displaying it during the 19th century. Erotic themes occur frequently on the outer walls of havelis and sometimes also in their bedrooms. They may occasionally appear even in *chhatris* and temples.

Sometimes a woman is shown displaying herself partly or wholly naked. Sometimes the pictures are more perverse. But the 20th century has seen a puritan backlash. A panel of both men and women indulging in bestiality on the south wall of the Gulab Rai Ladi Haveli in Mandawa (18) was torn off the wall in 1984. It is only one of many erotic paintings to suffer a similar fate in recent years.

By far the most common are discreet panels secreted somewhere on a wall above the street showing a couple making love. The local youth generally know just where they are! Most people overlook the erotica, so neatly are they placed. On the east wall of a Choudhary *haveli* in Fatehpur (5) there are a multitude of pictures. One, partly obscured by mud, shows the figure of a standing woman. Look carefully, and behind her is a donkey. On her left side its head projects, to be caressed by a man whose name is written above. To her right, its backside appears and receives very different attention from another man. He, too, is labelled, obscenely in mirror-writing! In another similar scene, high on the wall of a little *haveli* in Nawalgarh (not far south of 18), a man is shown about to spank the donkey's lover with his slipper. Perhaps the righteous fellow represents the painter himself, since he is labelled as a Kumhar, or potter.

There is a most amusing juxtaposition in the master-bedroom of the small *haveli* of Shiv Narayan Nemani in Churi Ajitgarh (1). This building was decorated in 1898 and someone selected suitable subjects for the bedroom – sex and royals! So, interspersed with the most explicit erotica are pictures of the British royal family, including Queen Victoria and Princess Alexandra. They are trying not to look! Unfortunately, this building is usually locked. In that same room there is an unusual painting of a naked couple making love. Generally, the partners are shown half- clothed, reflecting the real state of affairs in a society where there is little privacy.

Some paintings are jokes, appearing to be erotic when they are not. There is a good example on an outer wall in Nawalgarh (just north of 31). A man, standing, has both his hands to his crotch. He glances slyly at the viewer. He is holding out his .... no, it is just his finger!

8) Maps and Places

Amongst the most interesting murals are a handful which show towns, using a fascinating perspective that distorts reality to produce an accurate map as well as pictures of each individual building. These proved useful during our survey work, for once the picture itself could be dated it helped to place chronologically some of the buildings portrayed.

Three such murals are outstanding. Two are in Nawalgarh (1 & 8) showing views of that town. That in the Bala Qila, the main fort, is painted on the ceiling of an ill-lit bastion which is generally locked, the key being hard to come by. It is worth taking some effort, and a torch, since it also contains a very fine map-picture of Jaipur. The third is in the Sheesh Mahal of the palace in Sikar (5). It is full of little details of the everyday life of the town as it might have appeared in 1864, the year it was painted.

There are several map-pictures of Jaipur apart from that in the Bala Qila. A small one is on the ceiling of the Gopinath Temple in Sikar and must date from about 1850. In a *chhatri* to the north of Bowri Gate in Nawalgarh, another remains unfinished, the outlines sketched on the plaster. It is not alone; an unfinished Jaipur painting can also be seen on the walls of the Bakhtawar Mahal in Khetri (2).

Buildings and views of places inside and far outside Shekhawati turn up on walls from time to time. On the ceiling of the Shani Temple in Ramgarh (10) there are scenes of the annual pilgrimage to Lohargal, a local holy place. The pilgrims are shown visiting the *bowri* and the tank at the shrine. Other pilgrimages appear, particularly that to Badrinath, in the Himalayas, the earliest of which is in the Gopinath Temple in Sri Madhopur (c1770).

Buildings of Jaipur feature in some places. Most popular is Ishwar Lath, the tall minaret in the centre of the city, but Tripolia Gate and the city palace also appear. Local forts may attract the artist. There are several reflections of Mandawa fort on the *havelis* in that town.

In the 20th century, many improbable foreign views are depicted, copied from prints. Not least of these are various paintings of Venice by Balu Ram in Mandawa (10), a Tower of London and views of Calcutta on *havelis* in Lakshmangarh and several Muslim holy places in the Dargah of Faza Nazimuddin Suleimani in Fatehpur (25).

9) The Foreigners and their Contraptions

From the time of the inclusion of Walter Reinhard in the Ringus chhatri (c1770) until the middle of the following century, Europeans feature as military men, with or without supporting troops. In the middle of the 19th century the first of their alien machines start to appear, beginning significantly with boats. A paddle steamer in the courtyard of a Saraogi *haveli* in Fatehpur (3) is probably based on those carrying merchandise up and down the Ganges. In Ramgarh there are several sailing vessels in pictures of the holy man, Dadu Dayal, in the Poddar *chhatris* (2). Usually the painter is familiar enough with the subject to include a member of the crew surveying the scene with a telescope. Was he inspired by a print ?

The railway first reached India in the 1850s, but the earliest picture to include a train is dated 1872 and shows a long-funnelled locomotive. Before long it was to become a very popular subject, the ideal frieze to divide a wall horizontally. Occasionally there are erotic scenes in one of the carriages!

By the close of the 19th century, foreigners and their contraptions took a major role among the subjects – bicycles, cars, manned balloons and aeroplanes intermingling with camels and elephants. There are unveiled European women, with or without hats, children in prams and even, on a Churu wall (north of 3), a group of girls playing netball. The Latin script is put in where it seems appropriate, but that does not indicate any mastery of the tongue. The artist who copied the words "Made in Germany" took it either from his tin of paint or from some print he had. The word "Germany" occurs in several paintings where some "English" has been thought necessary. It is no coincidence that that nation was the major producer of cheap coloured prints as well as dyes and paints.

A regular supply of coloured prints reached the region through the merchants who handled imported cotton goods. The mills of Manchester and the Vale of Leven were in fierce competition for the Indian market. Especially in demand was dyed "Turkey Red" cotton piece goods. In order to gain the edge on their competitors some companies started to produce beautiful coloured picture-labels, often illustrating Hindu mythological scenes. These seem to have been designed in Calcutta but printed in Britain. Some of the best turn-of-the-century labels were printed by F. Steiner and Co. of Manchester, Wm. Stirling and Sons of Glasgow, and the importers Finlay Muir and Co. of Calcutta and Bombay. The merchants liked them, as

Opposite page:
Bissau (8): Like most of the foreigners shown in the murals, this man is probably a soldier. He relaxes rather uncomfortably on a cane stool with his pet bird on one hand. Interior of Ramlal Jainarayan Tibrewala Haveli. (c1890).

Left, top:
Sikar (5): It was well-known that both sexes of Europeans drank and they are often depicted bottle in hand. While this lady grasps her bottle and glass her little boy plays the concertina. His earrings are a local touch. A panel on the ceiling of the Chini Mahal. (1861).

Left, bottom:
Raghunath Temple, Sikar (8): Lieutenant Boileau is the only British official of the early 19th century to earn a named portrait. He came to Shekhawati in 1831 and 1835, leaving accounts of both visits. In Bikaner he gave the court artist a camera lucida to help him to paint full-face portraits like this one of himself. His short hair and lack of headgear would have struck the painter as odd but it is unlikely that he wore earstuds! (c1840).

The Guide

In this section I have picked out a selection of the best buildings, most of them painted, in each town. I have further marked a handful of buildings in the larger towns which strike me as being the most impressive for those who are not able to visit everything!

The numbers within brackets which occur throughout the text indicate the position of a monument in the list for that town; for example, Churu (5) refers to the fifth building listed for Churu, thus the Kanhaiyalal Bagla Haveli.

Almost all the buildings listed are under private ownership, many of them private houses. Naturally, the owners or tenants are under no obligation to allow access. The fact that this is rarely refused is greatly to their credit. Nowadays, some householders charge a nominal entry fee, which should encourage them to value their murals. It is normal practice to put a few coins in the shrine of a temple. Footwear is usually removed not only when entering a temple or mosque but also the inner courtyard of *a haveli*. The names given for *havelis* generally denote the merchant who built the house. The first names are often little known outside the family and therefore not very useful in locating a building. The last name is more helpful – except in Ramgarh, where most houses were built by a Poddar!

Following pages:
Churu (5): One of the best friezes in the region decorates this south wall of the Kanhaiyalal Bagla Haveli. It shows a procession with episodes from two folk tales, 'Sassi-Punu' and 'Dhola-Maru', at its centre. (c1880).

Hotels And Travel

Most visitors will approach Shekhawati from either Delhi or Jaipur. There is regular public transport from both directions and fairly good metalled roads serve most of the painted towns.

From Delhi:

Public transport: Personally, I prefer the train. There are connections to Jhunjhunu, Nawalgarh, Dundlod and Sikar from Delhi (not New Delhi) station. Churu and Ratangarh are on the main line from Delhi to Jodhpur and to Bikaner. I used to take the Bikaner Express (for years it has left Delhi sometime after 08.00 to reach Churu before 15.00) since it provides a chance of seeing the countryside gradually transform from rich farmland to desert. Change at Churu for the little train to Bissau, Mahansar, Ramgarh, Fatehpur, Lakshmangarh and Sikar, although the bus would be more convenient. Bus services ply to all the towns of Shekhawati, leaving from the Inter State Bus Terminal at Kashmiri Gate, north of the old city of Delhi. Best served are Khetri, Pilani, Jhunjhunu, Sikar and Churu and the towns that fall along those routes. Allow five to six hours for the journey. Check with the tourist office in Jan Path, New Delhi, for the latest timetables.

If you have a car there are two straightforward routes:

1) Via Loharu (once the seat of a Muslim ruler), entering Rajasthan near Pilani, then passing Narhad, Chirawa (the first extensively-painted town on this route and worth a visit), Bagad and Jhunjhunu (here, on the by-pass, is a pleasant halt, 'Midway Jamuna', for cold drinks, beer and snacks) to points beyond. Distance: Delhi to Jhunjhunu 215 km.

2) Via Narnaul (also once a Muslim capital), passing near Khetri (a diversion and the stiff climb to the fort above the town could be a rewarding break in the drive) and Singhana to join the above route at Chirawa. There is little difference in the length of these routes.

From Jaipur:

Public transport: There are several daily trains to Sikar, where the line branches to Churu and Bikaner via Lakshmangarh, Fatehpur, Ramgarh, Mahansar and Bissau or to Jhunjhunu and Loharu, via Nawalgarh, Dundlod and Mukundgarh. Buses from the main terminal at Sindhi Camp are faster and more regular, serving all the towns of Shekhawati. Most frequent are those to the district towns of Churu, Jhunjhunu and Sikar. Allow two and a half hours for the journey from Jaipur to Sikar.

By car there are two routes into Shekhawati from Jaipur:

1) The usual route is via Sikar. on the highway to Bikaner. Some 35 km out of Jaipur the road passes Chomu, where a diversion to Samode, with its palace-hotel, is worthwhile. The palace offers good accommodation at the dearer end of the market; it also contains some fine murals. (Reservations: Samode House, Gangapole, Jaipur 302002. Tel. 42407). Ringus, about halfway to Sikar, with its *chhatri* on the southwest fringe of the town containing a mural of the Battle of Maonda, is of interest to the specialist. Distance: Jaipur to Sikar 115 km.

2) Another road enters the region via Udaipurwati to Jhunjhunu. It parts from route 1 at Ringus and passes through Sri Madhopur. There, the fine painted Gopinath Temple is worth a visit. (A diversion eastwards to see the early 18th century murals in temples at Bagriawas, Nathusar and Lisaria is again for the specialist.) The road skirts Khandela (an attractive town amongst the hills, with two forts but few murals) and passes beneath the

hill-top fort at Kotri to Udaipurwati, Gudha, Barragaon and Jhunjhunu. Udaipurwati is only 27 km from Nawalgarh, but the first part of the road is not yet metalled and is passable only for four-wheel drive vehicles. Distance: Jaipur to Jhunjhunu 170 km.

For travellers using Shekhawati as a first step on a tour of Rajasthan the best onwards routes are to either Bikaner or Jodhpur.

Bikaner:

Public transport: Two main trains connect this city with Delhi via Churu. These are the Bikaner Mail and the Bikaner Express. Another runs between Bikaner and Jaipur, via Churu and Sikar. Regular buses connect the city with Churu, Jhunjhunu and Sikar and towns along those routes.

By car: The route from Sikar, Lakshmangarh and Fatehpur follows the main Agra-Bikaner highway. It joins the road from Churu at Ratangarh. Here there is a Rajasthan government establishment, "Midway Chinkara", which offers snacks, cold drinks and beer. Distances: Sikar to Ratangarh - 93 km; Churu to Ratangarh - 50 km; Ratangarh to Bikaner - 130 km.

Jodhpur:

Public transport: There are two direct trains between Jodhpur and Churu, via Ratangarh. The best is the Jodhpur Mail, but it leaves Churu at an unearthly hour in the morning! Bus services connect Churu, Jhunjhunu and Sikar (and towns along these routes) with Jodhpur.

By car: A good route to take is via Nagaur, an interesting old town with a handsome fort, its palaces containing excellent murals. The road from Churu passes through Ratangarh and Sujangarh to Didwana, where it meets the road from Sikar. Distances: Churu to Jodhpur - 384 km; Sikar to Jodhpur - 320 km.

Where To Stay And Where To Go:

To do it justice, Shekhawati warrants several days of a Rajasthan tour. At the time of writing there are seven towns in the region which can offer good-quality accommodation to tourists, and several new projects are planned. I have listed them alphabetically. All these hotels cater for the dearer end of the market. I have recommended three, one expensive, one less so and one moderate. If you are less particular, moderate accommodation is available in hotels near the railway stations of Sikar and Churu and near the bus stand at Jhunjhunu. There are government bungalows in Churu, Jhunjhunu, Sikar and Pilani. Elsewhere, if you are hardy and have a sleeping bag there is usually a *dharamshala* (see Chapter 4) nearby.

The latest information on tourist facilities in Shekhawati should be obtainable from the Government of Rajasthan Tourist Office in Jaipur, and also that at Hotel Shiv Shekhawati (see below) in Jhunjhunu.

Bagad:

Until Independence, the headquarters of a Muslim Pathan clan. Apart from the 19th century family house there is little trace of its passing. Bagad has proximity to Delhi to recommend it. A quiet, small town with few painted buildings, a fine joharo and a Muslim saint's tomb, its hotel will have to offer very good facilities to compete with others better situated .

The hotel occupies one of the town's large 1920s havelis . It is aimed at the upper end of the market. There are six rooms and, like most business-caste households it serves only vegetarian, food.

Itineraries from Bagad. Much as they would be from Jhunjhunu, allowing for the fact that Bagad is 14 km further from the important towns.

Dundlod:

Accessible by train and bus from Delhi and Jaipur. This is a quiet, attractive little place gathered around the fort and set back from the main road. Too small to be among the richest towns, it nevertheless has a collection of painted buildings. It is well-situated for visits to other towns in the area.

Dera Dundlod Kila:

This hotel is housed in the 18th century fort which dominates the town. It is run by Raghuvendra Singh, grandson of the last ruling Thakur, Harnath Singh, who wrote a history of the local Rajputs. There are 10 double rooms with attached bathrooms, and both vegetarian and non-vegetarian food is available. The prices are similar to those charged in Nawalgarh's Roop Niwas Palace, considerably less than Mandawa's Hotel Castle.

Reservations: Dundlod House, Civil Lines, Jaipur 302006. Cable - Dera Hotel. Telephones - Jaipur 66276 and Dundlod 98 and 68.

Itineraries from Dundlod: Having looked at the town, two others close by are worth a visit – Mukundgarh (4 km) and Churi Ajitgarh (a further 5 km). The most rewarding trips would be either to Nawalgarh (7 km), with its wealth of painted *havelis*, or to Mandawa (18 km) and on to Fatehpur (19 km) and Lakshmangarh (20 km), returning to Dundlod (25 km) via Mukundgarh. Another possibility after Mandawa is Jhunjhunu (24 km) and back to Dundlod (32 km).

Fatehpur:

Served by direct bus and train services from Jaipur. Until 1731 the capital of a Muslim dynasty of nawabs which left several monuments to its passing. The town contains some fine painted buildings and is particularly convenient for those travelling by road between Bikaner and Jaipur.

Hotel Haveli:

A small hotel built by the Rajasthan Tourism Development Corporation and only recently opened. There are 8 double rooms with attached bathrooms and also a 6-bed dormitory for the budget tourist. Vegetarian, non-vegetarian meals and snacks are available; also beer. The prices compare very favourably with those of the hotels in Mandawa. The hotel stands near the junction of the Bikaner-Jaipur highway and the road into Fatehpur from the south. It is on the west side of the road into the town, opposite a johara (19).

Reservations: Through the Rajasthan Tourism Devp Corp in Jaipur.

Itineraries from Fatehpur: The town is well-positioned for visits to Ramgarh (20 km), then Ratannagar (5 km) and Churu (10 km) to the north, or to Lakshmangarh (20 km) followed by Sikar (28 km) to the south. Another possible trip would be to Ramgarh (20 km), Mahansar (6 km), Bissau (6 km) and then continue to Jhunjhunu (38 km) for the night or return via Churu to Fatehpur (42 km). Other outings could take in Mandawa (20 km) and Jhunjhunu (24 km) with lunch at 'Midway Jamuna' or via Mandawa and the little towns beyond to Nawalgarh for lunch.

Jhunjhunu:

Once the capital for those Rajputs descended from Sardul Singh, this town is now a district headquarters. As such it is easily accessible, with rail connections to Delhi and Jaipur and regular buses to Delhi, Jaipur, Jodhpur and Bikaner. At present, the only tourist office in Shekhawati is situated in Hotel Shiv Shekhawati. As the highway from Delhi turns to avoid the town it ascends a hill. On top of this is a private establishment 'Midway Jamuna', serving hot and cold drinks, beer and snacks including eggs. It is under the same management as nearby Hotel Shiv Shekhawati.

Hotel Shiv Shekhawati:

Recommended. This is situated just off the by-pass that skirts the town. If you are travelling by bus or car ask for Khemi Sati Temple before you reach the town – the hotel is very close to it. From the railway or bus station take a scooter rickshaw or a horse-drawn *tonga*. This is a modern building with a courtyard shaded by a vine and a pleasant garden. The rooms are clean and well-maintained, the atmosphere friendly. It has a licence to sell alcoholic drinks and serves vegetarian food and eggs. This, along with the Tourist Pension at Nawalgarh, is the cheapest of the hotels listed.

Reservations: Hotel Shiv Shekhawati, near Muni Ashram, Jhunjhunu, Rajasthan 333001. Telephone - Jhunjhunu 2651. Cable - Shivotel.

Itineraries from Jhunjhunu: The town itself is very interesting, but it is also well-situated for sorties in all directions. A round trip could take in Mandawa (24 km) and from there either past Taen to Bissau (24 km) and Mahansar (6 km) then back to Jhunjhunu (44 km), or from Mandawa to Nawalgarh (25 km) with a look at Churi Ajitgarh, Mukundargh and Dundlod, returning on the main road to Jhunjhunu (39 km). Perhaps you could hire a jeep to make another round trip to Alsisar (23 km), Malsisar (5 km) and then along the desert track to Gangiyasar (16 km) and Bissau (7 km), returning directly to Jhunjhunu (38 km). Not so rich in murals would be a foray to Bagad (14 km), Chirawa (16 km), then either to Pilani (14 km) or to Singhana (30 km) and Khetri (12 km).

Mandawa:

A charming little town, it is situated right in the centre of the painted region and has become the hub of tourism through Shekhawati. Although there is no rail link, there are direct bus services from Delhi and Jaipur. There are some fine painted *havelis*, and the impressive fort, its ownership divided between the families of two erstwhile rulers, houses a hotel.

Hotel Castle Mandawa:

Recommended. The eastern portion of the fort belongs to Thakur Jai Singh, who succeeded to the title in 1923. His grandson, Keshri Singh, runs this portion as the largest hotel in Shekhawati. Like most of the forts this has expanded over the years to meet the requirements of the family, so that its apartments vary in age. Some of the older rooms contain excellent murals sadly in need of repair. There is a good view from the terrace over the little town to the desert beyond. An interesting museum displays a variety of family treasures including the ceremonial robes of a previous generation. Both vegetarian and non-vegetarian food are available. All 35 rooms have attached bathrooms. This is the most expensive hotel in the region, relying on its situation. It is also the most popular. You will find the manager, Arvind Sharma (who published the first edition of this book) both knowledgeable and helpful.

The owner of the western section of the fort has handed the franchise to one of India's largest hotel chains, but nothing has yet been done to develop this section. There is a little painted room, with a sketch of the fort as it was at the turn of the century, its courtyard divided by a wall. There is a fine view from the turrets. The telephone number of this section of the fort is Mandawa 23.

Desert Camp:

This is basically under the same management. Situated 2 km from the town on the road to

Nawalgarh it consists of a collection of 14 tourist chalets with all amenities. The tariff is the same as in the hotel.

Reservations: Mandawa House, Sansar Chandra Road, Jaipur 302001. Telephone - Jaipur 75358, Mandawa 24. Telex - 365 2342 CMDW IN.

Hotel Rath:

This new hotel was planned with no understanding of the market. With a tariff similar to that of Hotel Castle it was naturally quite overshadowed and seemed doomed. Now, under new management, it is attracting more custom. It stands beyond the eastern fringes of the town on the Dhigal Road, surrounded by an arid landscape. There are 25 good rooms with attached bathrooms. Vegetarian and non-vegetarian food is available. The prices are now more competitive.

Reservations: Hotel Rath Mandawa, Dhigal Road, Mandawa, Jhunjhunu District, Rajasthan 333704. Telephone - Mandawa 40 or 59.

Itineraries from Mandawa: Don't go anywhere before seeing the town itself – it has some beautiful *havelis*. The best round trip for a very full day would be to Fatehpur (19 km), Ramgarh (20 km) (there is a sandy track – jeepable – between Ramgarh and Mandawa), Mahansar (6 km), Bissau (6 km) and back to Mandawa (24 km) via Taen. Alternatively, you could spend a day visiting Fatehpur (19 km) then Lakshmangarh (20 km), perhaps returning via Mukundgarh (21 km) to Mandawa (14 km). A sortie to Nawalgarh (25 km) could be broken to visit Churi Ajitgarh, Mukundgarh and Dundlod. Another trip could take in Bissau (24 km), Mahansar (6 km), Jhunjhunu (44 km) and back to Mandawa (24 km). Churu could be added to the Ramgarh itinerary.

Mukundgarh:

Accessible from Delhi and Jaipur by train and bus. Amongst the smaller Shekhawati towns. It has a few painted havelis, some handsome wells and centres on a temple. Well situated to explore the region.

Mukandgarh Fort Hotel:

Large a turn-of-century building recently converted into a hotel. It aims at the upper end of the market, offering 46 rooms (5 single, 25 double and 16 suites) with both vegetarian and non-vegetarian food. Further information: Cross Country Hotels Ltd., 45 Community Centre 11 floor, Basant Lok Complex, Vasant Vihar, New Delhi 110057. Tel/Fax 6885344. Itineraries from Mukundgarh are similar to those listed for Dundlod, only 4 km away.

Nawalgarh:

Although Ramgarh can lay claim to the highest number of painted buildings in Shekhawati, Nawalgarh, which runs it a close second, has the better selection. A busy market town set back from the main road, Nawalgarh has direct rail links with Delhi and Jaipur. There are also regular bus services with both cities and with the neighbouring painted towns.

Roop Niwas Palace:

Recommended. A large country house with an attractive garden situated about 1 km east of the town in peaceful surroundings. This is the home of the Rawal Sahib of Nawalgarh, Madan Singh. Brother of Thakur Jai Singh of Mandawa, he succeeded to the estate by adoption in 1928. There are 21 pleasant rooms, all with attached bathrooms. Good quality vegetarian and non-vegetarian food are available. Pricewise Roop Niwas Palace, along with Dera Dundlod Kila, comes well below Castle Mandawa, but well above either Hotel Shiv Shekhawati or

Tourist Pension (see below). It is well worth the price.

Reservations: Roop Niwas Palace, Nawalgarh, Jhunjhunu District, Rajasthan. Telephone - Nawalgarh 8.

Tourist Pension:

A pleasant, clean and friendly establishment, more modest than its rivals, it is aimed at the budget tourist. Situated near Maur Hospital in the western part of the town, it is run by Ramesh Jangid, who speaks German as well as English. He arranges jeep trips and treks both within Shekhawati and in other parts of Rajasthan. There are five double rooms, all with attached bathrooms. The cheapest good-quality accommodation currently available in Shekhawati, it tends to be in demand!

Reservations: Ramesh Jangid, Hotel Tourist Pension, near Maur Hospital, Nawalgarh, Jhunjhunu District, Rajasthan. Telephone - Nawalgarh 129. Cable - Kapitaen.

Itineraries from Nawalgarh: The best round trip is to Mandawa (24 km), Fatehpur (19 km), Lakshmangarh (20 km) and back to Nawalgarh (32 km) by Mukundgarh, but it is rather a long outing. Less ambitious would be a visit to the three small neighbouring towns of Dundlod   (7 km), Mukundgarh (4 km) and Churi Ajitgarh (5 km) then on to Mandawa (9 km). Alternatively, Lakshmangarh (32 km) via Mukundgarh, Sikar (28 km) and back to Nawalgarh (29 km). If you want to escape from the standard painted towns why not visit Parasrampura (15 km), and then, if you have four-wheel drive transport, go on to Udaipurawati (12 km). From there you can visit one of the three little holy springs set amongst the hills, Shakambari (16 km), Kirori (6 km) and Lohargal (15 km). The last of these is the most impressive, with its spring-fed tank nestling beneath the rugged hillside. Nearby, Raghunathgarh, walled off in the head of a valley, is worth a look. There the stone elements of many Shekhawati buildings were, and are, shaped. High above, on the summit of the hills, is the most formidable of the local forts – but it is a stiff climb!

The Towns And Their Buildings

Alisisar

Samrath Singh, grandson of Kishan Singh, the second of those five sons of Sardul Singh, settled here in 1783. He founded the fort that year. Most of the buildings in the towns are made from *dhandhala*, the coarse grey hardpan. A characteristic of the red and blue paintings of Alsisar and neighbouring Malsisar is that the frame surrounding figurative panels is often of solid colour, unbroken by any floral designs. The town is about 25 km north of Jhunjhunu.

1) *The Fort.* Standing on a slight eminence at the western edge of the village, it is now derelict and in a state of collapse. It contains only traces of painting.

2) *Srilal Bahadurmalka Well.* A beautiful well with four *chhatris*, standing on the south-east side of the bus-stand. It was built in 1846. There are some good murals in the domes.

3) *Haveli of Harmukhrai Ramjasrai Tulsian.* A handsome little *haveli* built around 1850. The paintings are in ochres and of good quality, illustrating religious subjects and Rajputs. This building is generally locked. It stands about 30 m north of the west end of the bazaar, on the east side of the track.

4) *Temple of Lakshminath* (the Lord of Lakshmi, thus Vishnu her consort). A fine temple with little painting. It is situated about 40 m west of the bus-stand, a little to the north of the bazaar. Built by the Bahadurmalka family 1859-61.

5) *Temple of Satyanarayan.* Copies the architecture of the previous one, which is only 40 m to the south. The murals are not of very good quality but there is some attractive mirrorwork near the shrine. Built by Janki Das Kejariwal around 1875.

6) *Haveli of Jhabarmal Jhunjhunuwala.* A handsome *haveli* with good murals on outer and inner walls. There are two painted rooms, one of which was damaged by lightning a few years ago. In the north room subjects include the marriage procession of Rama and folk stories such as Binjo-Sorath, Dhola-Maru, Heer-Ranjha and Laila-Majnu. Built in 1877, it stands south of the bazaar a little to the east-south-east of the post office.

7) *Haveli of Madanlal Bahadurmalka.* Built around 1855, it is a good example of a single-courtyard *haveli* of that era. The open arches on the facade above the door are typical. Subjects on the south wall include Buddha, a snake charmer and jugglers. The footings of the building have been severely damaged by rising damp. It stands about 60 m north-west of the Satyanarayan Temple (5).

8) *Haveli of Tejpal Jhunjhunuwala.* Built in 1875, this is a good example of a *haveli* with both forecourt and courtyard. The building is locked but the key is available nearby. Some of the locked rooms are said to be painted. It is about 50 m south-south-west of the Lakshminath Temple (4).

9) *Johara* (sunken reservoir). Built by Mangalchand Marodia around 1865. It is situated on the northern fringe of the town and is generally dry. There is an enclosed section where the women would bathe.

Bagad

This town formerly had some importance locally as headquarters of the Muslim Nagad Pathans from 1456 until Independence. Several other small towns, including Ked and Narhad, fell under their sway. In the 1730s, when the Shekhawat Rajputs took over Jhunjhunu, their rule came to an end. They seem to have maintained cordial relations however, and the Nawab and his descendants remained in the town until Partition. The family then migrated to Pakistan, but their sadness is recorded in some very faint graffiti in pencil on the walls of their house. There were once some impressive and solid Muslim houses in the town. Their remains are still to be seen. There is no fort or town wall, but traces of earthworks on the western edge of the town probably indicate defences.

Bagad contains a number of large 20th century havelis, one of which has been opened as an up-market hotel.

1) *Fateh Sagar*. A *johara*, reservoir, built by a Brahmin, Fateh Chand Ojha, in 1877. It is a good example of its genre, with a ramp for cattle and an enclosed bath for women at its northern side. There is a little painting in the decorative *chhatris*. This tank is at the western edge of the town, not far north of the main road from Jhunjhunu to Chirawa.

2) *Pathanon ka Mahal* – (The Pathans' Palace). The present building was largely constructed by Taj Khan in the 1820s. The south-east corner is far older, probably dating from the 17th century, and contains traces of painting. Here the descendants of the Nawabs lived. When they finally left the town for Pakistan in 1947 they sold it to a local merchant. He intended it for a *dharamshala*, but it is rarely used. Several years ago one member of the Pathan family, returning on a visit from Pakistan, stayed here briefly. Did he see ghosts?

Bissau

On the partition of Sardul Singh's estate, this area came to his fifth and youngest son, Keshri Singh. In 1746 he founded Bissau on the site of a small village. He constructed the fort, gave land to the Banias for a bazaar (the northern part of the present market) in 1755 and completed a town wall in 1762. Of this wall little remains, although the western gate still stands. He encouraged the merchant community to settle in the town and they, in turn, brought prosperity.

Then came his grandson, Shyam Singh, whose name recurs in this book. He became Thakur in 1787 and succeeded in bringing notoriety to the town. Short of funds, he extorted almost two million rupees from the local merchants, who promptly left, taking business with them. He then became the focus of the dacoits of the region, organising raids, especially across the border into Bikaner State. One such foray almost led to a British invasion in 1812, for they thought, mistakenly, that it had been inside their territory. The merchants who had been robbed were sent with an escort to confront the Thakur. They met him in the fort. While he politely denied all involvement in the affair they were able to recognize their own stolen camels amongst those in the courtyard! He kept a small army, which included two French mercenaries as officers. One was sent with troops in 1809 to aid Ranjit Singh of the Punjab. The other lies in an unmarked grave in the town. When Colonel Lockett came in 1831, the town was utterly run-down and the merchants gone.

There is a local story about the arrival of the Shekhawati Brigade here. Convinced that this was a nest of robbers, they had come to slight the fort. Before they arrived, the Qazi, the Thakur's adviser, asked a merchant how they might prevent the destruction. He suggested that all the people should be ordered to appear in their finest clothes and richest jewellery. This they did. When the army arrived the Qazi pointed to the inhabitants and said: "You tell me that we are robbers and the town ruined. Look about you at the prosperity and confidence of the townsfolk." The British went away and the fort remained.

In actual fact, Shyam Singh died in 1833, two years before the Brigade was raised, and his heir, Hammir Singh, had favourably impressed Lockett. He brought the merchants back and set the town on the path to recovery.

Bissau is an attractive little town, rich in painted *havelis*. Dunes enclose it to the north and west. For 10 days in October, prior to the festival of Dassehra, the story of the *Ramayana* is acted out in the bazaar at twilight. This unique performance was started by a *sadhvi*, a woman ascetic, about 1880. She used local children as actors and made *papier mache* masks for them. The tradition continues, centered on a small *haveli* where masks and costumes are made and stored.

1) *Keshargarh*: The fort built by Keshri Singh from 1751 to 1755. The interior buildings owe much to later Thakurs. The handsome residential bastion on the western side is known as Hazari Burj. There are no murals but the view from the roof over the town and the desert beyond is good. The last Thakur sold the fort and it now houses a Bania family.

2) *Sarkari Chhatri*. The memorial of Hammir Singh, said to have been built by his concubine in about 1875. This *chhatri*, the best in the town, has paintings on its basement walls. There is a procession with a cannon and also guns mounted on camels, a man repairs shoes and a woman grinds flour. It stands beside the bus station.

3) *Kamra*. This is a little pavilion some 60 m west of Sarkari Chhatri (2). It was built as a *baithak* for entertaining guests etc. by a merchant of the Tibrewala family around 1900.

There are some paintings, including a few panels in the rooms. The wreckage of part of the town wall lies close to the north wall of this building.

4) *Jainarayan Gopiram Tibrewala Haveli.* A fine, heavily painted *haveli* dating from around 1885. At the north end of the facade, pictures include Laila and Majnu, Prithu Avatar of Vishnu milking a cow, and the goddess Ganga – the Ganges. It stands on the corner north-west of Sarkari Chhatri (2).

5) *Motiram Jasraj Sigtia Haveli.* Both the architecture and the murals of this *haveli* are good. There are several painted rooms, in one of which a man is shown tying his turban with the aid of a mirror whilst another does exercises. On the north wall Laila and Majnu are shown above the small window nearest the gate. Lower down, between the brackets, is an erotic version of the popular story of Krishna stealing the *gopis'* clothes whilst they bathe. Some 50 m east of the Tibrewala *haveli* (4) on the south side of the road.

6) *Govindram Girdarilal Sigtia Haveli.* Good murals remain on the south and north walls and in the courtyard, but those in the rooms are stunning. Every room on the second floor is painted to some degree, those on the eastern side being particularly good. That in the south east corner has pictures of the *Ramayana* battle and scenes from three love stories – Dhola-Maru, Binjo-Sorath and Laila-Majnu.

7) *Dharamchand Gulabrai Mertia Haveli.* Small *haveli*, built in 1880, with some good pictures on its facade and forecourt, particularly a panel of Dhola and Maru on the west side of the latter. Some 40 m east of Motiram Sigtia Haveli (5).

8) *Ramlalji Jainarayan Tibrewala Haveli.* The third *haveli* on the west side of the alley leading north from Mertia Haveli (7). In the forecourt are several nice paintings – note the well scene to the right of the door, also the elephant on the wall reflected on the side of the steps below. On the porch ceiling is a procession and a lady in a revealing blouse. The pictures on the exposed walls are overshadowed by those in the rooms, especially that in the south-west corner of the second floor. It has long been locked, preserving the colours. The west side of the ceiling shows the story of Krishna. The south, the birth of Rama and his brothers, then his *baraat*, marriage procession, setting out. The east shows the *baraat* continuing with deities among the party, whilst on the north they arrive at Janakpuri, Sita's hometown, for the wedding. Panels show merchants, rulers and Europeans. Mirrorwork adds to the beauty of the room. The paintings in the courtyard show Heer-Ranjha, Binjo-Sorath, Laila-Majnu, Sassi-Punu on horse back and another episode from this last love-story where the couple meet in a palace courtyard. A woman smokes a hookah.

9) *Panalal Sheodayal Singhania Haveli.* At the end of the road about 70 m north of Govindram Sigtia Haveli (6). There are good murals, a nice *baithak* to the right of the door and a picture of a European with a falcon on its wall. Dates from c1885. North of this across the road is a painted wall with erotics, a hunt and Britons with a cannon.

10) *Khyaliwala Haveli.* About 100 m north of Singhania Haveli (9) on the corner of the road, west side. This c1870 small building is well painted and has some good geometric designs in its forecourt.

11) *Bhagirath Das Kedia Haveli.* Thakur Shyam Singh brought this family to Bissau from Jhunjhunu. The *haveli* was built around 1845 and has some very individual murals in natural colours, particularly on the north (street) wall. Dhola-Maru, a Gangaur procession carrying the figures of the deities Gauri and Iser, uniformed troops of the Jaipur army and Europeans on elephants are all shown. The last may refer to the Lockett expedition which

Bissau (8): A view of a four-pillared well in an inset panel on the north side of the forecourt of the Tibrewala Haveli. On the left a pair of bullocks descend the ramp, drawing up a skin bag of water which the attendants will spill into the first of a system of channels. On the right a couple pull up their own pot. Animals come to drink at the troughs which surround the platform (c1880).

Bissau (15): The forecourt of Babulal Chetram Khemka Haveli is decorated with both religious and secular subjects. A rise in the ground level caused by the drifting of blown sand has partially buried two arches of a storage room. (Built c1860 but repainted around 1900).

Below:
Bissau (8): The entrance of Ramlal Jainarayan Tibrewala Haveli. In the niche above the carved door–surround sits elephant-headed Ganesh. Above him is a scene from the coronation of Rama, commonly placed in doorway arches. The porch leads to a blank wall pierced only by a little window. This spy-hole allows the womenfolk to identify any visitor. (c1880).

came this way in 1831. The building is an excellent example of the architecture of the earlier 19th century, especially as far as its internal layout is concerned. Some 50 m north-west of this building is a *haveli* dating from 1840 in a state of collapse, providing an interesting cross-section of the structure. There are some good murals in its forecourt.

12) *Harsukhdas Murlidhar Jhunjhunuwala Haveli.* A fine building with some good paintings dating from around 1860, it has the added advantage of being a student hostel and thus easy to enter. On the south wall is a procession, also religious pictures including idols in three arches, of Balram, Krishna and Subhadra. There is good woodwork in the courtyard, also two of the rooms on the east side are *chandani*.

13) *Nathuram Poddar Haveli.* The exterior of this building, erected in the 1890s, has been painted over with green wash, obscuring the murals. Good pictures remain, however, in the room above the entrance door. There is the *baraat* of Rama; Arjuna and Krishna, in their *rath*, chariot, confront the composite beast Ajaibgulmari, and goddesses representing the three rivers, Ganga, Jumna and Saraswati are all depicted. There are also a number of folk stories.

14) *Temple of Venkat Bihariji.* Built by a *paswan*, concubine, of Thakur Hammir Singh in 1852 just in front of the main gate of the fort. Religious paintings in ochre on the facade of the building.

15) *Babulal Chetram Khemka Haveli.* A fine *haveli* with many good paintings on its walls. Built around 1860, there are a few murals from that period on the south wall. The rest date from around 1900. On the north wall there are several panels at eye-level, one showing the lovers Binjo and Sorath. On the west wall there are friezes of trains and soldiers, also a small car. In the forecourt, pictures include Rama breaking the bow and a panel of the goddesses representing the three sacred rivers, Ganga, Jumna and Saraswati. In the upper courtyard the three main deities Brahma, Vishnu and Shiva are shown in a *rath* slaying demons. There are also female snake charmers. The carved woodwork is good. This *haveli* is about 50 m north of the fort on the south side of the road and stands on a corner.

16) *Baijnath Fatehpuria Haveli.* Dating from around 1845, this *haveli* bears good ochre murals. On the south wall a panel illustrates the story of Sohni and Mehwal. Sohni swims across the river to her lover supported by a pot. That worked well until her mother-in-law replaced the pot with an unbaked one, which dissolved. There is also an erotic panel. Large painted posters deface this wall. In the forecourt there are the five Pandava brothers, Dhola and Maru and the god/hero Pabuji bringing camels to Rajasthan. This *haveli* is about 100 m north of the Khemka Haveli (15) on the north side of the road leading from the western gate.

17) *Samas Khan ka Dargah.* A small Muslim tomb dating from around 1850 with several graves in the compound. On the south side of this compound is the unmarked grave of a French mercenary who was attached to Shyam Singh's local forces. European mercenaries became an important element in the infantry of Indian armies after the middle of the 18th century. They appear in contemporary murals (i.e. Churu (8) and Sikar (1)). The tomb is situated about 50 m along the first turning to the south, west of the Fatehpuria Haveli (16).

18) *Jorawarmal Poddar Haveli.* Easily overlooked, this fine building was constructed c1855 but much repainted c1900. There are good paintings in the *baithak* on the north of the forecourt, but this has recently been closed. Around the courtyard are eight *chandanis*, bedrooms open to the sky. There is even a painted room, with a horse made out of

BISSAU

100m

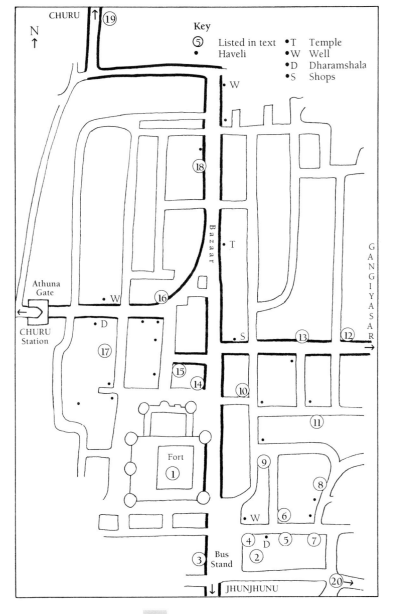

Key

⑤ Listed in text
• Haveli

• T Temple
• W Well
• D Dharamshala
• S Shops

women, and Krishna with Arjun facing the weird composite beast Ajaibgulmari. There are paintings in some of the *chandanis*. About halfway up the bazaar running north from the vegetable market on the west side.

19) *Jorawarmal Poddar Chhatri*. Beyond the North Gate – which no longer stands – the road runs north towards the Jatia Higher Secondary School. This *chhatri* is on the right before the school. It dates from around 1890 and has a little painting. Beyond it to the north is a fine well, also built by the Poddar clan and dated 1898.

20) *Dholpalia Johara*. This land was given by Thakur Hammir Singh in 1842 for the construction of the reservoir. Bhagirath Kedia Jhunjhunuwala financed the project from 1843 to 1846. Murals on a pavilion there are by the same hand as those on his *haveli* (11). The *johara* lies to the east of the town, some 100 m north of the Jhunjhunu road just before the turning to the village of Gangiyasar.

Opposite page:
Chirawa (8): On the south wall of Vilasrai Hemraj Seksaria Haveli Sudama, Krishna's pious and impoverished friend appears, his bag over his shoulder. His staff, beads and wooden sandals are common accessories of a holy man. (c1920).

Chirawa

The region fell in the portion of Kishan Singh, second of the five brothers, and became part of the Khetri Thikana. Bagh Singh of Khetri presented the village to his son, Abhey Singh, in 1788. He raised it to town status, building a mud fort, the ruins of which remain surrounding the police station some 300 m north of the Dwarkadish Temple (5). Under his control and that of his son, Bakhtawar Singh, the town thrived. For many years there was a mint here, producing coins from local and imported copper.

The greatest Bania family from this town is the Dalmia clan, perhaps second only to the Birlas of Pilani in wealth and variety of business interests. They came here from the south of Haryana, probably around 1800. A century later they were well-established amongst the richer Marwari families. There they remain.

Chirawa comes in the second rank of painted towns. It boasts two fine painted wells (6 & 9). There is also a characteristic style of painting, probably the work of one man and dating from the second and third decades of the 20th century. His pictures usually include a line of soldiers, or a band, marching. Each man wears a bulky uniform turban and his soft complexion will be coloured in more than one shade.

1) *Haveli of Ram Bhagat Dalmia.* A large mansion with paintings on its outer walls and in its courtyard. On the east wall two men are fighting rams; on the south are a snake-charmer, jugglers and wrestlers. The *haveli* was built in 1908 and stands on the corner of the fifth turning north as you enter the town from the main Jhunjhunu-Rajgarh Road.

2) *Manohar Lal Baid* (south) and *Jamnadas Baid* (north) Havelis. Built c1920, these stand side by side in the cul-de-sac immediately west of Ram Bhagat Dalmia's Haveli (1) and both are generally locked. They have good "Chirawa-style" pictures on their facades. On the north building two Rajputs sit in chairs in the door arch. In the doorway of the south *haveli* they are replaced by two Banias along with two *chowkhidars*, watchmen, with rifles. There are stucco elephants on the facade, another Chirawa speciality.

3) *Mangalchand Dalmia Haveli.* This c1920 building stands on the corner of the next turning west of Baid Havelis (2), on the same side of the main road. On the facade are two nice stucco elephants. Beneath one, two *seths* shake hands.

4) *Mohan Ram's Well.* Once a fine example of a large well of the c1820 period with arched *chhatris*, it has suffered improvement. Unpainted it stands on the south side of the street just after it makes a sharp double bend on its way into the town. Near here stood the old East Gate of the town. Today it is often described as having been built by Banjaras (gypsies), but there is little doubt that it is the same as Lockett described on his visit in 1831. He camped beside it and named the Bania "Mohun Ram" as the builder. The road running south from the well passes two painted *havelis*.

5) *Dwarkadish Temple.* About 50 m west of the well (4), on the south side of the street. This temple was built around 1910 by the Dalmia family and contains murals. In the forecourt two *seths* are labelled, one as Manna Lal Mhamia, the other as Marwari Bania. Within the *tibari* are scenes from the *Ramayana* and *Mahabharata*.

6) *Seksaria Well.* The main street continues west, then forks either side of a block of shops containing the Kalyan Temple, the hub of the town. This well is about 250 m along the road that leads south from the Kalyan Temple, on the west side. This way passes several *havelis*, one of which is typical of the early part of the last century, with a series of open arches along its upper facade. This well is one of the finest painted buildings in the town.

Above:
Chirawa (2): The facade of the *haveli* of Manohar Lal Baid showing the massive gates and the little doors which open through each leaf. Soldiers and merchants are shown in a style typical of 1920s work in this town.

Left:
Chirawa (3): Beside the gate of Mangalchand Dalmia Haveli a merchant rides a stucco elephant. Beneath him, two more Banias shake hands. (c1920).

In its north-east dome are a view of a *johara*, a scene at a well, and a rare picture of fireworks. The panels around the base of the dome show 22 incarnations of Vishnu. It was built around 1840.

7) *Nagar Chhatri*. On the east side of the road about 125 m south of Seksaria Well (6). There are paintings within the dome, including Rama's *baraat* complete with fireworks – surely inspired by the previous building (6). On the basement wall a European is shown loading a pistol – there is also an erotic. Built c1900.

8) *Vilasrai Hemraj Seksaria Haveli*. North of the well (6) take the first turning west; the first turning on the right leads to this *haveli*, which stands on a corner. There are good "Chirawa-style" paintings on its facade and south wall dating from around 1920. Another, older, painted *haveli* adjoins it.

9) *Jagdish Temple*. Continue west for some 100 m and the road joins the main street. About 100 m south-west along this street, past a painted shop, the temple stands on the north side. A handsome building with little painting, it was built by Seth Bajuramka around 1830.

10) *Poddar Well*. Follow the street westwards about 125 m from Jagdish Temple (9) and this well is on the north side of the road. A very good example of its kind, dating from the 1840s, its *chhatris* are painted within. That on the south-east shows scenes from the *Ramayana* while 22 incarnations of Vishnu decorate the panels. The south-west dome shows *rasamandala*, Krishna miraculously replicating himself so that each of the *gopis* finds him dancing next to her in the circle. The panels include Saraswati, Shiv and his sons, Ganesh and Kartikeya. In the north-west dome subjects include Raja Mordhyaj, who showed his piety by cutting his son in half to feed the tiger belonging to two holy men. The boy, of course, recovered from this experience. This street leads back to the Kalyan Temple.

11) *Bodia Kuan*. Remarkable only for its historic interest, it stands in the west of the town on the north side of the road leading to the Guga Temple and has been much restored. Two large carved stones stand beside it, one bearing a date equivalent to 1190 AD.

Churi Ajitgarh

Really two little places run together, it is situated about 9 km south-east of Mandawa on the Nawalgarh road. Churi seems to have been founded in the late 18th century. Two clans of merchants have dominated the town. First were the Kejariwals, who have left a little group of *chhatris* dating from the first decade of the 19th century to the east of Shiv Narayan's *chhatri*. Then came the Nemanis towards the close of the 19th century. Shiv Narayan Nemani was adopted from Chirawa and settled here. He then moved to Bombay to make his fortune. He was employed as a clerk by a Marwari firm there, but when he suggested improvements in the way they conducted business he was ignored. So he set out on his own as a broker and began the forward-buying of cotton in the city. He made vast profits.

1) *Shiv Narayan Nemani Haveli.* On the west side of the little bazaar, at its southern end. It was built in 1898 and has an inscription on its east wall which tells that Binja of Mukundgarh, an important painter in his time (see Nawalgarh), painted the building. On the facade, one panel shows a man clutching a *lingam* and protected by Shiva from Yamraj – the God of Death. Brahma, Shiva and Vishnu in a chariot with the sun and the moon as its wheels, oppose demons. There is also an erotic panel. This *haveli's* greatest claim to fame is a little room, unfortunately generally locked. On its walls two unlikely subjects are juxtaposed – the British royal family of the time, including Queen Victoria in old age, and erotics, some the most explicit in Shekhawati.

2) *Nagarmal Nemani Haveli.* Some 60 m north of Shiv Narayan's Haveli (1) along the bazaar is a cross-road. Turn left, then first right. Two *havelis* stand on the left side of the road. The first is Nagarmalji's. On the facade is a picture of the pursuit of the famous 20th century dacoits, Balji and Bhoorji, who were hunted to their deaths around 1930, when this *haveli* was built. There is a nice French soldier in the gateway. In the forecourt are pictures of two freedom fighters, Gokhale and Gandhi. The neighbouring *haveli* is painted by the same man. In the forecourt are a good car and a European couple with their child. Other painted *havelis* are in the next road to the west and also just east of the bazaar.

3) *The Kothi.* Built by the Nemanis around 1930, this palatial house stands to the west of Churi, between it and Ajitgarh. The *seth* has returned to live there and tends a herd of cows in its grounds. The large white marble *chhatri* of Shiv Narayanji stands east of the house.

Below:
Churi Ajitgarh (2): Copied
from some imported print but
with a touch of the local
idiom this French soldier
stands beside the doorway of
Nagarmal Nemani Haveli.
(c1930).

Above:
Churi-Ajitgarh (1): An unusual juxtaposition on the wall of the master bedroom of Shiv Narayan Nemani Haveli. The artist has chosen erotica and royalty for his themes. Here Princess Alexandra carefully avoids admiring the display next to her! (1898).

Churu

Churu is the administrative headquarters of the largest and most truly desert district of the three that contain the painted towns. Before Independence, it was the second town in the kingdom of the Maharaja of Bikaner. It is said to have been founded in 1563 by a Jat, who gave his name to the place. The fort was begun in 1739. Impressive sand dunes enclose the town, especially at its southern and western fringes. The desert results in extremes of temperature and it is said that of all places in the plains of north India, Churu can claim the highest summer and lowest winter temperatures. The maximum, in May or June, may exceed 48 degrees C., whilst before dawn in January it may drop below freezing point, ice occurring occasionally.

The town was an important centre for the 18th century caravan trade and supported several rich merchants. Prime amongst these were the Poddar family, who were much involved in the trade of woollen goods, particularly Kashmir shawls. The Thakur, Sheo Singh, alienated them by imposing a heavy wool tax. The Poddars remonstrated, then threatened, but they failed to move him. Angry, they approached Devi Singh, the Rao of Sikar. He encouraged them to move into his estate which lay across the border in the kingdom of Jaipur. There, 15 km south of Churu, they founded the town of Ramgarh.

Soon, Sheo Singh of Churu was in rebellion against his overlord, the Maharaja of Bikaner. This led to a siege of the town then to his suicide when the garrison capitulated. Surat Singh of Bikaner took the place in 1813 and gave orders for the destruction of the fort and town walls. After the suppression of a further revolt in 1818 the rule of the Thakurs ended and the town was administered directly by Bikaner.

When British officials came here in the 1830s, they found the place in a state of ruin, the bazaar closed. Business had been destroyed partly by the shift to Ramgarh and partly by constant raids by the barons of Shekhawati. The Maharaja tried to persuade the merchant community to return. The town revived, with the result that it can boast a large number of painted *havelis* and some fine temples.

Churu is directly linked by good bus and train services with Delhi (285 km), Jaipur (210 km), Bikaner (185 km) and Jodhpur (380 km). There are several small hotels near the station and bus stand, the best being the Delux hotel. There is also a government bungalow.

There is a small museum/cultural centre housed above a painted shop in the main bazaar (14) where a local historian, Sri Govind Aggarwal, worked for many years on papers of the Poddar family dating back to the 18th century. His book in Hindi, *Churu Mandal ka Itihas*, is the most comprehensive history of any region in the painted area.

1) *Malji ka Kamra.* 500 m east along the road from the railway station is a tall, red sandstone tower known as Dharamstoop. Here the road forks to Bissau and Jhunjhunu or, northwards, to the centre of the town. Follow the latter road for almost 1 km to the Girls College near which a turning on the left leads to the telegraph office. Beyond it, set back from the road through an arched gateway, is *Malji ka Kamra.* It is an Italianate fantasy of slender pillars and stucco built around 1925 by Malji Kothari. Once beautifully maintained, it has become a picture of neglect. It houses government offices and in some of its rooms are late murals.

2) *Kothari Havelis.* Slightly to the east of (1) on the north side of the road, an alley passes between two large *havelis*, built by the Kothari family of Oswal Jain merchants. Both date from the turn of the century. The way leads along the back of another Kothari *haveli*

dating from about 1870, then follows along its side, northwards. This *haveli* is often locked but the facade is handsome. Within, there are two courts, both of which were repainted by men from Bissau in 1933 in preparation for a family marriage. There is a good painted room, but it is always locked.

3) *Surana Double Haveli.* This stands immediately to the west of the northernmost Kothari *haveli* (2) and is sometimes known as the Surana Hawa Mahal (Wind Palace) on account of its "1111" windows. It was built in the early 1870s and is painted on the outer and courtyard walls. Some of the rooms are decorated. Two gateways lead through the shared forecourt of the building which is used as a public right of way. A very handsome example of local architecture with an excellent view from its roof. Nearby, to the west and south-west of this *haveli*, there are three more later *havelis* of the Surana family who are also Oswal Jains. Follow the road north from the east gate of the double *haveli* and you come to a *haveli* painted in 1945 with scenes of the bombing of an aircraft-carrier and a pit-loom in action.

4) *Surajmal Banthia Haveli.* About 100 m west along the road from the 1945 *haveli*, on the corner, south side. Built around 1925, there are some amusing paintings on its north wall. Jesus is shown rather unusually smoking a cigar; there is the one-eyed ruler of Punjab, Ranjit Singh, with bow and arrows, and two princes travel in a car. In the compound of this building to the south is a small painted building with large copies of western prints on its facade, some labelled in English. Opposite this *haveli*, on the north side of the road, is another *haveli*, now used as a Jain centre. This has some murals.

5) *Kanhaiyalal Bagla Haveli.* Follow the turning north just west of the Banthia Haveli (4). The road passes several painted *havelis* then, straight ahead, can be seen perhaps the finest frieze of its kind in the entire region. This decorates the south wall of the *Kanhaiyalal Bagla Haveli* built c1880. The frieze illustrates two well-known love stories, the ubiquitous Dhola-Maru, the lovers fleeing on their camel from the wicked Umra-Sumra, and, in front of them on horseback, Sassi and her lover, Punu, from a Punjabi tale. The mosque, the Jama Masjid, stands just beside the road and the *haveli* which adjoins it to the north-west is an example of a Muslim painted building. It is decorated with floral and abstract designs, no figurative work. The entrance to the Bagla Haveli is from the north, from the main bazaar.

6) *Temple of Ganga.* On the north side of the little square that surrounds the White Clocktower in the main bazaar. Built by the Lohia family of Banias around 1890, it is worth a visit.

7) *Balaji Temple.* Built by Kanhaiyalal Bagla (see 5) in 1891. A large, ornate structure when seen from the south or east, contrasting with the plainness of the more concealed north and west sides. An attractive little forecourt with a stucco figure of Durga on her tiger either side of the door. In the door arch is some fine gold painting showing the marriage of Rama and Sita on the right side and that of Krishna and Rukmini on the left. There are also good golden pictures in the porch of the shrine. There are well preserved pictures in the courtyard. On the shrine side, Rama, in the centre with his bow, confronts ten-headed Ravana and his demons. Amongst the subjects on the south side are both Black Bhairon and White Bhairon with trumpets and dogs. On the east side, the second panel from the south shows Laila and Majnu, whilst on the north are two pictures of Hanuman. In one he carries Rama and Lakshmana and in the other the mountain, Giriparbat. Another handsome temple, also built by the Baglas, stands to the north of Balaji Temple.(7).

8) *The Aath Kambh (Eight Pillar) Chhatri.* This was built in 1776 by the mason, Sukha Kumhar, from Khandela. Perhaps he also had a hand in the paintings. These are the oldest murals in Churu. The majority show incarnations of Vishnu, particularly Rama and Krishna. One damaged panel shows a Rajput with his court. This is probably Bakshi Ram Taknet in whose memory the *chhatri* was built. Another shows Nagas, martial ascetics, with a ruler. Towards the top of the dome is a little procession, with a Rajput on horseback approaching a Shiva temple containing a *lingam*. One of the men nearest this temple wears a hat and carries a musket. He is an early European mercenary. The basement of the *chhatri* is in very poor condition. Windblown dust has so raised the ground level that the arches that once entered the basement have long been blocked. This *chhatri* stands in the first lane turning west off the road running north from the *sabji mandi*, the vegetable market.

9) *Panna Lal Mantri Chhatri.* Some 200 m further north from Aath Khamb Chhatri (8), on the west side of that same north bound road. It was built over a Bania of the Mantri family in 1863. There are paintings on the basement and in the dome, the latter mostly of incarnations of Vishnu. North of this is a *chhatri* of the Bagla family dated 1853. Beyond this to the north-west is a handsome well, dry and neglected. The road leads on north to a *johara* and a *gaoshala*, a hospice for cows, (1.5 km), then continues to a recent holy place, Nathji.

10) *Jayadayal Khemka Haveli.* About 100 m east of the *sabji mandi* at the south end of Mantri Marg. This *haveli* has some good paintings on its outer walls. There are the procession of Rama's *baraat* and the lovers Sassi and Punu, on horseback. Inside is a painted room. The building dates from around 1870. Its footings have been hideously repaired with cement. On the opposite side of the road is a *haveli* with pictures of Dhola and Maru on their camel and Europeans opening an umbrella.

11) *Bajrang Lal Mantri Haveli.* Neighbouring the Khemka Haveli (10) to the north, this building dates from about 1860. Blue is just beginning to join the traditional ochres on the outer walls, but it is used sparingly. There are two painted rooms, that above the main entrance, repainted in about 1895, shows incarnations of Vishnu, a procession of soldiers with a cannon, a band and some wrestlers. The wooden ceiling in the porch is characteristic of *havelis* of this date and earlier. About 25 m north along the road on the west side is another *haveli* painted early in the 20th century. On the north side of its facade are two pictures copied directly from labels of the Finlay Muir Company which would have been attached to bales of British cotton cloth. One shows the Sikh gurus seated on a chequered floor; the other, the seated lovers Laila and Majnu. On the north side of the gate projection a merchant in a chair talks to a veiled woman.

12) *The Fort.* Founded in 1739, it is now in poor condition. It withstood a long siege by the army of the Maharaja of Bikaner in 1813. The story goes that when the defenders grew short of ammunition the ladies gave up their silver and gold ornaments to be turned into musket balls. When the fort finally fell, the Thakur, Sheo Singh, swallowed a diamond, so they say, and died. In the time of the Thakurs there would have been some good residential buildings in the fort. They have long gone. Now there is only a clinic, a temple and a police station.

13) *Poddar Haveli.* On the south side of the bazaar, some 50 m west of the fort gate, a fine building with an excellent carved beam in its porch. The family acquired the land in 1827, having been persuaded to return to the town from Ramgarh. The building probably

started soon afterwards, although the murals in the forecourt and courtyard date from around 1860.

14) *Nagar Sri.* This is a museum and cultural centre on the north side of the bazaar, above a shop. Here are collected paintings, sculpture, photographs and literature relating to the history of the district. The institution publishes its own magazine, *Maru Sri*, containing information on monuments, documents and historic events relating to Churu district.

15) *Shantinath Jain Temple.* Although the building is older it was decorated in 1935 by a Jaipur team. The paintings are partly in gold and show Jain holy places, saints and monks with Banias. A well stands in front of the temple, which is on the south side of the alley that runs behind the Poddar Haveli (13).

16) *Sita-Ram Temple.* Built by the Lohia family around 1890, it has some well-preserved red and blue paintings on its facade and courtyard walls. On the facade, south of the door projection, are Hanuman and Garuda, the bird which carries Vishnu. North of the door is Krishna, with his characteristic single-peacock-feather headdress. A panel in the courtyard (north side) shows Krishna playing Holi with red colour.

17) *Dharamshala and Temple* Built by Bhagwan Das Bagla. This is west of the Sita-Ram Temple (16) and about 100 m west of the cross road known as Subhash Chowk. It stands on the south side of the road. The *dharamshala*, once a fine caravansarai, has now become a school and has murals of moderate quality. The complex was constructed in the early 1890s.

18) *Sethani ka Johara* (The Reservoir of the Lady Seth) lies on the north side of the road to Ratangarh, behind a Food Corporation of India store, and some 5 km west of Churu. It was built by the widow of Bhagwan Das Bagla, one of the famine relief projects financed by merchants during the terrible *Chaupan Akaal*, the famine of 1899. They say that the great wealth that Bhagwan Das Bagla acquired in Burma was ill-gotten and that, as a result, all the male heirs have died young, as he did himself. Some good did come out of his wealth, for this is perhaps the most attractive and most efficient *johara* in the region, often retaining its store of rain water from one monsoon to the next. A peaceful place to which I often retreated during the five years I lived in Churu. The large antelope, the Nilgai (Blue Bull), turns up there occasionally and the water usually attracts some birds – waders, a duck or two or a Little Grebe.

19) *Seksaria Well.* A large well on the eastern fringe of the town, the best landmark being the *chhatri* of Jali Ram Poddar, which houses a Montessori School. Here water is still raised by a pair of bullocks, the great leathern bags spilled into channels to fill open reservoirs and cattle troughs before the water is carried away to irrigate the surrounding land. The well is in action both in the early morning and at evening. The *chhatri* commemorates a Bania who was one of those living in Ramgarh when Col. Lockett went there in 1831. Lockett names Jali Ramji as one of the contingent of merchants who came to him with complaints against the brigands. He died in 1833. The *chhatri* contains a little painting. As well as good floral designs there is a fish motif in the apex of the dome which is usually peculiar to Ramgarh.

CHURU

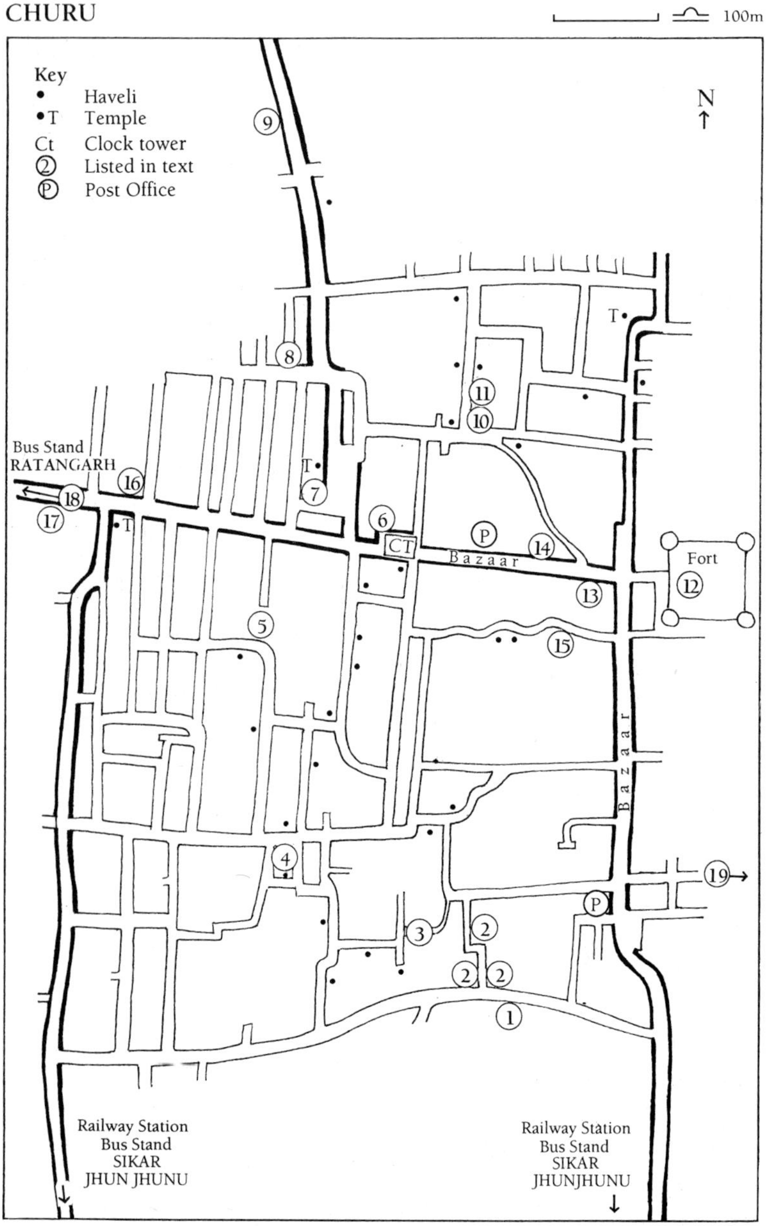

⊢————⊣ ◠ 100m

N
↑

Key
- •   Haveli
- •T   Temple
- Ct   Clock tower
- ②   Listed in text
- Ⓟ   Post Office

⑨

⑧

T•

⑪
⑩

Bus Stand
RATANGARH

⑯   T•
⑱   ⑦
⑰   •1   ⑥
    CT   B a z a a r   Ⓟ   ⑭
            ⑬   Fort
⑤   ⑮   ⑫

④

B
a
z
a
a
r

③   ②   ⑲
Ⓟ
② ②
①

Railway Station   Railway Station
Bus Stand   Bus Stand
SIKAR   SIKAR
JHUN JHUNU   JHUNJHUNU
↓   ↓

Churu: Everyone goes a little crazy at Holi. A boy dances in the bazar at night. He wears bells on his ankles and is accompanied by men playing *daphs*, drums characteristic of this season. Churu is locally famous for the quality of its drumming at Holi and Moharrum.

Left:
Churu (11): A detail in the master bedroom of Bajrang Lal Mantri Haveli. The marching soldiers are probably native sepoys whilst the two seated men who seem to menace each other with pistols would be their British officers. (c1895).

Below:
Churu (4): Overlooking the street on the north wall of Surajmal Banthia Haveli is an unusual example of Christian iconography. The painter has worked from some print of Jesus, recognising him only as a foreigner. To complete the picture he has thoughtfully added a cigar! (c1925).

Opposite page, bottom:
Churu: A panel in a *haveli* of the Banthia family just east of the vegetable market. Ganga Singh, Maharaja of Bikaner, stands beside his car. (c1925).

Top:

Dundlod (2): Low on the outer wall of the Satyanarayan Temple Krishna is shown rescuing his friends who have been devoured by a demon in the guise of a huge bird. Seizing both mandibles of the creature's beak he tears it in two. (1911).

Bottom:

Dundlod (3): The dome of Ram Dutt Goenka's *chhatri* is heavily decorated with red and blue paintings. The panel on the left shows Krishna playing Holi with the *gopis* and beneath him horse-headed Hayagriva is worshipped. The centre panel contains a court scene, whilst that on the right may be an episode from the *Ramayana*. (1888).

Dundlod

Dundlod, along with Bissau, came to Keshri Singh, the fifth of Sardul Singh's five heirs. He founded the fort in 1750. At the beginning of the 19th century, the Thakur, Ranjit Singh, was living in Jhunjhunu with his cousin, the infamous Shyam Singh of Bissau. In 1808, Shyam Singh murdered Ranjit Singh and one of his young sons with a view to seizing his lands; however, his youngest son, aided by some of his father's men, managed to escape. Eventually, the survivor, Sheo Singh, regained some of his property and settled in Dundlod. Much of the fort dates from his time. A branch of the Goenka family of merchants from Nawalgarh moved here after a dispute with one of the Thakurs of that town. Dundlod became their base when they joined the migration to Calcutta. There they became brokers and were extremely successful. When the patriarch, Ram Chandra Goenka, died in 1908, his two sons invited 7,500 guests to the village for the funeral rites, fed them all and gave each one rupee. This is just a glimpse of the enormous wealth these *seths* accumulated. The best Bania buildings in the town were all financed by this family. Part of the fort is open as a hotel, Hotel Dera.

1) *The Fort*. Though founded in 1750, much of the present building dates from 1840 onwards. The fort boasts a fine *diwan-khana*, a hall of audience. There are traces of murals dating from around 1840 on some of the outer walls. The best paintings are in a niche in one of the rooms. Probably the room was once smaller and other murals were destroyed when it was enlarged. Those that survive date from around 1840 and mostly depict incarnations of Vishnu. They were certainly the work of sophisticated Jaipur painters, not local masons.

2) *Satyanarayan Temple*. Built by Hariram Goenka in 1911, it stands at the north side of a small square some 50 m east of the main gate of the fort. There are some good paintings. One, on the projecting surface between the brackets on the west wall, depicts the painter himself.

3) *Chhatri of Ram Dutt Goenka*. This stands some 200 m south-east of the fort on the southern fringe of the town. Amongst the murals on the basement is one of the masons constructing a building. The *chhatri* is dated 1888. A handsome well stands a little to the west of the *chhatri*. Both were built by Ram Chandra Goenka.

4) *A group of Goenka havelis*. One stands on the north side of the road, three south of it on the south side of the little square containing the Satyanarayan Temple (2). The southernmost of these has an amusing erotic set high on the east wall. The smallest of the group, some 10 m north-east of the southern one, was the *haveli* the Goenkas built on their arrival from Nawalgarh.

5) *Chhatri of Shiv Bux Goenka*. This is set back on the southern side of the road at the eastern edge of the town and is surrounded by a *dharamshala*. It was built in 1903 at the cost of 18,361 rupees 11 annas. There are religious paintings in the main dome, but the secondary domes include folk tales, some of them labelled. "Hadi Rani" gives a sword to "Amar Singh", a man ploughs, a barber is shown at work.

6) *Jagathia Haveli*. This stands on the corner about 40 m north of Satyanarayan Temple (2). On the east wall is a good frieze of trains, dancers perform for *seths*, and a man beats his wife. The pictures in the courtyard show a farmer and a woman cooking *chapatis*. It was painted by Gopal of Dundlod in 1914. A couple more *havelis* stand close to the north-west of this.

Top:
Fatehpur (5): On the east wall of this doomed Choudhary *haveli* is an illustration of some long-forgotten tale of jealousy. The red and green ochre pigments are typical of earlier murals. (c1850).

Bottom:
Fatehpur (8): The *naal* gate on the facade of Jagannath Singhania Haveli. The deep ultramarine blue ground is typical of Fatehpur work of this period as is the picture on the left. This shows Vishnu and his consort Lakshmi seated on a lotus and bathed by elephants. An episode from a love story is shown above the gate. The pictures have been damaged by a leaking drainpipe. (painted c1885).

Left:
Fatehpur (10): A detail in the beautiful painted room in Mahavir Prasad Goenka Haveli. One man swings 'Indian clubs' whilst another uses a local type of chest-expander. Beside two wrestlers their turbans lie surrounding a small figure of Hanuman. (c1860).

Below:
Fatehpur: In the courtyard of a little Devra *haveli* on the south side of Municipality Road this panel illustrates the optimism of the erstwhile owner. Mother India stands in front of a map of her country and King George V hands her a document – Freedom. A group well-known heroes of the struggle for independence witness the event. (c1930).

Fatehpur

A settlement already existed on the site when Fateh Khan, one of the Muslim Kaimkhani Nawabs, chose it for his capital in 1451. He founded the fort and his successors added to it. Several important buildings remain from the time of the Kaimkhani rulers. Sheo Singh of Sikar coveted the town and, in alliance with Sardul Singh, he defeated the last Nawab, Sardar Khan, in 1731. The Kaimkhanis briefly retook the town during the 1740s, but they were again evicted. In 1799, the romantic Irish freebooter, George Thomas, came here with his Maratha allies. The Maharaja of Jaipur, Pratap Singh, brought an army against him which, although it lost the ensuing battle, caused him to retreat.

Hindu Banias flourished in Fatehpur even in the time of the nawabs. In the 19th century, some of the menfolk migrated to the cities and prospered. Amongst the famous families in the town were the Singhania, Poddar, Devra, Saraogi, Choudhary (who had played an important role in the commerce of Fatehpur under the earlier regime), Ganeriwala and, later, the Chamaria clans. Devki Nandan Khedwal in his book, *Fatehpur Guide*, describes the marriage of Puranmal Singhania in 1879. The groom was eight years old. His *baraat* set out for Ramgarh with five elephants and 800 camels, carriages and horse-buggies. The cost of the marriage was 125,000 rupees and to commemorate it his father gave a solid silver door-frame to the Lakshminath Temple in the town. If life was expensive, so was death; the family had spent 75,000 rupees on the funeral rites of Puranmal's grandfather only six years previously.

Today the walls of the town are gone and none of the old gates remains. A new source of wealth in recent years has been the Gulf, which has attracted many young Muslim masons. The town contains the oldest murals in Shekhawati and the local masons are given the credit for many of the earlier 19th century paintings in neighbouring towns, especially Ramgarh. The State Government has recently opened a new establishment, 'Hotel Haveli'. It is situated to the south of the town opposite a handsome *johara* (19) and close to the Jaipur-Bikaner highway.

1) *The Bowri, or step-well.* This building is in the process of being destroyed. It lies just to the west of the road at the central bus stand, invisible short of climbing some steps to a well behind the shops. It is one of the architectural feats of the region, for the water-table is deep in this desert. It was constructed in 1614 by Sheikh Mohammed of Nagaur during the reign of Nawab Daulat Khan. There was a Persian inscription to this effect until the antique business was encouraged in Shekhawati. It then disappeared. Local people used to refer to this *bowri* as the 17th Wonder of the World. They will still tell you stories of a robber who dwelt many years among its underground passages undetected. They talk, too, of a tunnel leading from there to the fort. The single arch which was built to retain the side walls proved insufficient when a *haveli* was built close to the southern side. The side collapsed. Forty years ago one could still walk down the steps to the water's edge. Now it has become a dumping place.

2) *Gopiram Jalan Haveli.* This has some amusing late murals including a European marriage party on the facade, the coronation procession of George V and some interesting cars on the south wall, and the Raja of Sikar along with members of British royalty in the forecourt. It dates from around 1912.

3) *Harnand Rai Saraogi Haveli.* Built and painted around 1850, some of the murals on the east wall were repainted in 1911 to celebrate the visit of George V and Queen Mary to Rajasthan. Amongst the more interesting earlier paintings a panel in the courtyard shows a Ganges paddle-steamer such as carried so much of the merchants' trade.

4) *The Lal Patthar (Red Stone) Haveli*. Such heavily-carved stone *havelis* are usually seen further west in Rajasthan. This one is exceptional. It was built by the Saraf family and has long been locked. The rise in ground-level caused by drifting sand has buried the gateway, the depth giving some indication of the building's age. It probably dates from early in the 19th century.

5) *Choudhary Haveli*. This has one of the most richly-painted interiors in the region but is, unfortunately, generally locked. It was briefly rented out, whereupon the antique industry took its toll of mirrors and woodwork. The south part of the building was constructed around 1850, the forecourt added c1880. On the east wall the difference between the pigments used on the two sections can easily be seen. There are some interesting paintings on that east wall including erotics which have been defaced with mud. One shows a dancing girl. A donkey, behind, projects on either side of her skirt. A man feeds the beast at one side, at the other ...... If you have the good fortune to find the door unlocked ask to see the interior. It will be visible to all fairly soon unless the footings of the walls are repaired.

6) *Chauhan ka Kuan (the Chauhan Well)*. This, though unpainted, is a fine well dating from the time of the nawabs, probably the early 18th century. The ruler had two wives of Hindu Rajput origin, one a Chauhan, the other a Rathor. Each built a well. The Rathor Well is just near the Makbara of Alef Khan (21) and bears illegible inscriptions in its shaft in both Persian and Sanskrit.

7) *Nand Lal Devra Haveli*. Built around 1880, this building has a large number of good murals. The ceiling of the porch has both paintings and mirrorwork. In the forecourt are large pictures of the Goddess of Fortune, Lakshmi, with her attendant elephants, on an ultramarine ground, typical of Fatehpur work of that time. The *baithak* off the south side of the forecourt has some fine painted panels on its ceiling, undoubtedly the work of Jaipur men. These must have impressed the rest of the Devra family since several of their later *havelis* in the town have local copies of them. Two such *Devra Havelis*, both built as famine relief projects during the catastrophe of 1899, stand only 60-70 m north of this.

8) *Jagannath Singhania Haveli*. Another of the gems of the town, this *haveli* backs on to the main road. The paintings on this back wall show an interesting contrast with those on the front. The former date from around 1855, the foundation of the building, whilst those of the facade and forecourt, rich in ultramarine, were painted c1880. Large pictures of Lakshmi with attendant elephants on a blue ground dominate the forecourt. There are some fine carved beams in the *tibaris*. The interior is locked and is said to contain painted rooms.

9) *Gania Sati Temple*. This commemorates the *sati* self-immolation, of a woman of the Choudhary clan. Most of the present building probably dates from the early 19th century, but some parts are older.

10) *Mahavir Prasad Goenka Haveli*. This little single-courtyard *haveli* must have been constructed in the 1850s. The paintings on its outer walls are not outstanding; those in the second-floor room are. This room is one of the best in Shekhawati, complete with mirrorwork. The pictures are varied in subject matter but include religious and folk themes. Paintings of women are combined to form the outlines of a horse and an elephant. Krishna is the rider. Elsewhere, men do exercises, their coloured turbans lying near them on the floor, and there is a man with monkeys. A second, less spectacular room adjoins this.

11) *Udai Ram Devra Haveli.* Immediately to the west of the *Goenka Haveli* (10), a two courtyard *haveli* dating from around 1885. There are some fine brass doors and good woodwork. In the forecourt are three pictures characteristic of Fatehpur - the large Lakshmi with elephants, a panel showing a blue *sadhu* (Kapildevmuni, another incarnation of Vishnu), a Rajput and a horse, and another showing an idol with a blue face which probably refers to Rameshwaram. The gate porch is impressive, with mirrorwork in its ceiling and a circle of Krishna dancing with the *gopis*.

12) *Gopiram Bhotika Haveli.* West of Udai Ram's Haveli (11) and about 40 m east of the Nagar Palika (Municipal Office). This c1850 *haveli* is generally locked but the ochre painting was worth a look, unfortunately the painted facade has just been demolished.

13) *The Fort.* This building is doomed and more of its architecture disappears each year. The area is at present very filthy, being used as a convenient lavatory for the bazaar. Much of the old palace of the nawabs dating at least from the 17th century is collapsing, and its fine carved stonework is being torn out to feed the antique market. These structures, if they remain, stand in the south-east part of the fort. The newer palace, which contained some 20th century painting, was demolished some 10 years ago. Even the older section shows traces of geometric and floral designs painted on its walls, more evidence that muralists were active in Fatehpur before the Rajput takeover. The outer walls and their four bastions were built during the third quarter of the 18th century. Chand Singh, the Raja of Sikar, demolished the older defences in search, so they say, of treasure buried beneath them by the nawabs. One of the few Kaimkhani monuments of Fatehpur, the demise of this historic building, like that of the *bowri* (1), will be regretted too late.

14) *Lakhoram Hariram Saraogi Haveli.* This dates around 1890. On the facade are two Lakshmis on a green ground. There are some good murals in the forecourt. On its east wall are some court scenes and on the north wall Krishna plays Holi with colour whilst above him the five Pandavas play the board game, *chaupad*, and lose Draupadi, a popular episode from the *Mahabharata*.

15) *Ram Gopal Ganeriwala Haveli.* Good painted *haveli* from around 1895. There is a fine carved beam over the gateway. In the forecourt, two panels are repeated four times. One shows Krishna riding on an elephant made up of women, and the second, Krishna playing his flute in three arches. The latter is an exact copy of a label produced by the Finlay Muir Company, which they attached to cotton piece-goods from Manchester. Above the centre of an ugly iron roof another incarnation of Vishnu is shown, Badrinath. The panel shows a figure and a temple in front of a hill.

16) *Bavan Tibari Haveli (The Haveli of the 52 Tibaris).* Built by the Ganeriwala family. Architecturally, this is one of the most imposing Bania structures in the town. The exterior is not so impressive, but the building is used as a student hostel, so a view of the interior is usually easy to obtain. The paintings of the facade are original, dating from around 1840. They are angular and unsophisticated, typical of the earlier exterior work, but they are not lacking in humour; note the small panel where five women carry water from a well. The man operating the well is using his team of bullocks to raise a skin of water from outside the frame of the picture. There is also a picture of Dhola and Maru. In the forecourt are some good geometric designs. The courtyard and the west wall have been partly repainted using artificial pigments.

17) *Dwarkadish Temple.* This stands on the east side of the main road at the south edge of the town. Built by the Poddar family in 1898, in the courtyard is a fine frieze of the *Ramayana*.

On the south side the island of Lanka is shown with ten headed Ravana, its demon king. He sets out for battle in his chariot whilst Sita, whom he has abducted, is shown as a small figure on a swing in a garden. Hanuman approaches her. On the east side Rama and Lakshmana, with their monkey and bear allies, advance, crossing the sea to Lanka. On the north, Rama's *baraat* sets out from Ayodhya and travels, with deities in the entourage, across the west side to Sita's palace at Janakpuri. In the *baraat* are Ganesh riding his rat, his father, Shiva, on his bull, and both Surya the sun, and Chandra, the moon. Rama is shown at the gate on his elephant.

18) *Ram Gopal Ganeriwala Chhatri*. This family of merchants were particularly successful in Hyderabad, in South India, as bankers. This marble pile was erected by Ram Gopal Ganeriwala over his father's cremation site in 1886. The family keeps it well maintained.

19) *Johara*. About 300 m south of the *Ganeriwala Chhatri* (18) on the east side of the road, this reservoir was built jointly by the Singhanias, Devras and Anat Ram Poddar of Ramgarh in 1854. On the opposite side of the road stands '*Hotel Haveli*'. Some 3 km south of this on the west side of the Sikar road is another such tank, built by Ram Gopal Ganeriwala as a relief project during the great famine of 1899.

20) *Harikrishandas Saraogi Haveli*. A large *haveli* with two courts a short distance to the south of the *bowri* (1). On the facade are false windows, decorative designs and soldiers. There are good beams over the entrance gate. A procession in a series of blue panels circumambulates the forecourt. On the north-west side of the forecourt the manner of laying out the pictures can be seen where construction lines made with taut string have left marks on the wall. The string was dusted with charcoal and this has been trapped in the wet plaster.

21) *Makbara (tomb) of Nawab Alef Khan*. A large, domed building, unpainted and dating from the close of the 17th century. This building has been preserved from the general decay by the fact that the Muslims treat it as a shrine.

22) *Two havelis built by the Bhartia family*. These both stand to the north of the town and date from around 1925. They set an example of how such buildings can be maintained, although unoccupied, when the owners, still wealthy, take an interest in their upkeep.

23) *Bhakhtmal ki Chhatri*. Double *chhatri* erected by the Choudhary family between 1840 and 1842. It stands next to the westernmost of the *havelis* (22). There are some good pictures of women with musical instruments and other panels in the domes.

24) *Jagannath Singhania Chhatri*. On the north edge of the town at the east side of the road to Churu. This was built as a memorial to his father by Jagannathji. The large *chhatri* is surrounded by a peaceful little garden, well-maintained by the family. Adjoining this to the north-east is a large well built by the same family. Follow the road some 100 m north and you enter Chamaria Colony with its college. The complex was built by the Chamaria family. The compound of the Chamaria Guest House, at the entrance to the colony, contains a functional model of the astronomical instruments constructed by Jai Singh II in Jaipur.

25) *The Dargah of Faza Nazimuddin Suleimani*. The tomb of a local Muslim saint and its associated buildings, on the southern edge of the town. The complex dates from 1863-1874. There are some good murals of Muslim holy places in a *tibari* beside the mosque.

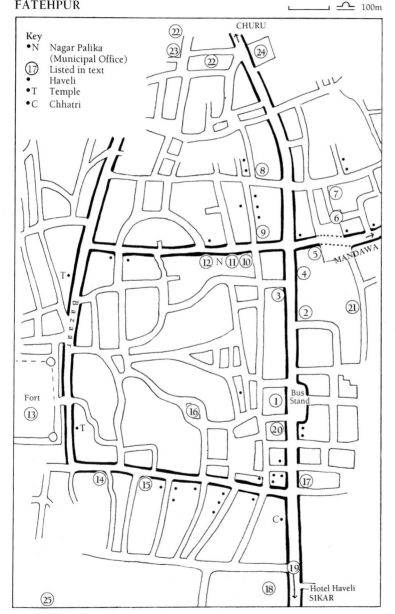

Gangiyasar

This place came in the portion of Zorawar Singh, the eldest of the five brothers. His son, Umed Singh, founded a fort there in 1755, and the little town dates from about the same year. In the 1830s it was thought of as a nest of robbers. Today, it is a quiet, attractive little village amongst the dunes. It is best known for the Mataji Temple, dominating a high dune to the south-east, where a holy man once dwelt. Each year in October, at the time of the Dassehra festival, there is a two-day fair at the temple. Stalls and merry-go-rounds are set up and people come from the surrounding villages to attend. In the late afternoon, the wrestling bouts begin. They are held in a natural amphitheatre made by a sand dune, before a large, all-male crowd.

1) *The Fort*. Founded in 1755, it is now derelict, gradually being devoured by the moving sand dunes. Above the two gates are no less than forty *torans*, the wood or metal tokens put up at the doorway of a building when a groom arrives to marry a daughter of the house. There is little painting.

2) *Mataji Temple*. This has been much renovated. A small, domed Shiva temple above the *samadhi*, a building that marks the grave/cremation site of the ascetic who once lived here, contains some paintings dating from around 1760, the date of some graffiti on the wall. In the porch, Rama, with cannon and muskets, attacks Lanka. In the temple are Dhola-Maru, the holy man on an elephant with Nagas armed ascetics, some large serpents and religious pictures.

There are several painted *havelis* in the town, none of them outstanding. There are also some 18th century *maths* and *samadhis* of holy men who probably led a group of Nagas in the village.

Gangiyasar: A large crowd of men watch the wrestling competition which is the highlight of a fair held each Dassehra at the Mataji Temple (2). A massive sand dune provides a grandstand for the audience.

151

Gudha

Once one of the most important towns in Shekhawati, time has passed it by. It stands beside a rocky outlier of the Aravalli Hills which is topped by a small temple. It was held by the Nagad Pathan rulers of nearby Ked until, in 1645, Jhujhar Singh seized it from them. The Gopinath Temple probably dates from the 17th century, but the murals within it are 19th century. Those on the vaulted ceiling on the north side are the oldest (c1840) and show scenes from the life of Rama and Krishna. They are in poor condition. There are several good *havelis* with interesting paintings. Most impressive is that of Girdarilal Modi, in the east of the town, which was built around 1860.

Gudha: On the outer wall of a *haveli* in this small town a soldier drives a galloper gun. Over his shoulder he has the ramrod with which to load his weapon. (c1890).

Jhunjhunu

The date of the town's foundation is uncertain, but it seems that it took its name from a Jat ruler. Mohammed Khan, the first of the Kaimkhani nawabs, occupied it around 1450, and his descendants held power until 1730. In that year the last Nawab, Rohella Khan, died in Singhana on his way to Delhi. Sardul Singh, a Shekhawat Rajput who had once been his *diwan*, first minister, seized Jhunjhunu in a bloodless coup. The town became the capital of an extended Shekhawati. When he died in 1742, his estate was divided amongst his five surviving sons. The town was also partitioned and each of the five had a *pied-a-terre* there. Their *chhatris* (1) stand with others of the family towards the east of the town.

In 1835, when the British raised the Shekhawati Brigade to suppress the brigandry prevalent in the area, Jhunjhunu presented an obvious base. Major Forster, the Anglo-Indian commander, lived here for several years as virtual ruler. He seems to have made himself popular, constructing a sector of the town just east of the town still known as Forsterganj. There he built a mosque and temple. His infant son is buried under a little pyramid beside the Dargah of Kamaruddin Shah (22). His wife appears briefly in the annals of the Mutiny of 1857. She was immensely fat and refused to jump from the walls of Delhi as the British fled. She was pushed by her fellows and succumbed from the fall. Two families of merchants, the Tulsians and the Khaitans, flourished in the town at least back to the 18th century. The latter family is known throughout India for the electric fans that bear its name.

Jhunjhunu, standing in the shade of its conical hill, Kana Pahar, is attractive with winding alleys and surprising monuments. A scramble to the top of the hill in the evening provides an excellent view of the town and its surroundings. There is good accommodation at Hotel Shiv Shekhawati in the east of the town, just off the main road from Delhi, near the Midway Jamuna, which serves cold drinks, beer and snacks. The Midway also offers two rooms in a pretty garden. There are other hotels near the bus stand. Today, Jhunjhunu is a district headquarters with direct train links to Delhi and Jaipur and buses to Delhi (215 km), Jaipur (185 km), Jodhpur (440 km) and Bikaner (235 km).

1) The memorial *chhatris* of the Shekhawat clan. These date from 1740-1840, and include those of six of Sardul Singh's sons, including Bahadur Singh, who predeceased him. The *chhatris* are now used as a school and whitewash has obliterated some historic murals. One has recently been revealed as the wash has fallen away. It shows a battle scene, perhaps Baswa-Rajgarh (1782). No one is sure which *chhatri* is whose, the inscriptions having been obliterated. There are traces of painting connected with religious rituals on the inner walls of some of these memorials.

2) *Mohanlal Ishwardas Modi Haveli.* On the north side of Nehru Market, this building dates from 1896. Some paintings of Edward VII and George V over the gate, and half-finished cars in the forecourt must have been added later. The painter's name, Nawalsar Khan, is mentioned in an inscription.

3) *Kaniram Narsinghdas Tibrewala Haveli.* At the western end of Nehru Market and dated as 1883. There are paintings on the outer and inner walls of this *haveli*. In the forecourt a train and soldiers are shown. There is also a European with a little dog, a *munim* pays workers, and carpenters work. In the courtyard are some folk tales, including Laila-Majnu, Sassi-Punu and Amar Singh and Hadi Rani. The painter signs as Suleiman.

4) Two *makbaras* raised over Kaimkhani nawabs. To the east, that of Nawab Samas Khan (reigned 1605-1627). To the west, that of Bhawan Khan, built by the last Nawab, Rohella

Khan. North-east of Bhawan Khan's tomb on the north side of the road is the entrance to *Chhe Haveli*, Six Havelis, which are poorly painted.

5) *Nuruddin Farooqi Haveli*. Continuing west along the road from the Samas Khan Makbara (4), this *haveli* is about 100 m away on the corner. It is an excellent example of a Muslim painted *haveli*, with no figurative paintings, only floral and decorative designs. A fine building with two courtyards, a handsome porch and good beams in the second floor rooms.

6) Tomb of Makhdoom Husain Nagori and others. South of the Farooqi Haveli (5) at the edge of Pirzada Mohalla, an ancient Muslim sector of the town, is a mosque and an interesting collection of tombs. The oldest of these is that of Makhdoom Husain, which has three domes and is so ancient that centuries of blown sand have buried it deeply in the ground. It was probably built in the 16th century over a Sufi saint.

7) *Khetri Mahal*. Architecturally, amongst the finest buildings in Shekhawati. Wherever possible, marble pillars take the place of walls, allowing the maximum flow of air through the building. When new, these pillars would have provided a pleasant contrast to the buff plaster of the walls, but the years have dulled their whiteness. A ramp ascends through the building, allowing one to take one's horse up to the roof. There are conflicting accounts as to when this palace was constructed, but it seems that Bhopal Singh, founder of Khetri and grandson of Sardul Singh, built it around 1770. Today, it is used as a hostel, but the students leave the haunted upper rooms empty. There are two small panels of flowers in the building, typical of Jaipur work of the late 18th century. The view from the roof is exceptional, the busy little town laid out below and the Badalgarh (11) rising like a ship above it. Note the households of dyers and printers, Muslim by faith, at work beneath you. Col. Lockett mentions them when he came here in 1831. As he went through the town, his elephant broke a pot of dye and he threw a silver rupee down to the dyer as recompense.

8) *Surajgarh Haveli*. This was built by the Thakur of Surajgarh in the early 19th century. As much a fort as a *haveli*, it has no murals. The building figured in a dispute that came before the Jaipur court in 1837. One member of the family wanted to park his elephant in the forecourt, but another objected. The argument became bitter so, in order to have his own way, the second man shot the beast! Today the building is used as a screen printing centre.

9) *Gopinath Temple*. Built by Sardul Singh c1735, it integrated some of the structure of the Nawab's palace. The ochre painting around the doorway and in the courtyard is original. That inside, near the shrine, dates from c1890. This temple is about 100 m south-east of the fort Badalgarh (11).

10) *Bissau Mahal*. Built by Keshri Singh, youngest son of Sardul Singh, c1760, this is another beautiful little palace. There were paintings in some of the rooms, but they have been whitewashed over. One ceiling still retains some floral and bird pictures. It was here that Shyam Singh of Bissau murdered his cousin and one of his two sons in 1808. The other boy escaped with a servant, who hid him in a cave and then took him to Khetri by camel. The survivor, Sheo Singh, became Thakur of Dundlod. This building is now used as a school. The area around it is known as Nau Mahal (Nine Palaces – for such there once were). It stands some 50 m south of Badalgarh (11).

11) *Badalgarh*. This, from the exterior at least, must be one of the most impressive forts in Shekhawati, its high walls raised on a rocky hillock above the town. Built by Nawab Fazl Khan or his predecessor at the close of the 17th century, it was intended to house the horses and camels which were so vital to warfare in this region. The interior is an

anticlimax. The walls enclose little apart from a poor modern statue of Sardul Singh bearing no resemblance to contemporary paintings, but there is a plan to found a museum here. The view from the walls is good. Above, on a foothill of Kana Pahar, stand the ruins of another fort, Shyamgarh, built by Shyam Singh of Bissau around 1810. The British saw it as a potential threat and destroyed it in 1834.

12) *Sri Bihariji Temple.* Perhaps the finest 18th century temple in Shekhawati, it was built by four merchants from Khetri in 1776. There are important contemporary murals probably by the same painter as those of the *Aath Kambh Chhatri* in Churu (8). The lower walls have been marred by ugly modern religious plaques. Within the temple, on its upper east wall, one sees Sardul Singh (top) with his five sons as youths seated before him. Beneath are pictures of each son presiding over his own court. On the west side are incarnations of Vishnu above the shrine. The south shows scenes from the *Ramayana* – dominated by the battle for Lanka. Rama, Lakshmana and Hanuman fight against the demons of ten-headed Ravana. A procession crosses the north wall – probably of the Maharaja of Jaipur.

13) *Zorawargarh.* This fort was founded in 1741 by Zorawar Singh, the eldest son of Sardul Singh. The old residential quarters are in the north-west corner. It now contains government offices and the town jail. It stands about 70 m north west of the *Modi Haveli* (2).

14) *Bhikala Kuan.* This well was constructed by a Bania, Hansa Ram, in 1680-1682. The inscription mentions Aurangzeb as the ruling Emperor. The shape of the corner domes is quite unlike any others in the region, but then there are only a handful of wells so old.

15) *Tulsian Havelis.* This group of *havelis* on the east side of the main road to the Rani Sati Temple (23) and Churu are reached through an arched gateway. Several such arches leading into older *haveli* complexes used to exist in the town, probably to make the group a defensive entity in the absence of town walls. To the south-east of the standing buildings is the ruin of an 18th century haveli of the family. The rest date from 1843 to 1864, the pair on the east side of the group being the oldest. These have good paintings on the facades.

16) *Tulsian Bowri.* One of the two important clans of merchants in the town during the 18th century, the Tulsians sank this step-well. It appears to have no inscription, but probably dates from c1790. The Tulsian Bowri is set back from the east side of the road about half way between the *havelis* (15) and the massive Rani Sati Temple (22). This *bowri* was in a filthy state when I last saw it.

17) *Khaitan Bowri.* This *bowri* was built around 1790 by Girdarilal Khaitan, but it remains unfinished. There is a story concerning its origin. The rival Tulsians had completed their step-well and it became a popular place to go and bathe. One day a member of the Khaitan clan had just completed his bath and put on his clean clothes when a Tulsian boy jumped into the water and splashed him. He remonstrated with the youth, who replied that if he was so fussy, he should build his own *bowri*. So he did! They say that an accident occurred during the last stages of construction, killing eleven men. The merchant stopped the work and it was never resumed. It stands about 100 m west of the main road slightly to the north of the Tulsian Bowri (16). There is a plan to restore this *bowri* – a project which requires expert guidance!

18) *Lakshminath Temple.* Built in 1919 by Ram Vilas Khaitan, this impressive building has a few murals, signed as the work of a Jaipur man. It is about 100 m north-east of the fort, Akheygarh (20).

Opposite page, top:
Sri Bihariji Temple, Jhunjhunu (12): Around the dome of this temple, one of the finest of 18th century Shekhawati, Krishna dances with the *gopis* in a *rasamandala*. On the left side of the panel Sardul Singh is depicted with his five sons. In the lower part each son is shown presiding over his own court. (1776).

Below:
Jhunjhunu (2): The facade of the painted *haveli* of Mohanlal Ishwardas Modi, one of the best in the town. It was built in 1896 but the pictures were added over the following decade. The quality of the woodwork has started to decline.

Opposite page, bottom:
Jhunjhunu (9): Children watch as I photograph in the Gopinath Temple. Around the ceiling Krishna and the *gopis* dance. The paintings are in the red-and-blue dominated colour scheme so common in late 19th century work but the temple itself dates from the mid-18th century.

19) *Vilasrai Khaitan Haveli* c1900. A *haveli* with two courtyards raised on a high plinth above the road. On the facade are soldiers and religious themes. There is a handsome *baithak* on the left as you enter the forecourt and above its entrance are panels showing Rama's marriage. Interestingly Ravana is in attendance. There is also depicted the episode in the *Mahabharata* where one of the Kaurava brothers tries to strip Draupadi, but her sari, thanks to Krishna, becomes miraculously endless. Beside the *baithak* entrance is an amusing little picture of a *seth* being carried in a covered chair. In the gate arch are some good religious panels and there are pictures as well as a carved beam in the porch. Adjoining this *haveli* to the north is another built by Vilasrai's son. In its courtyard are scenes from the *Mahabharata* and some views of Jaipur.

20) *Akheygarh*. Best located by asking for Lakshmi Talkies, the cinema which is located within the walls of this fort. Founded by the third of the brothers, Akhey Singh, it was incomplete when he died. It passed to his brother, Nawal Singh, who finished the construction around 1760. It must then have been the most formidable of the fortresses in the town. Though dilapidated now, it remains imposing.

21) *Mertani Bowri*. The oldest and finest of Jhunjhunu's three step wells. It is said to have been built in 1783 by Sardul Singh's widow, Mertani. She must have been a very old lady by that time. Handsome though it is, a British official visiting the town in 1831 reported of the well that:.. "When first made, the water was so bad, or rather poisonous, that those who drank of it, expired they say in less than two hours. Bleeding in the temple was the only cure, and even that operation was useless, unless performed immediately after the water had been drank". In the extreme south-west of the town – Recently it has been drastically restored.

22) *Dargah of Kamaruddin Shah*. A complex standing at the foot of Kana Pahar to the south-west of Surajgarh Haveli (8) housing the tombs of several pious men revered by the Kaimkhani community. The buildings were constructed in the mid-19th century and include a mosque and a *mehfilkhana*, concert hall. Behind the *madrassa*, Koran school, there is a pathetic little pyramid erected over Major Forster's infant son who died in 1841.

23) *The Rani Sati Temple*. This massive, ever-expanding temple dominates the north-east corner of the town. Built by the merchant community, it clearly reflects the enormous wealth passing through their hands and is the main point of pilgrimage for Marwaris coming back to their homeland. A big *mela* fair, is held by the temple in August, attended by crowds from all corners of the country. Until this century this was merely a small shrine marking the site where a young widow committed *sati*, immolated herself on her husband's pyre, in 1595. The Bania community, to which she belonged, has chosen to sanctify her. Sati, although long banned, still takes place occasionally. A case in Sikar district as recently as 1987 caused a national furore and the government attempted to curb all Sati celebrations such as this temple's fair.

24) *Kandelia Well*. Beyond the Rani Sati Temple (23) to the north the road to Churu takes a very sharp turn to the west. At this point another road turns off eastwards. This large well stands a little way along the eastern road, on the left. It was built in 1921.

25) *Ajit Sagar*. This *johara*, beneath a hill, usually contains some water and is a pleasant retreat from the town. It was built by Jitmal Khaitan in 1902. For the energetic it makes a pleasant cycle trip from the town. Instead of turning east to the well (24), or west towards Churu, continue northwards for 2 km. The tank is on the left side of the road. Steps lead to the temple on top of the neighbouring hill, giving a good distant view of the town.

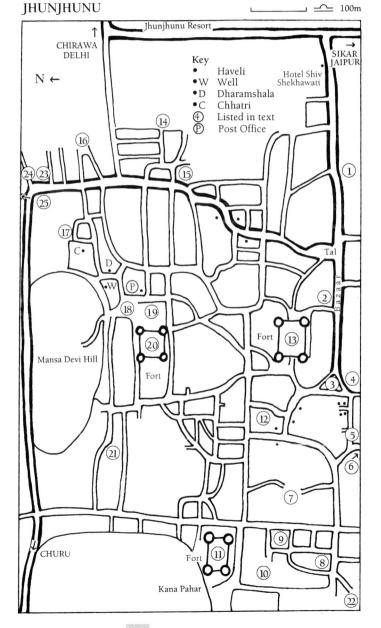

Ked

A pretty little town overlooking the dry, wide ribbon of sand which constitutes Shekhawati's apology for a river, the Katli Nadi. For two centuries this place fell under the Nagad Pathan rulers of Bagad. Sardul Singh's grandfather is said to have evicted them in the late 17th century, but an inscription in the old *chhatri* shows that they were still in power in 1695, long after the old man died.

1) The *chhatri* of Rajmal Choudhary, who was the ancestor of many of the Kedia family of Banias, known throughout India for their electric fans. The *chhatri* was built in 1695 and has early paintings of horsemen, elephants and arabesques. Another inscription tells how it was repaired by his descendants.

2) *The Fort*. Another, more probable, tale says that Sardul Singh's half-brother took the town and its fort in 1720. It is a small redoubt with a fine view to the hills and plain. Within the walls are two domed buildings – were they once tombs?

3) *Dargah and Bowri*. The former is the tomb of a relative of the Muslim saint buried at Narhad. Near it is the *bowri*, which is in a poor state of repair.

Khetri

This hilly tract of Shekhawati came to Kishan Singh, second of the five brothers of the Panchpana. His son, Bhopal Singh, founded the fort and the town in 1756. Khetri was to be the second richest *thikana*, estate, in Jaipur state, and its rulers bore the title of Raja. The town is built at the head of a steep-sided valley running back into one of the hills. A wall crosses this valley to defend the old town from assault. Bhopal Singh encouraged Banias to come and settle here and form a bazaar. Commanding a pass through the hills, the town flourished on transit trade. The most important merchant families were the Choudharys and the Sahas.

The summit of the hill overshadowing the town is surrounded by a high wall. This constitutes the fort, Bhopalgarh. The stiff climb is well worth the effort, not merely for the view but for the opportunity to see the buildings within the walls. A track has just been opened which is passable by jeep. Pandit Jhabarmal Sharma published a Hindi history of the town, *Khetri ka Itihas*.

1) *Bhopalgarh*. The formidable walls of this fort several times defended the Raja from his enemies. Major Forster took it in 1844, soon after the death of Raja Sheonath Singh. The Rani, Bhatiyaniji, had turned out the minister, Ram Nath. He reinstalled him. In 1857, the Jaipur army attacked the fort with 35 guns but failed to take it. It is entered by three gates and the walls enclose a small village, now largely derelict, a temple and two palaces, the Bakhtawar Mahal and the Moti Mahal.

2) *Bakhtawar Mahal*. This handsome palace, being built along and above the fort wall, can be seen from the town. It takes its name from the Raja, Bakhtawar Singh, who constructed it during the 1820s. Until the last Raja died in 1987, it was kept locked. Now it has passed into the hands of the Rajasthan Government. The door has been smashed open and soon the fine building will be despoiled. Inside the doorway steps lead down to a rain-water store which collected all the water that fell on the building. On the right hand side of the courtyard is a high arched *darbar* hall, on the left side the screened women's apartments. On the second floor, beside the hall, there is a *sheesh mahal*, a room covered with mirrorwork, and a *rang mahal* (a painted room). The pigments used in the latter have deteriorated, those that are lead-based becoming black. Some of the panels are historically interesting, showing Raja Bakhtawar Singh in his court, with the individuals named. Several are men who met Col. Lockett and are recorded in his report. The painting was probably still in progress when the Raja died in 1829, since some panels are unfinished. One such is a picture of Jaipur City, part drawn but not painted. In another, a court scene, the courtiers are left as white silhouettes. On the roof is a little classical pavilion, an early sign of western influence in the local architecture. The view from the roof down on to the town and over the hills is magnificent. On the crest of the hills, away to the east, Baghor Fort can be seen.

3) *Moti Mahal* (the Pearl Palace). This is the older palace built by Raja Bagh Singh at the end of the 18th century. There were no doors. Screens would have hung in their place. From the roof one looks down on sand dunes built up against the hillside by the prevailing winds. To the north of the palace is a large bastion containing apartments. Col. Lockett describes meeting the Raja there in 1831: "..a little slave-girl, about 9 or 10 years of age presented herself at an outer door.... (she) disappeared but returned almost immediately with the young Raja in her arms, who was nearly as large and perhaps as heavy as herself.....As the little *budarun*, slave-girl, seemed much oppressed by the weight of her charge we proposed to retire."

4) *Gopal Temple.* Built by Hanuat Ram Choudhary, who appears in one of the court paintings in Bakhtawar Mahal. (2), it contains good murals in very poor condition. It stands on the south side of the east end of the newer section of the bazaar (that part outside the walls), perhaps 200 m east of the Nagar Palika (Municipal Office). It was built around 1825.

5) *Raghunath Temple.* Known as Hari Singh's Temple, it was built by Sobhag Singh of Niradanu around 1865 and stands on an eminence just to the east of the Gopal Temple (4). This building contains some very fine murals, mostly of religious subjects. Others show a man ploughing, another printing cloth and the saint, Kabir, working at his loom.

6) Johara built by Panna Lal Saha in 1871. This huge tank is situated behind the Nagar Palika. Here the Raja, Ajit Singh, greeted the great religious reformer, Swami Vivekanand in 1897. The sculptures set in the walls around the tank must derive from an ancient ruined temple nearby.

7) *Ram Nath Purohit Haveli.* This massive building stands on the hillside in the south-east corner of the walled town. He was the minister whose ejection caused the battle of 1844. He probably built this place in the 1840s. It was long used as a jail but now stands empty.

8) *Thakur Hari Singh's Bastion.* A massive bastion at the west end of the town wall which encloses a *haveli* within its walls.

There are some handsome unpainted temples in the town including that of Raghunathji built by Chandawatji, a Rani of Bakhtawar Singh, in 1827, that of Gopinathji built by Ranawatji, mother of Raja Fateh Singh c1850, and that of Ganga built by the merchant, Panna Lal Saha, in 1855.

Top:
Khetri (5): The ceiling of this temple bears scenes from the life of Krishna. In the pavilion Yashoda, his foster-mother, suckles the blue baby Krishna whilst Rohini feeds his brother, the white baby Balram. (c1870).

Bottom:
Khetri (3): The Moti Mahal was built in the hill-top fort by Raja Bagh Singh in the late 18th century. When Col. Lockett came here in 1831 three dowager *ranis* inhabited the fort. One lived in this palace but the youngest, mother of the infant ruler, was housed in the large bastion on the right.

Lakshmangarh

This town was founded by Lakshman Singh, Raja of Sikar, in 1806 as a new merchant centre to benefit from the boom in caravan trade at the time. The unsettled state of the region soon worked against it. It was plundered by Kan Singh Saledhi not long after its foundation, so the Raja surrounded it by a wall, passed by nine gates, no trace of which survives. He also constructed an impressive little fortress on the rocky hillock which rises from the west of the town. Col. Lockett describes the place in 1831: "I walked through the Town of Luchmun Gurh in the evening, and found it like most of the other towns in Shekhawutee, built in the Jyepoor style, with long wide streets intersecting each other at right angles and numerous shops (I was told 800) but all shut up and deserted. It was built ... for a mart, but the merchants and bankers who settled in it, on the recommendation of the Seekur Chief, had soon occasion to repent it. His exactions were constant and heavy, and on one occasion he had the whole Sahookars (Banias) mulcted to an enormous amount, on the plea of state necessity . ...the Sahookars fled ...".

This town is, in fact, far more "Jeypoor style" than any other in Shekhawati. Not only is it laid out on a grid plan but the main bazaar opens out at intervals into three squares which are also cross-roads, in imitation of the *chaupads* of Jaipur. The town recovered after peace returned to the region, but its great *havelis* were financed by trade through Calcutta rather than through Shekhawati. The Poddar family, known as Ganeriwala (they came from the village of Ganeri), completely dominated the merchant community of the town during the mid 19th century. They built many of the finer monuments that grace the town. Some of the family had already established themselves as prominent bankers in the distant city of Hyderabad in South India. Most of this town was constructed of brick, which has proved to be very vulnerable to decay caused by salts carried up the walls by rising damp. Amongst the local industries is bright tie-dye work.

1) *The Fort.* This dominates the town, moulding itself on to the great boulders of the hill that rises on its western fringe. It was built largely from the rock blasted from the hill top during the laying of its foundations. The design reflects the local response to increased artillery power. The 18th century forts are usually square or rectangular, their straight walls vulnerable to a lively cannonade. At the turn of that century, an agglomeration of rounded bastions became more popular, being more resistant. This fort was not just for show. It was attacked by the Jaipur army in 1825 and the marks of their bombardment show clearly on the north-east face. The buildings within the fort are not striking, but the view from the top makes the climb well worthwhile. The building now belongs to a Bania family.

2) *The Char Chowk Haveli* (the Haveli of Four Courtyards). This is a magnificent double *haveli* built by Murlidar Ganeriwala during the 1840s. The plan can be well seen from the walls of the fort. It was built in two stages, the southern portion with a *naal*, compound, along its north side, was completely and painted first. Probably the northern section was an afterthought, but when it was constructed the *naal* became a passage between the two. From above, one can seen the *chandani* and *pedkala*, little structures on the roof above the stair-wells. Probably the fine *loi* on the outer walls of the southern *haveli* was applied when the last layers were too dry, with the result that much of the painting has fallen away. The north section is generally locked, but it contains a small room decorated with erotic paintings. Not only an architectural gem, this building has some interesting

pictures on its walls, most of them religious. On the facade is a faded picture of a European officer on an elephant. Perhaps this was Col. Lockett, but it is more likely that it represents Major Thoresby. He came here in 1841 and became involved in a dispute between two of the Ganeriwalas, both of whom he found good company. A hint that the paintings date from around 1849 comes from the giraffe on the facade. In that year the Maharaja of Jaipur imported such a beast for his menagerie. It obviously caused a stir and its picture appears in several towns.

3) A row of shops on either side of the bazaar, handsome buildings but lightly painted, constructed by the Ganeriwalas around 1845.

4) *Temple of Radha Murlimanohar*. Another Ganeriwala construction of around 1845. This temple stands in the middle of the northernmost *chaupad* of the town. Notable for its architecture rather than its paintings. There are some nice stucco figures of deities on its outer walls.

5) *Sanwatram Chokhani Haveli*. A fine painted *haveli* from around 1900, red and blue dominating its colours. On the facade are incarnations of Vishnu, also Ardhanareshwar, a half-male, half-female figure which combines Shiva with Parvati. On the southern wall are pictures of a boar-hunt and also a massive chariot pulled by an elephant, such as existed in Jaipur at the time. There is fine woodwork on the building but the interior is unfortunately locked.

6) *Girdharilal Ganeriwala Haveli*. Girdharilal came from Ganeri, settled here and built this *haveli*. It is now sunk in the ground, the ground level having risen through the accumulation of wind-blown sand. One panel on the facade shows four uniformed soldiers, probably the Jaipur army. There are some nice geometric designs amongst the ochre paintings.

7) *Chetram Sanganeeria Haveli*. This Bania's name indicates that he came from the town of Sanganeer, just south of Jaipur. There are soldiers on the facade and on the west wall a couple on a sofa, a *dholahinda* (a little Ferris wheel), a depiction of Krishna and Radha on a swing seat; farmers plough, businessmen do their accounts, carpenters saw and the Rajputs hunt. In the courtyard, a water-carrier is shown with a merchant. The building is rich in good murals. That opposite, to the north, also has some good pictures.

8) *Rishikesh Harbhajandas Ganeriwala Haveli*. Another fine example of an 1840s *haveli* with ochre murals. On the facade are the five Pandavas, heroes of the Mahabharata epic, carrying spears, swords and shields.

9) *Chhatri of Lalchand Choudhary* (the family were known here as Churiwala). Built in 1856. Within the dome are labelled paintings of incarnations of Vishnu. Some of the murals have been whitewashed over, but an attempt has been made to remove the layer – a hopeful sign! Neighbouring this memorial is a double *chhatri* built by the same family in 1847.

10) *Jamnadas Jawahar Mal Pansari Haveli*. The south wall is covered with paintings. In the centre is a Raja of Sikar riding in an open carriage. There is a marriage with the couple standing on a raised platform. A man rides a motorcycle. There are several named folk tales, one being Nehalde-Sultan – Sultan holds his shield over Nehalde's head as an umbrella. At the bottom of the wall the small panels, though faded, are worth a look. Beneath this wall there is usually an encampment of the nomadic ironworkers known as Lohars, with their distinctive carts. It is said that when the fort of Chittor fell to the Mughals in the 16th century, the swordsmiths of the garrison set out to become tinkers,

Lakshmangarh (10): The south wall of Jamnadas Jawaharmal Pansari Haveli is rich in interesting pictures. The Raja of Sikar, in his landau, is shown in procession whilst beneath him are several scenes from folk tales. The shops or storerooms in the base of the wall are a common feature of these *havelis*. (c1915).

Above:
Lakshmangarh (11): On the facade of Shivlal Ramnarayan Pansari Dharamshala the British use a motorized pump to raise water from a well. Playing with the architectural features the painter has perched two more men on top of a stucco arch. Perhaps one intends to dislodge the other! (c1900).

Right:
Lakshmangarh (20): A prosperous merchant in all his finery poses on the facade of Mahadev Prasad Jalan Haveli. With his jewels and sash he is certainly a man of rank. (c1920).

Lakshmangarh (18): On the wall of a *baithak* built by the Rathi family a foreign lady listens to the gramophone. The decorative designs used are quite as alien as the subject! (c1912).

vowing never to settle until the Rana of Mewar was once more established in his fortress. But the Rana moved his capital to Udaipur, never returning to Chittor – so the Lohars continue to wander! The *haveli* dates from about 1915.

11) *Shivlal Ramnarayan Pansari Dharamshala*. Built c1900, a good example of a painted *sarai*. On the facade south of the door is a train, and beneath it a lady tells a man to let go of her hand, since she is shy. North of the door are pictures of a well with a motor pump and even a little man with a cannon perched above a window. In the courtyard are more pictures including a woman applying a spot of colour to the forehead of a Rajput's horse, another episode in the Sultan-Nehalde tale.

12) *Girdharilal Churiwala Haveli* c1900. A good single-courtyard painted *haveli*. On the top right hand side of the facade the moon travels in a *rath*, a chariot, pulled by deer; the sun follows in a horse-drawn *rath*. Sheltered in the arches of the lower facade a woman ties her turban in front of a mirror.

13) *Shyonarayan Kyal Haveli* c 1900. Another heavily-painted single-courtyard house. There are some erotics neatly placed on the outer walls. At the north end of the facade Krishna is shown with his brother, Balram, and sister Subhadra, in the form that they are worshipped as Jagannath (Lord of the Universe) at Puri in Orissa. At the south end Ranjha is shown sitting on a hill minding his cattle while his beloved Heer approaches with food. Under the arches of the facade a woman removes a thorn from her foot – a theme popular for centuries with Indian artists. The porch has a painted ceiling, Krishna and the *gopis* dancing in the *rasamandala*. On the south wall Rama and Lakshmana go for a ride in the *rath* with Hanuman driving. There is also a good picture of Surya (the Sun God) in his rath. On the east wall are a farmer and his wife – and a couple of erotics. The painter, Banna Chejara, has signed his work.

14) *Ram Parasrampuria Naria Haveli* c1910. Again, heavily painted. On the east wall are an elephant *rath* and Dhola-Maru. On the south, a merchant in a black coat with his wife, a Gangaur procession, with women carrying the images of Gauri and Iser to a well, erotics and farmers. At the west end of this wall a woman says to a European: "I can give you much pleasure". On the north a man is in the act of making his camel kneel whilst his wife tells the child to hold on. A *seth* sits in a chair writing whilst a woman peeks from her veil beside him. The painter signs himself as Lakshmi Narayan Chejara.

15) *Ram Chetram Sikaria Haveli* c1890. On the facade a man ties his turban, a scene at the well, and a train. The dome of the porch is painted and has mirrorwork set in it. There are two merchants on the wall, wearing long coats and flying kites – spot the kites! An attractive courtyard with Surya and Chandra (the sun and the moon) in their respective *raths* on the upper wall. There is a painted *baithak* off the forecourt.

16) *Chunnilal Harinarayan Jajodia* (Dalia) *Haveli*. 1902. Generally locked, but with good paintings on the outer walls. Upper facade has portraits of ruling princes of India, the north wall shows a Gangaur procession. Panels show deities and women. The painters often use their space with imagination — note the little man above the window posed to avoid a cavity in the wall. He reaches down to take his hookah from a woman standing below!

17) *Satyanarayan Jajodia Haveli + Nohra + Shop*. c1885. A *nohra* is an enclosed piece of land where cattle are kept and firewood stored. There are some nice red and blue paintings, most of them religious.

18) *Baithak* built by the Rathi family. c1912. European women listen to the gramophone and

use a sewing machine on the west wall. On the facade there are several stencil copies of a popular print of Krishna.

19) *Mahavir Rathi Haveli.* A handsome small *haveli* dating from around 1900. There is mirrorwork set in the upper facade. In the arches on the lower facade *seths* and Rajputs sit in chairs.

20) *Mahadev Prasad Jalan Haveli.* On the facade are some copies of paintings by the artist Ravi Verma. A little panel shows a man with elephantiasis with two dogs. A *seth* is shown in a fine yellow coat. On the west wall is a cyclist. The east wall has ruling princes of India, George V and some rabbits; also, much faded, a view of the town in which the fort is just distinguishable. Built c1920.

21) *Raghunath Temple.* Built by Bidawatji, the senior Rani of Raja Lakshman Singh of Sikar, the founder of the town, in 1825. There are some ochre murals.

22) *Gumaniram Kanhaiyalal Ganeriwala Johara* and *Tibari.* This is situated on the western fringe of the town about 100 m south of the road and the same distance south-west of Todi College. Constructed in 1842, this is a fine tank, but there is little painting. There is another *johara* on the eastern edge of the town near the Mukundgarh road, built as a famine relief project by the Chokhanis in 1898.

LAKSHMANGARH

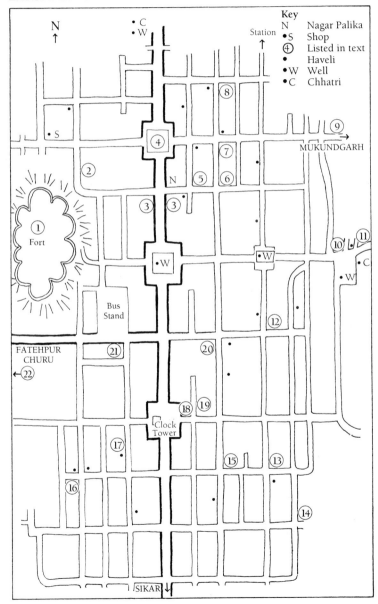

Lohargal

A small place of pilgrimage right at the foot of the steep Aravalli Hills. Here a spring emerges from the ground and fills a little tank, which is the centre of devotions, surrounded by temples some of which date back to the early 17th century. The place was a religious centre long before that. It is reached along a track that leaves the Sikar-Udaipurwati road at Golana. This passes a fine step-well with a temple beside it. Both date from the early 19th century. The village itself is set amongst dark mango trees. High above, requiring a stiff climb, is a little shrine, Barkhandy. From there one gets a beautiful view of this part of Shekhawati ... provided the day is clear. There are two other similar holy places, Shakambari and Kirori, both reached from near Udaipurwati.

Lohargal: One of three small centres of pilgrimage along the foot of the Aravalli Hills in Shekhawati. Each marks a spring, which here fills a little reservoir, Surya Koond, where people come for ritual bathing. The rocky hills rise abruptly behind the temples.

Mahansar

This village fell in the portion of Nawal Singh, fourth of the five sons of Sardul Singh. The fort was founded in 1768. In the early 19th century the Thakur seems to have been tempted from time to time by the rich caravans that passed nearby. There is a record of a protracted legal battle at the Jaipur court in 1825. Some Poddars from nearby Ramgarh accused the Thakur of hijacking 16 of their camels laden with cotton. Eventually the beasts were returned and relations must have improved for, when Anat Ram Poddar's son had a disagreement with the Raja of Sikar he chose to desert Ramgarh, in the Sikar *thikana*, and settle 6 km east in Mahansar. Here he set up the headquarters of his business, trading in chintz and opium.

Between 1836 and 1851 the Poddars built six monuments which can boast some of the most accomplished mural work in Shekhawati. Their descendants still live in the town – those who are not based in Calcutta. They tell how their ancestor invested much of his wealth in two ship-loads of opium. Both were lost at sea. He had not taken the precaution of insuring his cargo, so he was ruined. Thus they explain the absence of any major buildings put up by their clan after 1851.

The charms of this little town far exceed its size and make it well worth a detour.

1) *The Fort.* Founded in 1768 but, like most others, continually expanded and altered. There are murals on the inner buildings, but the best are the few panels in the gateway arch (perhaps dating from the late 18th century), all of which relate to incarnations of Vishnu, and those in a room above the gate (c1820s). The latter are very good but in poor condition. The view from the highest tower over the town and the desert beyond is interesting.

2) *Raghunath Temple*, known locally as the Barra Mandir (the Big Temple), is among the largest and most handsome temples of its kind in the region. It was built between 1844 and 1850 by Harkanth Rai Poddar and his family. At the east end of the building is a structure intended to be the foundation of a great tower. The loss of that opium cargo, they say, prevented its completion. There are excellent paintings both in the courtyard (one shows Ram Raj, the wonderful era when the cow and the tiger will peacefully drink together) and on the outer walls. The latter, in red and green ochres, are fine two-dimensional pictures in the best traditional manner. A side shrine contains some marble idols of Shiva and his family. The view from the roof is good.

3) *Shiva Temple.* Built by the Poddars in 1839 it stands some 80 m north of the Raghunath Temple (2) on the west side of the road. Small, but it has good murals, especially the guards at either side of the door.

4) *Sone ki Dukan* (The Golden Shop). This fine little building, adjoining the Shiva Temple (3) to the north, was put up by Harkanth Rai Poddar and his family as the *baithak* and head-office of his business. The exterior is attractive, with its white marble pillars and pierced screens on the upper facade. The pigments that were used on the outer walls were abruptly changed for some reason. Those on the facade have faded badly, whilst those on the sides – the usual ochres – are still clear. The change can best be seen under the eaves. But the importance of this *baithak* comes from its interior – the keys may be available from a shop beneath the Barra Mandir (2), run by a descendant of the builder. The place has wrongly been described as a jeweller's show-room. Its name comes from the liberal use of gold in the paintings on the walls and ceilings and its shop-like layout. The vaulted ceiling is in three sections: the south bears the story of the *Ramayana*; the central,

Left:
Mahansar (1): In a room above the gateway of the fort this foreigner has been added to older paintings. He is surely one of the early British officers to visit Shekhawati, perhaps Col. Lockett (painted c1840).

Below:
Mahansar: This tiny town as seen from the tower of its fort (1). On the right is the Barra Mandir (2), in the centre a two-pillared well and to the left of this are the Shiv Temple (3) and the remarkable Sone ki Dukan (4), both seen from the rear.

Mahansar (4): One of three vaulted ceilings in the Sone ki Dukan (the Golden Shop), perhaps the finest painted room in Shekhawati. The central carpet-like design is surrounded by panels showing incarnations of Vishnu. This building was constructed by Harkanth Rai Poddar around 1850 as the head office of his opium and chintz business.

Top:
Mahansar (4): On the vault of this section of the ceiling the whole of the epic *Ramayana* is illustrated. Here Rama and Lakshmana accompany the sage, Vishwamitra, to his hermitage. There they destroy the demons who have defiled his sacrifices. (c1850).

Bottom:
Mahansar (5): Above a *tibari* three-arched chamber, are some fine panels painted in earth colours. On the left, ten-headed Ravana and his demons confront some of Rama's monkey army. Rama and his ally Hanuman advance in the central panel whilst on the right the creation of Brahma from a lotus springing from Vishnu's navel is depicted. The basement of a Poddar *chhatri* dated 1836.

24 labelled incarnations of Vishnu; the north, episodes from the life of Krishna. The walls are covered with fine floral designs, bowls of fruit and religious texts in gold leaf. Do not overlook the fine carved beams. Completed around 1850.

5) *Sahaj Ram Poddar Chhatri*. This stands on the western edge of the town, just north of the road leading from the bazaar towards Ramgarh. It was built in 1836 and bears some excellent ochre paintings on its basement walls. On the north wall is a procession, the small figure on the elephant being, surely, the young Raja of Jaipur, Ram Singh. On the west side are some seated Rajputs with their full pleated skirts. On the south, horsemen hunt. On either side of the steps are some fine religious panels, including Vishnu lying with Lakshmi at his feet while Brahma is born from a lotus growing from his navel; the demons and the gods churning the ocean; Rama with his bow riding in his *rath* and Ravana also in a *rath*, with his demon army. About 200 m west of this *chhatri* is a *johara* built by the Poddars in 1846.

6) *Tola Ramji ka Kamra* – Built by Tola Ram Maskara c1920. Local people often prefer this to the Golden Shop. It contains a number of early 20th century prints and stands opposite the post office. South of the post office is a small painted *haveli* with labelled paintings signed by one Binja. One of the panels above the street shows two men seated in chairs. They are Boileau (who came to Bissau in 1831) and the Qazi, the administrator in that town.

7) *Poddar Haveli*. About 150 m south-south-east of the south-east corner of the fort. This handsome mansion contains some good maroon paintings, particularly in the courtyard and porch.

There are other interesting painted houses in the town. It is an ideal place to walk about and explore for yourself.

Malsisar: Outside the great gates of a *dharamshala* in the main street of this town a camel stands tethered. This building is only lightly painted as are most caravansarais.

Malsisar (3): The *samadhi*, burial place of Prem Giriji, an important holy man of the town. Krishna and the *gopis* encircle the mirrorwork centre of the dome. Two panels amidst the floral designs show (left) a combination of Shiva and Krishna and (right) another figure which is half Shiva, half Parvati. The central panel, presided over by Ganesh, illustrates incarnations of Vishnu. An imported glass ball hangs from the dome. (c1850).

Malsisar

Malsisar came in the portion of Zorawar Singh, the eldest and most prolific son of Sardul Singh. His son, Maha Singh, settled here in 1752, and founded the fort 10 years later. It is recorded that he brought a merchant with him, who built a *haveli* and a temple. His son, Thakur Prithvi Singh (1770-1822), encouraged more Banias, including members of the Banka, Marodiya, Kedia, Latha, Loharuka and Saraogi clans. Some of these must have prospered since there are considerable buildings in their names. The town became one of those involved with the dacoity in the region and the Thakur was spoken of as a member of Shyam Singh of Bissau's gang. Because of this the Shekhawati Brigade paid the place a visit in 1836 and blew up one wall of the fort – which was soon repaired. The people of Bissau have another story. They say that the Brigade came to Bissau with orders to fire eight shots at its walls. So impressed were the British by a ruse played on them (see Bissau) that they were reluctant to use the shots on the walls of Bissau. The Qazi suggested that they might use them on the walls of Malsisar instead. So they did. A holy man, Prem Giriji, arrived here in the 1820s, and the Thakur became his devotee. He was to be the first of a succession of *gosain* to settle here. These *gosain* were Brahmins, many of whom lived a semi-monastic life and became warriors, fighting for their local ruler.

Malsisar is about 6 km north west of Alsisar and the two little towns can be combined for a very pleasant trip from Jhunjhunu. At present, the road to Gangiyasar is not yet metalled and is passable only for local buses and jeeps. The road extends each year and soon, no doubt, Malsisar will be equally accessible from Bissau.

1) *The Fort.* Commenced in 1762 but, as with all forts, continually improved. There are some nice ochre paintings on the walls of the inner buildings dating from around 1855. It is now in the hands of a Brahmin Trust.

2) *Johara.* Dug some 2 km north of the town on the east side of the road, this is another example of a relief project, in this case jointly funded by the Thakur and local merchants during the terrible Chaupan Akaal, the famine of 1899.

3) *Samadhi* (burial place) of Prem Giriji. About 0.5 km south of the fort, this building stands in a compound with other small, domed *samadhis* of his successors. The interior of Prem Giriji's *samadhi* has fine murals and mirrorwork. The style indicates that this was painted by the same Jaipur team who decorated the Sone ki Dukan in Mahansar. The subjects are mostly religious, but there is also a glass painting of Prem Giriji with Thakur Prithvi Singh. Built about 1850 – the outer paintings are later. This building has wrongly been described in various publications as a Gopinath Temple. The *samadhi* of Moz Giriji, nearby, also contains good paintings.

4) *Banka Well.* This stands a little to the west of Prem Giriji's *samadhi* (3) on the north side of the road. The four pillars lean markedly away from the shaft. This appears to do no harm. When I suggested to an old man that they were on the verge of collapse he smiled and told me that they had been like that since he was a little boy. Built c1895.

5) *Jokhi Ram Jhunjhunuwala Well.* On the eastern fringe of the town, a fine well with some painting, built c1890.

6) *Banka Johara.* On the west side of the road to Alsisar, beyond the south edge of the little town.

There are several painted *havelis* in the town, mostly along the road between the fort and the *samadhis*, but also along that running northwards from the Banka Well (4). A Kedia *haveli* beside the bus stand used to have some interesting murals on its facade, dating from the 1820s. It was improved by whitewash.

Mandawa

Nawal Singh, the fourth son of Sardul Singh, inherited this place and raised it to town status by the foundation of a fort in 1756. The family did not settle here until the very end of the 18th century, when Nawal Singh's grandsons, Padam Singh and Gyan Singh, moved in from Nawalgarh. The town was originally walled, but little trace remains of the defences. The only gate to survive, Sonthliya Gate, at the east end of the bazaar, is a very recent construction.

In 1828, the fort held out successfully for more than a week against the united forces of Jaipur and the Rao Raja of Sikar. They had first attacked Nawalgarh, but, despairing of success, suddenly struck camp and headed for this town, hoping to take it by surprise. The Nawalgarh Thakurs learnt of the move and quickly sent reinforcements to their relatives. These troops entered the fortress under cover of night. The batteries opened fire the following morning but, fortunately for the defenders, serious disagreements broke out between factions in the attacking army. This ended in violence, some men were killed and the siege was lifted.

Lockett came here on 6th May 1831 and leaves one of the earliest references to the painted buildings of Shekhawati: "The town of Mundawah though small, is built in the Jeypoor fashion, with fine pucka houses and wide streets at right angles. The buildings are in general handsome and the upper stories of some of them painted in a very neat manner."

In the early 19th century, two merchant families dominated the business community – the Dhandhanias, from the village of Dhandhan, and the Harlalkas. One branch of the former clan, descendants of one Bhagchand Dhandhania, were known as Bhagchandka. Both families left fine old buildings. Other prominent Bania families were the Ladias, who can lay claim to what is perhaps the finest painted *haveli* in Shekhawati (18), the Chokhanis, the Sonthliyas, Sarafs and Goenkas. Ram Nath Goenka, the owner of the *Indian Express* chain of newspapers, has a *haveli* just north of the bus stand on the east side of the little park.

A local man, Balu Ram, was one of the last painters of note in the area. Active around 1940, he has left an interesting collection of murals, many of which are inspired by, or copied from, western prints. The fort houses Hotel Castle Mandawa, which also offers suites in a rural setting at its Desert Camp. A new building, Hotel Rath, stands on the eastern edge of the town. In the town there are several shops selling souvenirs. At one of these, Chhe Chokia, in the main street, Ram Ratan Sharma, a carver of sandalwood, plies his craft. Mandawa has bus connections with Delhi (240 km), Jaipur (165 km), Jhunjhunu (24 km), Fatehpur (20 km), and Nawalgarh (25 km).

1) *The Fort.* Founded in 1756, but the oldest residential buildings date from about 1800, after Padam Singh and Gyan Singh moved in. Some of the rooms are decorated with fine murals, but these are mostly in a poor state of repair. They date from around 1830 and some of the figurative panels were added over earlier floral designs. Here and there, where damp has damaged the pictures, traces of the earlier decoration can just be seen. The artists would have been itinerant professional muralists brought in from Jaipur. The subjects are very variable. Apart from the customary religious scenes, there are pictures of hunts, women musicians, a Gangaur procession, a labelled *ragamala* and even such subjects as fairgrounds. The family have opened a museum, which contains an interesting display of items, including the formal robes of some of their ancestors.

2) *Sonthliya Gate.* The rather lurid eastern gate of the town, built in the 1930s by the Sonthliya family. On top of it is a figure of Krishna with a cow on either side. A room above the gate contains some murals by Balu Ram (c1940), some having a flavour of the

Mandawa: On the wall of a Saraf haveli a British officer sits in his armchair surveying the world through his telescope. Telescopes are often associated with foreign ships in the murals. (c1890).

Below:
Mandawa (9): A child peeps through a window in the south wall of the Goenka double *haveli*. The pictures show a *bhishti*, water-carrier, laying the dust in front of a horse dragging a gun, a falcon sitting on a soldier's wrist and an aggressive procession. (c1890).

Page 186:
Mandawa (6): On the east wall of this *haveli* of the Newatia family traditional subjects contrast with those that were then topical – the unattended car and an interesting early plane. (c1920).

Page 187:
Mandawa (16): In the forecourt of this beautiful *haveli* an elephant painted on the wall is repeated on the side of a little flight of stairs. Above them merchants and foreigners sit in armchairs. (painted c1890).

work of Douanier Rousseau. Others are portraits carefully copied from photographs. One of these shows Jai Singhji, one of the two present Thakurs of the town.

3) *Rameshwarlal Sundarmal Akhramka Haveli.* A handsome and richly-painted house dating from c1880. The subjects include hunting and folk stories. On the south wall is a long frieze showing a Rajput ruler meeting a British officer, probably a reference to one of the visits paid to the town in the 1830s and 1840s. Krishna is shown playing *chaupad.*

4) *Balkrishan Sriram Saraf Haveli.* c1890. A large mansion with interesting pictures. A shop projects on to the street from the west end of its facade. On the facade is a large faded ship – an unusual subject. On the east wall is a procession, a train, carpenters sawing, erotics and even a panel of a woman giving birth between the northernmost brackets!

5) *Group of Bhagchandka Chhatris.* These are just east across the road from the Saraf *Haveli* (4), the entrance being on the main road to Jhunjhunu. The *chhatri* nearest the road is dated 1852 and has a little painting on its outer walls – also a nice pair of stucco elephants either side of its door. In the compound beyond are a line of three *chhatris* on a single basement, in danger of collapse. One contains murals in poor condition dating from the early 19th century.

6) *Bansidhar Newatia Haveli.* c1920. The east wall of this building has some interesting paintings. A merchant family waves farewell to an early aeroplane, a boy telephones, there is a bicycle, and a car is being restrained by "Professor Ram Murti Nayar", a famous strong-man of his time. Beneath are more traditional subjects. The older *haveli* (c1850) to the north has two Europeans with telescopes and even a giant rat on its facade!

7) *Bhagchandka Haveli.* Built perhaps in the 1820s, this is a handsome example of an early 19th century *haveli*, part buried by the rising ground level. It is not heavily painted, although a couple of panels by the door are good. It illustrates the tragedy of the lack of any guidelines on the preservation of these buildings. A Congress poster depicting Mrs. Gandhi has defaced one of the panels (political posters and slogans are a menace to these pictures, but I have heard of no suggestion by any party that their use be controlled!) The upper facade, which retained some nice geometric patterns, has been, recently, brightly painted over. A new tin roof has been attached to the facade, damaging the plaster.

8) *Hanuman Prasad Goenka Haveli.* A fine painted building, the work by one Harsa of Mukundgarh. A nice array of carved wooden windows. On the south wall there are Banias seated in small chairs, dressed in white and wearing their characteristic little turbans. The west end of the house with the *baithak* was never completed and has been left unpainted. Some erotics. On the facade, over the door, Shiv riding his bull, Nandi, meets Vishnu on an elephant, and the heads of the two beasts merge. c1900.

9) *Goenka Double Haveli.* These two *havelis* share a common forecourt and the paintings on one side are mirrored by those on the other. Large panels of elephants and horsemen cross the facade. The paintings on the north and south walls have been protected from the worst effects of weather and remain in very good condition. A panel on the north wall depicts the *Ramayana*, another, a man hand-printing cloth. The murals date from around 1890.

10) *Nandlal Murmuria Haveli.* c1935. Another example of Balu Ram's work, much of it straight copying from contemporary prints etc. The subjects include views of Venice, trains, cars, a copy of a painting by Ravi Varma, Nehru on horseback, Gandhi and George V.

11) *Thakurji Temple*, built by Harnand Rai Goenka c1860. The outer walls have some interesting murals: masons build a temple, jugglers perform, and uniformed soldiers are

shot off the mouths of a cannon – probably a reference to the suppression of the Mutiny of 1857.

12) *Goenka Chhatri*. Built by Harnand Rai Goenka around 1855. There are excellent murals on the basement and in the domes. Those in the domes are mainly religious, relating to incarnations of Vishnu. There is an odd painting on the west wall, whilst on the south a mason labelled "Kalu Khan" is shown carrying his spade. This may be a self-portrait of the painter. The little figure of Ganesh which till recently stood over the gateway has been smashed. Not iconoclasm – just an inefficient attempt at theft for the antique market!

13) *Harlalka Chhatri*. Double *chhatri* built by Bhagwan Das Harlalka 1841. Very good murals, mostly depicting incarnations of Vishnu. This *chhatri* now houses a middle school – a common adaptation for such memorials, and seemingly a sensible and sensitive one ... as long as the kids can't touch the paintings! The painter of this *chhatri* (13) and the well (14) was also responsible for some of the fine work in Mahansar (i.e. the *chhatri*) (5).

14) *Harlalka Well*. This magnificent well can still be seen in action in the early morning and evening, irrigating the patch of land surrounding it. There are good murals within the domes. In the north-east *chhatri* a panel shows the lovers Laila and Majnu; there is a *fakir* with long hair and a girl with a yoyo. In the south-east, wrestlers with Indian clubs. In the north-west there is a picture of the ideal age, Ram Raj, when cow will drink beside tiger, also Chandra, the moon, in his chariot, fights a demon. Built around 1845.

15) *Kedarmal Ladia Haveli*. A double *haveli*, the northern section built in the early 1900s, the southern in 1915. There is a fine painted *baithak* in the north-east corner of the building, the work of Jaipur artists. The paintings on the outer walls were by Govardhan Chejara and are not of a very high quality. The lead-based pigment used for the faces has deteriorated to make them black. High on the north wall is an erotic panel, whilst a horse, lower on the same wall, has partly been constructed using a compass-arc.

16) *Mohanlal Saraf Haveli*. Probably built around 1870, but painted towards the close of the century. This is a very handsome building, heavily painted in blue and red. On the south wall, exposed to the sun, most of the pictures have faded completely. On the facade, Dadu Dayal, a disciple of Kabir, is shown in white clothes above a window. There are also wealthy Banias seated in chairs whilst a satirical panel shows a woman putting on her skirt after a visit from a holy man. In the forecourt, as well as mirrorwork there are pictures of a goldsmith, a carpenter and also the three deities representing the sacred rivers, Ganga, Jumna, and Saraswati.

17) *Lakshminarayan Ladia Haveli*. Built in 1851, but mostly painted in the 1890s. On the west wall there are some good religious panels between the brackets, one of which shows the composite beast Ajaibgulmari. There are also two large horsemen, perhaps representing the dacoits Dungarji and Jawahirji, who gained a reputation for robbing the rich to help the poor. When one was arrested and put in Agra jail by the British the other took a small force and released him! A frieze shows Rajput and British notables meeting, a faded erotic, and a scene at a well.

18) *Gulab Rai Ladia Haveli*. Probably completed around 1870, its present murals date from the 1890s. This building is undoubtedly one of the finest in Shekhawati. The walls are covered with very good work, the subjects many and varied. On the facade there are several scenes from the life of the merchant, Gulab Rai, with Mandawa Fort in the background. There are also Europeans working some kind of machine, a train and the familiar elephants and camels. Splashes of blue wash here and there undoubtedly denote

censorship. The late 19th century was very open to erotic art and such pictures were commonly strategically placed on the outer *haveli* walls. Recently there has been a backlash of prudery and murals have suffered. Beneath a window at the east end of the south wall there used to be an amusing erotic. Too many people noticed it, and it was scraped off in 1984. Others survive under the projecting cave of the facade, or on the south wall. There, a little train runs beneath an elephant – but what is going on in the third coach from the rear! Another picture shows an interesting connection. Between the brackets low on this wall at its east end is a picture of a man climbing a tree out of hell. Nearby stands an elephant. This is an exact copy of a label produced by F.Steiner and Co., a Manchester manufacturer of red-dyed cloth such as the merchants so often handled. In the forecourt there is mirrorwork above the door. In the *baithak* on the south side there is also a portrait of Gulab Rai by Balu Ram, copied from a photograph. There is said to be a good painted room in the *haveli*, but it is locked.

19) *Chokhani Double Haveli.* A handsome building dating from around 1910 with some interesting pictures.

20) *Sneh Ram Ladia Haveli.* Built in the early 20th century, some of its outer murals are dated 1907. On the facade is a picture of a man being bathed before his marriage, and in the *baithak* on the south side of the forecourt are some amusing pictures by Balu Ram (1940). On the south wall a merchant listens to his gramophone and Sultan rescues his lover Nehalde, out of a *sati* fire. Beneath this *haveli* is a handicraft/souvenir shop with a wide selection of goods.

21) Two *havelis* built by Tanu Manu Saraf in the late 19th century. Both are painted with good pictures. On the south wall of the south *haveli* is a procession, probably of the Jaipur army. In the forecourt, mirrorwork, a scene at a fort, Europeans having a party and two copies of labels attached to cotton goods, one a variant of that seen on Gulab Rai Ladia Haveli (18). On the facade is a train and a woman with two cobras. There is also a nice train on the north *haveli*. The walls of both buildings have been recently repaired in traditional materials, a far better solution than the usual cement.

22) *Two small Chokhani Havelis.* Both built about 1840. These have murals in natural ochres on their outer walls. Apart from religious subjects there are soldiers, hunters and wrestlers.

23) *Majisa ka Kuan.* A fine well built by the wife of Thakur Gopal Singh between 1848 and 1851. There is little painting but a short distance to the west stand the *chhatris* of the local rulers. Of these the most interesting is a double *chhatri* probably erected over Thakur Gopal Singh and Thakur Ram Pratap Singh around 1860. There are some fine murals within the domes.

24) *Chokhani Johara.* Known as Alkhia Johara and built around 1845, it stands to the east of the Nawalgarh road, some 2 km from Sonthliya Gate. The Desert Camp is not far away on the opposite side of the road.

MANDAWA

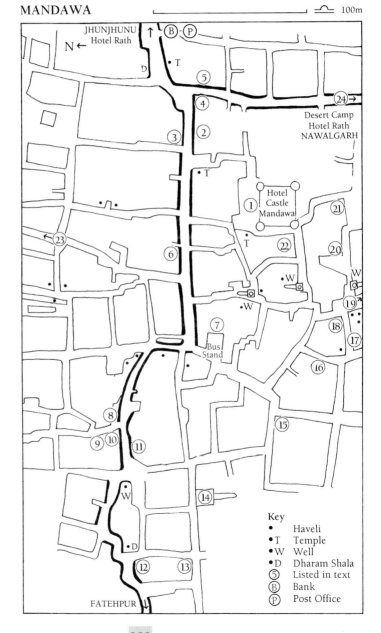

Key
- • Haveli
- •T Temple
- •W Well
- •D Dharam Shala
- ⑤ Listed in text
- Ⓑ Bank
- Ⓟ Post Office

Mukundgarh

This town was founded in 1860 by Mukund Singh, one of the Thakurs of Nawalgarh. The streets are laid out on a grid plan, centering on the temple of Gopinath. As usual, Banias were encouraged to settle in the town and activate a bazaar. Prominent amongst the merchants were the Ganeriwala and Kanoria families. The town is about 5 km north of Dundlod and 7 km south-east of Churi Ajitgarh. The three could be combined for an outing. Recently the fort has been opened as a hotel.

1) *The Fort.* Founded in 1859 by Mukund Singh, but much of the building dates from the turn of the century. Not a handsome building and lacking in any murals.

2) *Gopinath Temple.* Founded in 1861. Its design is of a type that was more common in the 18th century, with a single tower over the shrine. Perhaps it was inspired by the Gopinath Temple built in the heart of Nawalgarh by Nawal Singh. The murals date from around 1895 and those in the courtyard are quite good, probably the work of Binja of Mukundgarh. Outside the temple on the north side is a well from which the priest could draw his water without leaving the precincts. This temple is the central feature of the town.

3) *Shiv Dutt Ganeriwala Haveli.* About 150 m south-west of Gopinath Temple (2) on the corner, west side, of the second road running south. The building is now largely whitewashed, but a room contains paintings of moderate quality, including some erotics behind a door. Built c1870.

4) *Venugopal Temple.* This was built by the Ganeriwalas around 1865 and stands some 100 m west of Gopinath Temple (2) on the north side of the road. There are some good murals in the chamber in front of the shrine.

5) *Jagannath Rai Ganeriwala Haveli.* c1865. A fine double *haveli* about 100 m south-south-west of Gopinath Temple (2), on the east side of the first road running south, west of the temple (2). There are some good paintings.

There are a number of other painted *havelis* in the town, mostly to the south of, and not far from, the bazaar. There are also a couple of fine wells on the western edge of the town, but they have little painting.

Opposite page
Mukundgarh (2): In the courtyard of the Gopinath Temple a man is shown bending a bow. Despite the unusual beard and hat this probably represents Rama who by breaking a bow won Sita's hand. The artist was probably Binja of Mukundgarh. (painted c1900).

Narhad

In 1600 this was still one of the most important towns in the region. Now, set back from the main road between Chirawa and Pilani, it is a little village known only for its *dargah*, the tomb of a Muslim saint. There are still traces of its former glory. Whenever excavations are made it is not uncommon to turn up ruins or even statuary. One relic which still survives is a small well situated just beyond the village to the right of the track. The oldest of its kind in Shekhawati, it has a *chhatri* at each corner of its platform. Each dome is supported by four pillars made of a sandstone which has proved good for sharpening blades. Some of them are almost worn through! The well is used as a supply for pumped water and two *chhatris* have suffered alteration as a result. An inscription dates the building to 1506.

Nawalgarh

Nawal Singh, the fourth of the five brothers, founded this town in 1737. There was already a village on the site and the Kaimkhanis had a fort nearby. He built a fort and the temple of Gopinath and surrounded the site with walls. All three survive. The walls and bastions enclosing the town were constructed of stone fragments and have lasted particularly well. The original gates were rebuilt in the early part of the present century. The place boasted three forts. Neither Nawalgarh nor Mandawa were amongst the rulers who turned to brigandry. They had managed to keep their estates relatively undivided and thus remained quite prosperous. In the early 19th century Nawalgarh was ruled by four *thakurs*. Boileau describes a visit to the town in 1835: ".....a flourishing city neatly fortified with walls of masonry and boasting of four jolly looking Thakoors ... While engaged with my theodolite on the highest bastion of the citadel I heard a loud noise in the court below where one of the Thakoors was seated and I afterwards discovered that he was discussing Jhootha Ram's circular calling for assistance against the British. While the letter was being read to him the Thakoor, who was as usual under the excitement of opium, was continually interrupting the clerk and bawling out in a most incautious manner the passages which particularly struck his fancy... to the great amusement of his hearers..."

Nawal Singh encouraged some Jaipur merchants to settle here. The Patodia family claim to be among the first. Since the town was successful and the rulers relatively benevolent, the Bania community thrived, and more families came to join them. The Murarka clan were prominent amongst the early arrivals. They say that they came at the request of Nawal Singh in 1756. Two of their early *havelis* still stand about 100 m south-east of the Bowri Gate. Both were handsome buildings, though one is now in a state of collapse. From this town arose that branch of the Choudhary clan which is known throughout India as Goenka. Many other Banias flourished, the names of some clearly giving their origins – i.e. the Jaipurias and the Sanganeerias.

At the west end of the south side of the square which surrounds the Gopinath Temple often a small group of men collects. Here they indulge in a popular pastime – speculation on the weather. Much money depends on a drop of water falling from a certain piece of roof there, for only then is it recognised to have rained. It rarely does, of course, but on those occasions some people make a small fortune! There is only one *thakur* in the town now, the last ruler bearing the title Rawal Sahib. He is the brother of one of the Thakurs of Mandawa and came here by adoption. He offers excellent accommodation at his country house, Roop Niwas Palace, situated about 1 km east of Poddar Gate. This was completed by the present Rawal Sahib in the 1930s and is surrounded by a pleasant garden. More modest is the Tourist Persion in the west of the town. Surjan Singh Jhajhar has published a Hindi history of the town.

1) *The Bala Qila*. The main fort of the town, founded by Nawal Singh in 1737 but with later additions. Today, with the *sabji mandi* just in front of it, buying and selling of vegetables and grain takes place in a corner of the fort. Within the south east bastion is a circular, domed painted room dating from 1850, but with additions into the present century. On the ceiling there are fine views of Jaipur City and Nawalgarh as they were at the time. The painter was surely a Jaipur man, probably the same as decorated the Golden Shop of Mahansar and the *samadhi* in Malsisar. This bastion belongs to the Mukundgarh family and although the key is available at the time of writing it is often difficult to acquire.

Left:
Nawalgarh (8): This map-picture of Nawalgarh is taken from the south, as if from the interior of the Bala Qila (1). It decorates a ceiling in another fort, the Fatehgarh. On the right the Fatehgarh itself is shown, with horses and camels tethered in its compound. In the centre of the town the Gopinath Temple (2) is the dominant building, standing in the middle of the busy bazar square. (c1840).

Below:
Nawalgarh (27): The facade of Mohanlal Saraogi Haveli boasts several fine motor vehicles amongst it murals. (c1930).

Right:
Nawalgarh (30): On the side of one of the eight *havelis* which constitute Aath Haveli this woman holds her baby as she tries to do her make-up in front of a mirror. (c1910).

Below:
Nawalgarh (7): The builder of this mansion, Anandi Lal Poddar, was deeply involved in the struggle for Independence. Now his house has become a school. The frieze at the top of the wall shows a Gangaur procession, women carrying images of the deities. Below the dark carriages of the train the five Pandava brothers attend the *chaupad* game at which their shared wife, Draupadi, was lost. (c1920).

Adjoining this fort to the south is another, the Barragarh, which contains government offices.

2) *Gopinath Temple.* A typical 18th century Shekhawati temple founded with the town, it has been much restored and the present murals are undistinguished 1930s work.

3) *Four Dungaichi Havelis.* These were built around 1890 and have some interesting paintings on their outer walls, many of them the signed work of Binja of Mukundgarh, a popular painter at the time. The Goddess of Learning, Saraswati, appears on her peacock on either side of the door arches. She is a common feature of Nawalgarh *havelis*. On the north wall two large horsemen with spears and muskets are the Robin Hood-like Shekhawati dacoits, Dungarji and Jawahirji. There are also seated merchants in white *dhotis*, a woman peering from behind a barred window and, suitably out of the way, some erotics. The facade by the doorway is interesting since it is constructed at an unusual angle to the door – another not uncommon feature of Nawalgarh *havelis* of that time.

4) *Kalyan Temple.* A large and handsome temple built by Kalyan Singh in 1902 and containing a fair amount of contemporary murals, mostly religious. In the gate arch are rulers.

5) This group of monuments built by the Chokhani family in the 1840s and 50s is a good example of the five buildings each merchant aspired to construct. There are two temples, a *haveli*, *a chhatri* and on the opposite side of the compound a small *dharamshala*, with a fine well to the north. Both the larger temple and the well bear some contemporary murals. To the north of these, on the east side of the road, is an enormous 1930s *haveli* of the Bhagat family.

6) *Radheshyam Murarka Haveli.* Built around 1900, this *haveli* also has an oddly-aligned facade. On the west wall is a procession, Dhola and Maru, and even Jesus looking down from between the brackets. There are named folk-stories on the facade and also two men playing a *daph*, a drum, above a window left of the gate. Daph-playing is popular before the spring festival of Holi. There is also mirrorwork.

7) *Anandi Lal Poddar Haveli.* c 1920. The founder of this *haveli* was an important member of the Congress when it was working to evict the British. The building now houses a higher secondary school bearing his name. It has some good painting. In the forecourt are trains, cars, a Gangaur procession and people bathing in a tank. There is also a picture of the Pandavas playing *chaupad* in which they lost Draupadi in the *Mahabharata*.

8) *The Fatehgarh.* Often known as the Kachhia Garh, this fort was probably a late 18th century construction. It was once surrounded by a circular moat and mud walls, but both have disappeared. Today, only the residential buildings stand, the northern section in the hands of a Brahmin family, the southern with a family of Muslim dyers. The paintings on the outer walls are not remarkable but there is a *tibari* off the courtyard of the northern part which has some paintings dating from about 1845. As well as processions and religious pictures there is an interesting view of the town at one end of the ceiling vault. This is an accurate map of the walled section taken as though from above the courtyard of the Bala Qila, of which only the gate is shown. Near the Gopinath Temple, people are shown at the bazaar, even some merchandise which is perhaps awaiting a camel caravan to carry it away. Several of the buildings can be recognized, including the well and *chhatris* that stand outside Poddar Gate. The east side of the painting is taken up by the Fatehgarh itself, with horses and camels tethered in its courtyard. When the town was painted in the bastion of the Bala Qila (1) some years later, the artist was no doubt

responding to the wish of a rival branch of the family, for he centered his picture on the Bala Qila and showed the Fatehgarh as a tiny place out in the jungle! There is also some mirrorwork in this room.

9) *Shyonarayan Bansidhar Bhagat Haveli*. Architecturally handsome, this mansion is heavily painted. On the facade are a steamship, train and Yam Raj, the God of Death, coming to fetch a man who clings to a lingam for protection. In the forecourt a Gangaur procession and a horsedrawn tram. In the courtyard, Brahmins eat sweets. The paintings date from around 1900 and some are in the style of Binja of Mukundgarh.

10) *Pannalal Mansingka Haveli*. The south wall of this *haveli* adjoins the road and bears pictures of a Gangaur procession as well as some large, named, folk tales including Amar Singh (on horseback) and Hadi Rani (standing above window with a sword), Binjo-Sorath and Heer-Ranjha. There are also paintings on the facade of the *haveli* and the *nohra* which adjoins it. They date from the 1900s.

11) *Ram Kumar Chokhani Haveli*. On the east wall of this *haveli* is a good picture of Dhola and Maru on their camel pursued by the dacoits led by Umra-Sumra. Maru turns back to let fly some arrows. On the south wall there is a procession with large elephants and some uniformed soldiers with a band. An obliterated panel between the brackets must have shown an erotic scene. On the building opposite an erotic has been partially destroyed. The building north of the wall bearing Dhola-Maru has two pictures of the Gangaur procession high on its facade. c1900.

12) *Mohanlal Mukanlal Murarka Haveli*. c1905. The murals here are poor, with the invasion of an unpleasant yellow pigment. The forecourt is worth seeing. It is crossed by a little covered walkway sustained by six pillars.

13) *Gangadas Jamnadhar Goenka Haveli*. c1905. Standing on the corner at the crossing of the main road and two *cul-de-sacs*, another fine mansion. On the facade, a train, the Goddess Ganga, some large Rajputs and a picture of Arjuna and Krishna in a *rath* as they go to battle, a scene from the *Mahabharata*. In the forecourt panels show Saraswati on her peacock, also the three major deities Brahma, Vishnu and Mahesh (Shiva) together. On the south wall are several large scenes from folk stories, some of them labelled – Sultan is shown with Nehalde and three other women at the west end, further along, Amar Singh and Hadi Rani and also an elephant *rath* – a vehicle that actually existed in Jaipur.

14) *Mohanlal Mithuka Haveli*. This was built around 1910 and stands on the corner opposite the previous *haveli* (13). On the facade are some labelled stories, horsemen and a fairy playing a sitar!

15) *Jodhraj Patodia Double Haveli*. Painted in 1903. The Patodias claim to have been among the first merchants to have settled in this town. This is a fine painted building decorated with a variety of subjects. On the facade peacocks dance in the rain, four rats ascend a string held by a European, a man loads his musket and the boar incarnation (Varaha) of Vishnu holds the earth, drawn up from the bottom of the sea, on his snout. As you enter the gate into the forecourt on the wall in front of you there is a large figure of Lakshmi with attendant elephants. From there, two doors lead into the separate houses. The painters were Partha Chejara and Hanuman Chejara. Opposite this *haveli* are two houses with paintings and mirrorwork, one (to the south) signed as the work of Binja of Mukundgarh.

16) *The Chhatris of the Rajput rulers*. The four to the west of the group date from 1824 to 1845. Unpainted but for patterns and perhaps a deity, they are in a poor state of repair.

Top:
Aath Haveli, Nawalgarh (30):
A couple, just married, walk
out in the rain. She is tied to
his scarf and covers her face
entirely with her veil.
(c1920).

Bottom:
Nawalgarh: On the south wall
of a *haveli* belonging to the
Jangid family tailors are
shown at work. Perhaps they
are preparing the young man
for his wedding. This
building is about 100 m south
of the waterworks in the
southeast of the town.
(1921).

The larger memorial to the east was built in 1902 and in its dome has a portrait of Chandra Singh, whom it commemorates. There is an interesting Shiva temple in the centre of the basement. This building is used as a school – my favourite adaptation of these monuments.

17) *Goenka Four Havelis*. Four *havelis* constructed as a unit around a single court. Architecturally interesting, most of the walls are unpainted, being finished in the buff plaster, *loi*. There are some pictures in the gate arch and a large Ganesh at the north exit. c1900.

18) *Goenka Haveli*. Many murals, mostly religious and often labelled decorate this building. On the facade men look out from false windows, a popular Nawalgarh theme.

19) *Hariram Kedwal Haveli*. In the forecourt are a nice train (faintly, in Hindi, on one of the trucks the goods are addressed to a prominent merchant of Dundlod) and a Gangaur procession. On the south wall are a large Dhola-Maru, an elephant *rath* and Rajput soldiers.

20) *Lakshminath Temple*. A large temple built by Ram Kumar Jaipuria in the 1890s. There are some good, mostly religious, murals in the courtyard.

21) *Jokhi Ram Kanoria Well*. Built around 1860, this is the best well in the town, with paintings in its corner domes. Another, older, built by the Jaipuria family, stands a little to the east. It also has some painting but its *chhatris* are arched rather than domed.

22) *Kushali Ram Chhauchharia Haveli*. A very handsome *haveli* situated just outside Nansa Gate, the south gate of the town, on the east side of the road. There are paintings in natural ochres. The facade has recently been damaged by the insensitive construction of a row of shops. Built c1855.

23) *Lakshminarayan Temple*. Known as Saraswaton ka Mandir, it stands opposite the previous *haveli* (22). Small but interesting, with some good mural work. Said to have been built in 1827, but the paintings on the outer walls date from 1848.

24) *Ganga Mai Temple*. Built by the Chhauchharia family in 1868, this temple stands some 200 m south of Nansa Gate near where the road turns sharply to the west. On the vaulted ceiling in front of the shrine there is a set of 24 incarnations of Vishnu. There is also a picture of the *Ramayana* battle and a merchant at his accounts. On the outer wall near the road there is even an erotic, not common on a temple.

25) *Jawaharlaldutt Laduram Sanganeeria Haveli*. A handsome mansion with two courts, boasting beautifully-preserved red and blue paintings on their walls. In the forecourt on the north side is a frieze of the Gangaur procession and either side of the door Saraswati on a goose. On the east wall of the forecourt two bulls fight. There is a good painted porch with illustrations from the stories of Rama and Krishna, as well as a scene from the *Mahabharata*. The carved woodwork is of good quality.

26) *Banwarilal Jivrajka Haveli*. c1890. On the facade of this *haveli* is a Gangaur procession, a hand-pump, a station complete with train, a man with his coat over his head against the cold and even an erotic. Under the canopy to the left of the gate is the Jagannath incarnation of Vishnu – the three idols Balram, Krishna and Subhadra – being worshipped by Brahmins. There are good paintings in the porch and forecourt, but the courtyard is generally locked. There is said to be a good painted room.

27) *Mohanlal Saraogi Haveli*. Built around 1910, this *haveli* was painted c1930. The pictures on the facade should prove interesting. There are Europeans with cars and lorries, a bus, a tent and a viaduct, even a couple of western lovers on a park bench, he in his boater.

There is also a copy of a famous Ravi Varma painting showing the saint, Vishwamitra, being seduced by a very scantily dressed Menaka. Ravi Varma was a South Indian artist who turned to Victorian romantic realism to portray Hindu myths and legends.

28) *Dungarsidas Jhunjhunuwala Haveli*. A fine building, well painted. In the forecourt a Gangaur procession heads for a *johara*, which has been whitewashed out. Perhaps the bathers in the tank were shown naked and the puritan revival decided they must go! The Maharaja of Jodhpur, Takhat Singh, is shown hunting, a family of merchants, Brahma rides a seven-headed horse drawing *a rath* in which Shiva is firing a bow with Vishnu as the arrow, at a demon. There are also several folk tales. On the north wall is a procession, also a train. Built c1895.

29) *Kesardev Murarka Haveli*. c1890. This building has long been locked but the paintings on the facade and its architecture indicate that it might be worth looking inside if you find it open.

30) *Aath Haveli*. Designed as a complex of *aath*, eight, *havelis*, only six were completed. The paintings are amusing rather than good, including such pictures as European women in a bath, riding side-saddle or driving a car, trains and other more traditional subjects. Built around 1910.

31) *Surajmal Chhauchharia Haveli*. Built around 1870 but the paintings date from c1890. Amongst the pictures on the east wall are some Europeans travelling by a balloon (the painter improvises a little on the technology) and men struggling with a machine, perhaps a pump. Brahma and Saraswati are depicted at either side of the gate. There is an interesting little facade on the north side of the alley which runs along the north wall of this *haveli*. On this is a large picture of Binjo and Sorath, he playing his *veena*, and a man on the right side of the wall stands holding his .... finger. Another piece of humour by the painter Binja.

32) *Shivchandra Saha Haveli*. c1920. A large *haveli* with some amusing murals on the east wall – a fire engine, angels, a European girl standing on horseback, another as an acrobat balanced on a pole and a third putting curlers in her hair. In the gate arch are George V, an English railway station with a train and a bridge over a river. About 75 m south along the road from here on the east side is another large *haveli* with some good cars on its facade.

There are a number of painted *havelis* in the vicinity of these last two buildings, so it is a good place to look around.

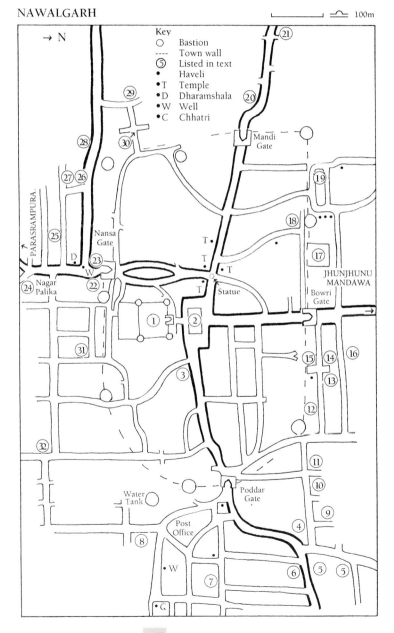

NAWALGARH

100m

Key

○ Bastion
---- Town wall
⑤ Listed in text
• Haveli
•T Temple
•D Dharamshala
•W Well
•C Chhatri

→ N

PARASRAMPURA

Mandi Gate

Nansa Gate

JHUNJHUNU MANDAWA

D
W

Nagar Palika

Statue

Bowri Gate

Water Tank

Poddar Gate

Post Office

W

G

Parasrampura

In this little village, Sardul Singh, later to become father of the five sons who held the Panchpana, settled with relatives. Here he made his home and here he returned to pass his last days. The village stands just east of a wide, sandy *nullah*, a dry river bed, with a small fort on its western bank. Two buildings make it worth a detour. The trip could be coupled with a visit to Udaipurwati and the little holy place of Lohargal.

1) *The chhatri of Sardul Singh*. Completed and painted in 1750. The inscription tells that it was built by his widow, Mertani, and the five sons "in the reign of the Emperor Ahmad Shah". It consists of a large dome supported by 12 pillars and raised on a simple platform. Beautiful, lively paintings seem to envelop you on stepping up between the pillars. These are undoubtedly some of the finest murals in the region. Apart from religious panels showing incarnations of Vishnu, there are scenes from the life of Krishna and also from the *Ramayana*. Sardul Singh is shown in court, with his five sons, also on an elephant hunting a tiger. He is depicted as a plump man, rather pop-eyed. In one scene he smokes a *hookah*. Several of the episodes shown must refer to incidents in his life which would have been familiar to men of this region long after he died but which have now been forgotten. A small scene of the torments of hell is characteristic of the period.

2) *Gopinath Temple*. Built by Sardul Singh in 1742, the year he died. The paintings are very fine and particularly interesting in that the painters were called away literally overnight. Tradition says that they were summoned to paint the temple, but that as soon as the *chhatri* was completed they were asked to decorate that. For some reason – probably problems with payment – they never returned to the first job. The work remains half-complete, clearly indicating the painters' methods. The ceiling was decorated piece-meal, so that there is no trace of sketching where the painters were not actually at work. There are rough lines in charcoal in places, but the pictures were drawn first in red ochre and the colours filled in one at a time. There are Persian-style angels, religious subjects, pictures of Sardul Singh and his five sons and another scene of hell. This building is typical of its period in Shekhawati.

Pilani

The village was included in the share of Nawal Singh, the fourth of the brothers. Later, there was a further division, so that the little fort is now divided between the Rawal Sahib of Nawalgarh and the Thakur of Mukundgarh. A new school has been built within the fort, but the walls remain. Pilani has a few painted *havelis*, some of them in the style of Chirawa. The importance of the town rests on one family, the Birlas. In the 18th century they were settled in Budholi, near Sikar. One of the family made the move to Nawalgarh and his son, Sheo Narayan, settled in Pilani. It was he who, moving to Bombay in the mid-19th century, laid the foundations to the family fortune. His son, Baldev Das, and grandson, Ghanshyam Das, founded the Birla Institute of Technical Sciences here, which has made the place the most widely-known Shekhawati town in India.

For its painted buildings Pilani is undistinguished, but a museum in the old Birla mansion sets an example to other rich local businessmen of what can be done with a painted *haveli*. It includes a wide collection of pictures of members of the family, the clothes they wore, a wedding *mandap*, a marquee, utensils for *puja*, religious rites, horoscopes and the decorative finery that was put on a *seth's* horse, bullock, camel or elephant on formal occasions, and even a fine silver *howdah*. There is also a *baithak* kept as it would have been in earlier days, with white sheets spread over the floor and great bolsters against which the men would recline. From the ceiling hangs a glass chandelier, one of the many Belgian imports, and a traditional *punkah*, the old swinging fan operated by hand (or, more usually, foot). This museum is a useful preparation for, or finale to, a visit to Shekhawati.

There is a rest house at Pilani, and even a little Chinese restaurant at Connaught Place on the college campus.

Raghunathgarh

Set back from the Sikar-Udaipurwati road at the head of a steep-sided valley right amongst the hills. A wall crosses the valley to defend the place from assault. There are a few minor painted houses here, but it is more important as the centre of a quarrying industry which provided many of the stone elements for the buildings of Shekhawati. The masons are still hard at work. Crowning the hills and invisible from the town is a large fort which the British, coming here in the 1830s, described as the most formidable in the region. There is barely a track leading up to it today. The way climbs past three small redoubts, the first of which rises just above the town to the south.

Ramgarh

Still known as Sethon ka Ramgarh (the Ramgarh of the Wealthy Merchants) to differentiate it from other Ramgarhs in the country, this town has an interesting history. It lies some 16 km south of Churu but, before Independence, was divided from it by a frontier. Churu was in Bikaner state whilst Ramgarh was in the *thikana* of the Rao Raj of Sikar, in Jaipur state. During the 18th century, the Poddar clan rose to become the principal merchant family in Churu, trading particularly in woollen products. The Thakur of Churu, short of funds, decided to impose a new levy on the wool trade, much to the anger of the Poddars. They remonstrated. He insisted. Then they presented him with an ultimatum: either withdraw the tax or they would abandon the town. He called their bluff and they left to found the town of Ramgarh in 1791 with the support of the Raja of Sikar.

There is another story, however. The Raja's wife was the sister of the Thakur of Churu, then a very prosperous trading town. One day she came to stay with her brother. In the women's quarters of the palace her sister-in-law goaded her with the fact that the Raja owned no such prosperous town as Churu in his domain. When she returned to Sikar she set about her husband, finally declaring that she would neither eat nor drink until a new merchant town was founded in Sikar *thikana*. The Raja, for the sake of peace, summoned one of the Churu Poddars and together they came to an agreement to establish this new town.

Whatever the truth, the rise of Ramgarh completely eclipsed Churu, which was in any case suffering from a dispute with the Raja of Bikaner. Britons visiting both towns in the 1830s describe Churu as run-down, its bazaar totally closed, whilst Ramgarh, despite the dacoits, was flourishing. Major Thoresby, travelling this way from Mandawa in 1841, describes it thus: "The first appearance of Ramgarh when descried among the sand *tibas* or ridges, which is not until approached within less than half a mile, is singularly striking and seems to give reality to a vision drawn from eastern romance. The buildings are all constructed from *kunkur* grey hardpan,... numerous handsome houses of the *seths* some of which are on a magnificent scale, ornamented and painted in various devices outwardly; the neat high wall and gateways and the *cupolard chhutrees* in the suburb in contrast with the desert around, altogether exhibit a scene deserving to be allied with enchantment".

The town was new then, and rising fast towards its peak of glory at the close of the century. It has faded. Of the walls little remains, though three gates still stand. But there is still more than a breath of the Ramgarh Thoresby described. This town boasts more paintings than any other in Shekhawati.

1) *Ram Gopal Poddar Chhatri*. Built in 1872 over Ram Gopal's grandfather. Architecturally the most opulent of all merchant *chhatris* in the region, it contains some good paintings, particularly in the dome. The latter is dominated by three themes – the *Ramayana*, the life of Krishna and a set of *ragamala* panels illustrating the musical modes. On the basement, where squatters have set up house, the paintings include an ancient train, a chained rhinoceros and a scene at a well, all on the southern side. This building bears a total of no less than 500 pictures.

2) *Group of Poddar Chhatris*. These stand on the south side of the road on the western edge of the town. They are enclosed in two main compounds, one of which is usually locked. That nearest the town is entered through an arched gateway. To the right of the entrance is a double-*chhatri*, now used as a school. This was the work of Chejara Ali in 1858. In the domes are panels of incarnations of Vishnu, also one of Dadu Dayal, a follower of the

great teacher, Kabir, shown with a ship. His intercession was often requested by the merchants in their insurance schemes. Opposite this *chhatri*, to the east, is another dated 1872. This has a series of labelled *ragamala* panels in its subsidiary domes. A battered *chhatri* to the south-west of this bears the date 1844 and has geometric designs on its outer walls, incarnations of Vishnu within. South of this is a last *chhatri*, dated 1861, again the work of Chejara Ali, with panels in the dome of labelled incarnations of Vishnu as well as one of Dadu Dayal.

On the eastern side of the compound are two *tibaris* now used for fodder and with paintings on their facades. These show a procession of trousered soldiers, probably British, meeting skirted Rajputs. South of the double *chhatri* is a double temple, with two courtyards, and two shrines. There are paintings on the facade and in the courtyards, but most impressive is the double vaulted ceiling in front of the shrine in the northern section. One vault mostly illustrates the *Ramayana*, the other the life of Krishna. This building also seems to have lost woodwork to the antique trade. The neighbouring compound contains another single *chhatri* built in 1833, and a double *chhatri* built in 1861, both painted, the former with the primitive figurative work not uncommon so early in the century. Further west still, near a mosque, is a triple *chhatri* of the Poddar clan dating from around 1890 and the work of another Muslim mason, Fateh Khan. The oldest surviving Poddar memorial in Ramgarh stands about 300 m north-east of the Ram Gopal Poddar Chhatri (1) and is a triple *chhatri* dating from 1827 with interesting murals on the pavilion next to it, soon doomed to collapse.

3) *Natwar Niketan.* A fine temple built by Anat Ram Poddar and family in 1844 at a cost of Rs.20,000, according to its inscription. The murals include huge elephants, camels and horses on the outer walls. There are also some paintings in a dome on the roof. Architecturally, this temple is only rivalled in Ramgarh by the Ganga Temple (9).

4) *A Poddar Haveli.* Small and heavily painted in natural colours, the geometrical designs so popular in the mid-19th century predominate. c1850.

5) *Ram-Lakshman Temple.* The original temple must have been built early in the 19th century, but blown sand gradually inundated it. A new structure was built on top of the old around 1860 and that in its turn was painted. The old temple, now the cellar, has a painted interior. Many years of enforced darkness have beautifully preserved the colours, which predate the imported chemical pigments and include indigo and cinnebar. They were probably painted around 1820. Most of the subjects are religious. At either end of the vaulted ceiling are incarnations of Vishnu, whilst on the sides are scenes from the *Ramayana*.

6) *Parsuram Poddar Haveli.* Fine geometric motifs on the facade; on the north wall peacocks, also fish designs which are typical of Ramgarh and rarely seen elsewhere. Opposite these, on the north side of the road, are more pictures, including a train.

7) *Dalsukhrai Jayadayal Poddar.* c1880. A good painted *haveli*. On the east wall is a train, Dhola-Maru and the god-hero Ramdevji on horseback holding a spear. There is also the three-fish motif peculiar to Ramgarh. In the forecourt are elephants, guards and religious pictures. East across the road, a chained rhino and a train.

8) *Madanlal Govardhandas Poddar Haveli.* This pretty *haveli* dating from around 1840 has suffered at the hands of the antique trade. The window frames were ripped out and the door replaced by a new one. Now an old door has been restored. The original woodwork no doubt graces some urban drawing room! There are some nice murals on the facade. At

Ramgarh (2): In a dome of the double *chhatri* in the western compound of these Poddar memorials a merchant is shown praying to Dadu Dayal, a disciple of the great teacher, Kabir. His intercession was sought to protect merchandise. Off the shore a foreign ship lies at anchor in a fish-filled sea. Goods are being lowered from its deck. (1861).

Opposite page, bottom:
Ramgarh (5): Rama with his army of monkeys and bears prepares to cross the sea to attack Lanka, Ravana's capital. Behind him comes his brother, Lakshmana, and Garuda, Vishnu's vehicle. Buried in this room by drifting sand the pictures have retained their brightness and even indigo has been preserved. (c1820).

Left:
Ramgarh (8): Rama and Sita travel in a handsome *rath* with Lakshmana as their driver. Above them two merchants are pursued by an armed bandit – a not-uncommon event in the early 19th century. (c1840).

Below:
Ramgarh (near 8): On the outer wall of a *haveli* built by Banarasi Das Poddar a man rides his bicycle, a primitive model. (c1930).

the north end Rama and Sita go for a drive in a *rath* and nearby men on a camel are pursued by a horseman. Beneath them a European couple, he with a pistol, are threatened by rising damp. A guard stands on either side of the door projection.

9) *Ganga Temple*. The finest temple in Ramgarh, built by Ramchandra Shivdutt Poddar in 1845 at a cost of Rs.32,000. There are some good pictures on its outer walls and between the brackets of the courtyard. An adjoining little *dharamshala* has had all its woodwork torn out for antiques. Ramgarh monuments have been particularly badly damaged by this recent wave of destruction.

10) *Double Chhatri* Built in 1870. The south dome, dedicated to Ramji Das Poddar, has some unusual stucco figures on its sides.

11) A group of Poddar buildings around a compound. These include a Ganesh Temple (1860) which is rarely open, two *chhatris* and a *dharamshala* (c1845) all with paintings, most of them religious.

12) *Shani Temple*. Built by Gurudayal Gangabaksh Khemka in 1840, but the painting, rich in ultramarine, is probably somewhat later. The murals are many and varied. On the porch ceiling is shown a pilgrimage to Lohargalji, a local holy-place, with pilgrims bathing in the tank there and passing the fine *bowri*. There are episodes from the life of Shaniji, the Saturn God, and also Prahlad, one of which shows a potter at work firing pots from which two tiger cubs escape. There are also more usual religious and folk subjects. One of the pair of large mirrors at either side of the courtyard disappeared several years ago.

13) *Kesarwala Poddar Haveli*. This *haveli*, built and painted around 1855, shows how well the ochre pigments resist fading. On the facade are good geometric designs, elephants and horsemen.

14) *Bashashwarlal Poddar Haveli*. This is a remarkably fine double *haveli* and must date from the 1830s. There are good ochre paintings, including floral designs typical of the period in the forecourt. Opposite it across the road is the fast disappearing ruins of one of the first *havelis* constructed in the town. This displays several features of the time – unpainted plaster finish, some wooden ceilings and the use of red sandstone in the fabric. At the south end of this *cul-de-sac* is the *haveli* of Tarachand Ghanshyamdas Poddar, a particularly prosperous section of the family, which contains a painted room. The building is generally locked.

15) *Sureka Dharamshala*. c1890. Over the gate Shiva is shown with the Ganges flowing through his hair. On the facade there are also portraits and religious panels. This is a fine *dharamshala* with massive iron gates opening into a courtyard with *tibaris* for travellers. There are good red and blue paintings of religious and folk themes.

16) *Two Ruia havelis*. Built around 1890 and painted with red and blue portraits of Britons and Indians. The Ruia family became increasingly important in the town as the century progressed.

17) *Hanuman Temple*. Built by the Ruias about 1885. This is known as the Lal Kuan Mandir (The Red Well Temple), presumably because the well which adjoins it to the north was once painted red. An interesting building with a passage passing along and beneath it, probably used for a processional *rath*. The vaulted ceiling in front of the shrine was once finely painted, but has suffered badly from percolating moisture. The pictures show scenes from the *Ramayana* and the life of Krishna. On the north wall a train and a row of soldiers form a good frieze.

18) *Kanoria Haveli* c1855. Another *haveli* painted in natural ochres. Apart from religious and

geometric designs a frieze of soldiers marches across the wall. The windows of the upper facade are attractive. The lower panels in the courtyard have been whitewashed.

19) *Anat Ram Poddar Double Haveli*. These are two of the Aath (eight) Haveli built in this part of town by Anat Ramji in the 1830s and 1840s. In the forecourt are elephants, religious and folk pictures and also several of the fish motifs peculiar to Ramgarh. On the south wall are false windows and erotics. On the west wall, high up, is the giraffe that Col. Sutherland purchased for the Maharaja of Jaipur in 1849 and which frequently intrudes on to the walls of the time!

20) Another of Anat Ramji's eight *havelis*. This has good geometric designs as well as horses and elephants on its facade. A biscuit bakery in the forecourt, the creation of an earlier tenant, hardly enhances its appearance. In the *chandanis* there are some good floral designs typical of 1830s work.

21) *Jagannath Poddar Double Haveli*. Architecturally a handsome building, built around 1845. The two *havelis* are connected only by a second-floor corridor crossing the narrow passage that runs between the two buildings. In the forecourt paintings show Krishna dancing with the *gopis* and Dhola-Maru. On the south wall a woman spins. On the west are wrestlers, guards, horsemen and Europeans.

22) *Shops*. The shops of the main bazaar and also that running north from it towards the old Churu Gate, are the best series in Shekhawati, although each varies considerably in quality and age. There are some fine examples on the north side of the main bazaar at its western end. These include a two-storied building near the bus stand known as the Kothi. Some of the shops are painted within, or have paintings in a room on the second floor.

23) *Three joharas*. Ramgarh has three such reservoirs. Most easily accessible is that built by Anat Ram Poddar on the north side of the road which turns into Ramgarh from the main Churu-Sikar road. Another, also built by Anat Ramji but more ambitious as well as more efficient, is about 2 km west of the above johara along the Dhandhan road. The third is about 1 km north of Churu Gate along the old Churu Road. It was built by Ramchandra Poddar in 1866 and has an enclosed bathing place for women.

Opposite page, top:
Ramgarh (1): The Ram Gopal Poddar Chhatri must be the most ornate of its kind in Shekhawati. This picture shows the view up into its dome. On a turquoise ground scenes from the lives of Krishna and Rama are depicted. Beneath these Krishna alternates with the *gopis* in a *rasamandala*. The panels around the rim depict other incarnations of Vishnu. (1872).

Opposite page, bottom:
Ramgarh: The funeral procession of a *sethani*, a wealthy lady, passes by the bus stand. She is accompanied by peacock feather fans and shaven-headed mourners. In the background one of the *chhatris* (2) can be seen.

Below:
Ramgarh (14): A handsome double *haveli* built by the wealthiest branch of the Poddar clan probably during the 1820s. Some fine floral designs decorate its facade.

RAMGARH

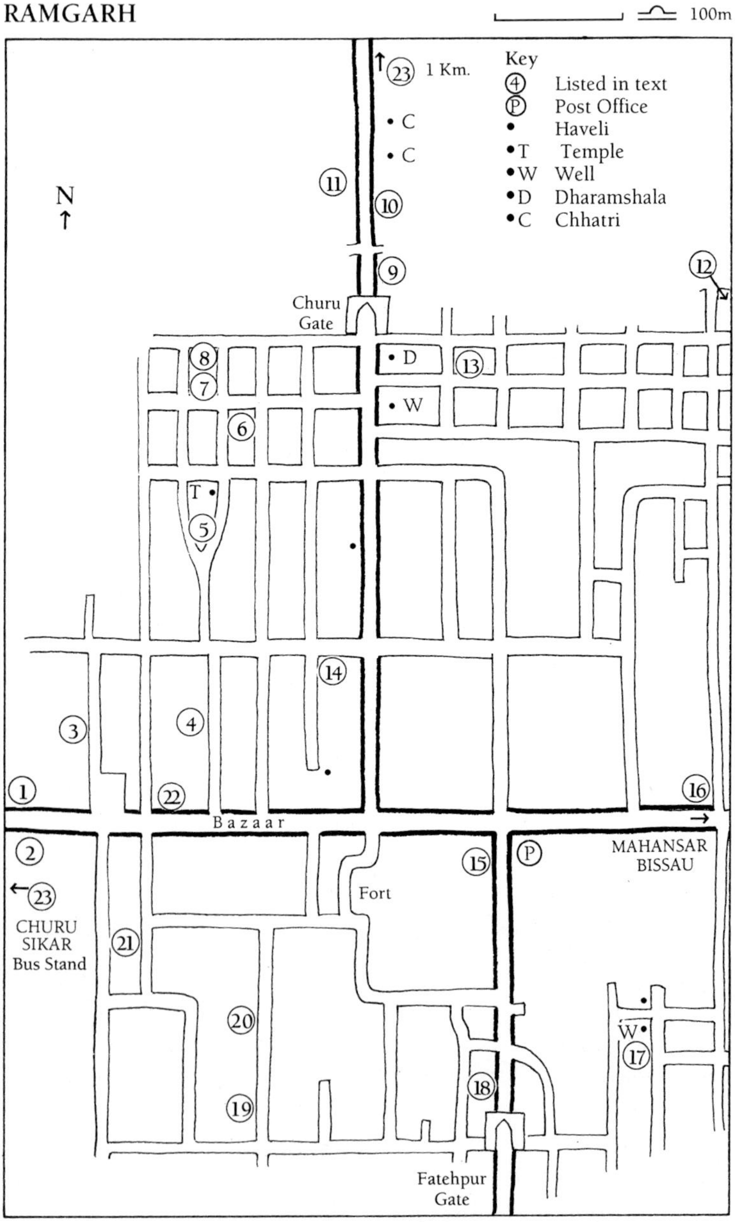

100m

Key
- ④ Listed in text
- Ⓟ Post Office
- • Haveli
- •T Temple
- •W Well
- •D Dharamshala
- •C Chhatri

N ↑

㉓ 1 Km.

•C
•C

⑪
⑩
⑨

Churu Gate

⑧
⑦
⑥

•D ⑬
•W

T•
⑤

⑫

⑭

③
④

①
㉒

Bazaar

②
←㉓

CHURU SIKAR Bus Stand

⑮ Ⓟ

MAHANSAR BISSAU

Fort

⑯

㉑

⑳

W•
⑰

⑲

⑱

Fatehpur Gate

Ratangarh

Like Churu, Ratangarh is not in Shekhawati but across the border in old Bikaner state. It was founded by Surat Singh of Bikaner in the late 18th century but it was his son, Ratan Singh, who brought it prosperity. To establish its place on the commercial map he called in Jeevan Ram Poddar, a merchant from Churu. That was in the 1820s. Since then the place has borne Ratan Singh's name. It stands 50 km south-west of Churu and 40 km west of Fatehpur on the main road from Jaipur to Bikaner. The bazaar is laid out in the form of a cross, its axes north-south and east-west, with some painted shops along it. There are a number of good painted *havelis* in the town. Some of the best are along the south section of the bazaar. It is also worth walking through the backstreets in the south-east and north-east sectors of the town, or along the alley that runs parallel to the north-south bazaar but just to the west of it. At the western edge of the town there is a good *johara* built by the Chandkothia family. The original fort has fallen into ruin and the walls have gone, but for a couple of short stretches. Near the town, on the main Bikaner-Jaipur road, is Midway Chinkara, a Rajasthan Tourism establishment serving snacks and cold beer.

1) Double *chhatri* of Jeevan Ram Poddar and his wife. This stands in the grounds of the Poddar Guest House at the north end of the bazaar on the west side. It dates from around 1850 and there are paintings in the domes. A contemporary Hirawat *chhatri* stands just to the east of it, on the opposite side of the road.

2) *Bansidhar Poddar Double Haveli*. A fine building on the north side of the first turning west off the north limb of the bazaar. Built at the close of the 19th century it is now shared among many descendants. In the forecourt are pictures of wrestlers, Krishna as a baby on a leaf, a man massaging a horse. The north courtyard has paintings, but the south is whitewashed.

3) *Thard Haveli*. On the west side of the southern bazaar, just south of the first turning to the west, is a good *haveli* of the Thard family, opposite the Raghunath Temple. This is said to have 300 wooden window and door frames. There is some painting. c1860.

4) *Vaidnath Taparia Haveli* Neighbours the Thard Haveli (3) to the south. An interesting house with some good paintings, mostly religious, but including a train and a station in the forecourt. c1900.

5) *Maganlal Taparia Double Haveli*. A little further to the south on the east side of the road. Some interesting murals in the forecourt, including trains with cutaway panels – one reveals a horse as the source of power, the other, more topically, shows the sun! Built 1893.

6) *Dhansukhdas Bhuwalka Double Haveli*. Immediately behind the Vaidnath Taparia Haveli (4) on a little road parallel to the bazaar. There are some mirrorwork designs set in the plaster and some paintings in the upper rooms of the north section. In the courtyards, religious paintings, Rajputs and trains. Built around 1905.

7) *Bhuwalka Haveli*. North of the above double *haveli* (6) is a crossroad on the north-west corner of which is another painted *haveli* with some good murals. These include Krishna in a palanquin made of women, the folk stories of Heer-Ranjha and Sassi-Punu, Arjuna and Krishna in a *rath* meeting the composite beast Ajaibgulmari and foot-soldiers with a cannon – all on the facade.

Ratannagar

A merchant of Bissau, Nand Ram Kedia, had a dispute with the local Thakur, so he left that town and founded this one. Just inside Churu district, it was on the old border between Jaipur and Bikaner states. The site might have been a master stroke in 1800, but by 1860 the borders were losing their significance and the town never flourished. Today it is almost a ghost town, its shops and *havelis* firmly locked. The painted buildings, worth a visit in passing, are mostly in the eastern part of the town. There is a pretty little *chhatri* built by the Gadodia family around 1880 on the east side of the main road to Churu at the northern edge of the town.

Opposite page
Ratangarh (5): In the forecourt of the Taparia double *haveli* an elephant, steered by Hanuman, carries Rama and Lakshmana towards the door. Above them Europeans man a station as a train approaches from the side. (1893).

Below
Ratannagar: High on the north wall of Gangabux Chandgothia Haveli the Maharaja of Bikaner, Ganga Singh, goes out in his car. This long-reigned monarch commonly appears in murals. (c1925).

Ringus

Situated on the main road from Jaipur to Sikar, this town has a few unremarkable painted *havelis*. It merits inclusion only on the strength of one *chhatri*, that of Bakshi Ram Khandelwal, which is coupled with a temple of Janki Ballabhji. It stands on the south-west fringe of the town and is partly made from white marble. Within the dome, painted in natural ochres, are some fine 18th century murals. For the most part they depict the Battle of Maonda (1767) and events connected with it. The army on the right hand side of the conflict is that of Jaipur, complete with the five-coloured flag of the state. Har Sahai and Gur Sahai, who led the army due to the illness of the Maharaja, are shown on elephants. Some of the barons are also named. On the Bharatpur side the Maharaja is shown, also on an elephant. His infantry is led by the German, Walter Reinhard, who is labelled by his nickname, Samru. The hats identify European mercenaries and they can be seen among the infantry in both armies.

Apart from the battle and scenes of the armies arriving at a city there are arched panels around the sides, showing religious subjects and a picture of Bakshi Ram Khandelwal with attendants. Lower still are some long, rectangular panels, one of which has a fine picture of a battle between two Sikh armies.

Sardarshahr

Some 50 km west-north-west of Churu in old Bikaner State, this town was raised from village status in 1831 and given this new name. The local merchant community are mostly Oswal Jains. Some of them built massive painted *havelis*, mostly a little west of the north-south bazaar in both the north and south parts of the town. A small fort stands at the east end of the main bazaar and houses government offices.

1) *Anoop Chand Birdichand Jammer Haveli*. Founded in 1873, but building progressed in stages and the paintings date from the early 20th century. To reach it, turn south at the clock-tower in the main bazaar, take the first right turn and this *haveli* is on the south side of the road, covering the area between the first and second intersections. On the east wall a scene of horsemen pursuing cows comes from the saga of Pabuji, the Rajasthani god/hero credited with bringing the camel to Rajasthan. In the forecourt are copies of English prints complete with "gilt frames" and in the adjoining *tibari* is a nice scene of a party in a garden. There is some excellent carved woodwork. The wall north across the road from this *haveli* has some amusing pictures, including a ship with its name copied from the artist's tin of paint: "Made in Germany" the wrong way up.

2) The double *haveli* of Chandmal Budhmal Nahata. c1900. A massive building, its entrance is about 100 m south of the back of the previous haveli (1) on the same side of the road. There are murals on the outer walls and also in the *baithak* on the north side of the forecourt.

3) *Jammer Haveli*. About 50 m south of the Nahata double *haveli* (2) on the south-west corner of the intersection. On the east wall Bhima shakes a tree in which the 100 Kaurava brothers are concealed and they fall like fruit. This is a Rajasthani embellishment to the *Mahabharata* epic. Pabuji is also shown with his camels. The murals date from c1900, but the building is older.

Sikar

The Shekhawats who ruled Sikar were distant cousins to those five brothers who shared the Panchpana. They descended from Tirmalji, the brother of Bhojraj, the great great grandfather of Sardul Singh. Two dates are given for the foundation of Sikar. In 1687 the region came under the control of Daulat Singh and he may have planned a town here, but 1724 is more generally given as its birth. In that year his son, Sheo Singh, seems to have started the building in earnest. He completed the palace, the fort and the first town walls. There is abundant evidence that this was a far more ancient site, and a well near the Fatehpur Gate which has a stele bearing the date 1278. Remnants of temple stonework appear during excavations and are built into the walls at Nani Gate and in the *bowri* (3). There are important early sites nearby, including the Harash Temple which dates from the 10th century and is the only protected monument in the three districts covered by this guide. Until well into the present century, the town remained small, largely confined within its still-surviving walls. These had been extended southwards in the mid 19th century, doubling the walled area and accommodating thereby many of the large Bania *havelis*.

The ruler of Sikar received the title of Rao Raja early in the 19th century and figured as the most important and wealthiest baron in Jaipur State. The *thikana* had been enlarged by Sheo Singh, supported by Sardul Singh, when he evicted the Kaimkhani Nawab of Fatehpur and seized his lands. Later, Devi Singh further enlarged it at the expense of his neighbours. He also built a handsome fort, Deogarh, some 8 km south-east of the town, during the 1780s. Lakshman Singh, his heir and the first of the family to bear the title Rao Raja, founded Lakshmangarh. The Biyanis were the main merchant family. The *havelis* of Sikar do not rival those of the towns to the north or those of Jhunjhunu district. This is the headquarters of Sikar district, connected by direct rail and bus to Jaipur (115 km) and Delhi (280 km). There is a decent hotel, the Natraj, and the Somani Dharamshala, both near the railway station. A Hindi history of the town has been written by Jhabarmal Sharma.

1) *Chhatri of Devi Singh*. He died in 1795 and the *chhatri* must have erected shortly afterwards. The dome contains 80 painted panels, the work of Lala Ram Chitera. The pigments have suffered with age and the pictures are in fairly poor condition. Most of the murals are religious but quite a number show scenes from the life of Devi Singh, many of the individuals shown being named. In a Gangaur procession no doubt referring to Jaipur, the painter's hometown, Europeans are depicted, each wearing a characteristic hat and labelled "faranghi". The memorials of other rulers adjoin this.

2) A handsome well built by Devi Singh's mother at the same time as the *chhatri*. It is unpainted.

3) *The Bowri*. The condition of this step-well is an example to those who control the others in the region. A trust keeps it well-maintained and clean. It was built by Gopal Singh Ugrawat around 1750. Three memorial steles dating from this time stand against the wall within the gate. There is no painting, but an interesting feature is the integration in its fabric of carved masonry which must have derived from an ancient temple nearby.

4) *Jain Temple*. Founded in 1860, but since enlarged. There are paintings in a domed ceiling showing some Jain scenes. There are also several good figures of Jain Tirthankars derived from other, more ancient, sites.

5) *The Mahal*. This was founded by Rao Raja Ram Pratap Singh around 1845, but was built in stages. The ground floor was the *adaalat*, or court. Above it, now largely used as a

transport office, is the Chini (China) Mahal and above that the late 19th century white marble section known as the Makrana Mahal (Makrana is the local source of white marble). A Sheesh Mahal, containing mirrorwork and generally locked, stands at the western end of the second floor. Another section of the new palace is accessible through the gateway to the old one. This is the Badal Mahal, now used as a student hostel. For its murals the Chini Mahal is outstanding. It takes its name from its painted designs imitating imported blue and white china tiles, a colour scheme later copied on several *havelis* in the town. The painter signs himself as Ramsukh Birdichand of Jaipur. The subjects include views of the palace and the *johara* (21), a Pathan horse-dealer, panels on the ceiling showing Indian and European portraits, and a procession with the Rao Raja Madho Singh on an elephant. The paintings are dated 1861. It is unfortunate that they are unprotected in this busy office. In the Sheesh Mahal is a beautiful view of the town and a portrait of Rao Raja Madho Singh, with a top-hatted British official. In the Badal Mahal is another picture of Madho Singh, this time watching dancers in his court. These paintings are the undoubted gems of Sikar. This *mahal* is mostly in the hands of an Aggarwal trust.

6) *Jamoon Mahal*. The old palace, built by Sheo Singh in the early 18th century, but largely renovated by Devi Singh at the end of that century. It has long been locked and there is little in the way of painting. The mirrorwork of a Sheesh Mahal has been applied over murals, but a portrait of Devi Singh remains there. In a courtyard some of the best sculpture from the ancient Harash Temple, as well as its beautiful Pali inscription, lie stored. They were put there when the building, the Mahamandir, which once housed a museum, was sold after Independence. There they remain, abandoned and unseen.

7) *Gopinath Temple*. Started by Sheo Singh in the 1720s, but the main building was redecorated by Devi Singh around 1780 and the ceiling in the mid-19th century. The new painting and porcelain tiles around the doorway are misleading. The murals in the temple include portraits of three 18th century rulers of Sikar, the last being Devi Singh, a picture of Deep Singh fighting a tiger and an interesting view of Jaipur city. Most of the pictures, however, are religious and many of them have been labelled. This would have been the work of a Jaipur artist.

8) *Raghunath Temple*. Known as Rathorji ka Mandir, since it was built by Rathorji, one of Lakshman Singh's widows, about 1840. The murals of the courtyard are mostly religious, but include some folk tales. On the upper storey there are more paintings – a battle scene, a man with a bear, a picture labelled "fairy standing in a garden" and also an interesting labelled portrait of Lt. Boileau, who came here first with Col. Lockett in 1831. It is interesting because it is a full-face picture, unusual at that time. Boileau recounts how, on a visit to Bikaner in 1835, he presented a "camera lucida" to one of the princes so that he could teach the court artist to paint full-face portraits, rather than the usual side-views. Perhaps, Boileau started his crusade for the full-face here in Sikar!

9) *Chhotalal Sodhani Haveli*. A good painted *haveli* built in 1884. On the south end of the facade the local cavalry rides. In the entrance are dancing girls, repeated on the cusps of the arch. In the forecourt are false windows above the door and amongst the religious subjects two panels from the *Mahabharata* on its north side.

10) *Murarka Haveli*. Built c1850. Paintings in rooms on the roof, mostly of religious subjects.

11) *Biyani Haveli*. c1865. A handsome *haveli* with some good paintings. Above the little *baithak* at the north end of the forecourt are a decorated room and a little temple with mirrorwork, scarred badly where antique dealers have torn out glass-covered pictures.

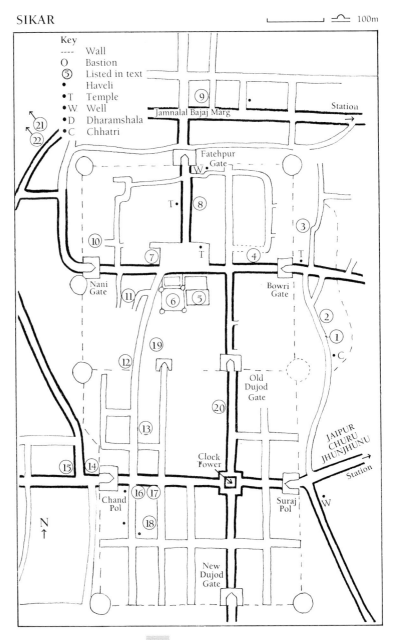

SIKAR

100m

Key
---- Wall
O Bastion
⑤ Listed in text
• Haveli
•T Temple
•W Well
•D Dharamshala
•C Chhatri

Jamnalal Bajaj Marg

Station

Fatehpur Gate

Nani Gate

Bowri Gate

Old Dujod Gate

JAIPUR CHURU JHUNJHUNU

Clock Tower

Chand Pol

Suraj Pol

Station

New Dujod Gate

N

12) *Deen Dayal Biyani Haveli.* The road passes through the forecourt of this building which is decorated in blue and white, inspired by the Chini Mahal (5). At this point one passes from the original walled town into the extension built by Bhairon Singh. Paintings dated 1900.

13) *Somani Haveli.* Painted in red and blue. Most of this *haveli* is generally locked.

14) *Madan Mohanji Temple.* Built by Balabux Biyani c1895. A good temple with paintings on the walls and in the dome.

15) *Govind Devji Temple.* Opposite Madan Mohanji Temple (14) across the road and in similar style. Built by Hiralal Biyani in 1888. On the south wall, wrestlers, a scene at a well and Dhola-Maru.

16) *Balabux Biyani Haveli c1900.* Paintings of moderate quality, including a painted room. On the north wall oval panels show mythological and religious figures, defaced by posters.

17) *Jivan Ram Biyani Haveli.* c1870. The oldest of the three buildings (16 – 18). The paintings on its south and west walls are hidden by the later *havelis*. On the east wall, at eye-level between the brackets, a musician, probably the famous Tansen, plays to some Blackbuck.

18) Another nice single-courtyard *haveli* of the Biyani family. c1890.

19) *Jubilee Hall.* 1897. Built by Rao Raja Madho Singh to celebrate the diamond jubilee of Queen Victoria's accession to the throne. There are portraits of rulers, including those of Sikar, as well as religious panels inside the hall. It is now used as a girls' college.

20) Haveli with five shops built by Somani the family. c1880. On the facade are paintings of Laila-Majnu and Dhola-Maru, as well as the goddesses Ganga, Jumna and Saraswati, representing the three great rivers (the last, mythical) that meet at Prayag (Allahabad).

21) Johara built by Pokar Ram Biyani around 1860 and situated some distance to the north-west of the town beside Nehru Park. A painting in the Chini Mahal (5) shows this tank during the Gangaur celebration filled with swimmers. An excellent example of such a reservoir, but unpainted.

22) *Chhatri of Pokar Ram Biyani.* 1878. This stands close by his *johara* (21) and is painted. In the dome is a portrait of Pokar Ramji. On the basement, amongst the religious subjects are a train, hunting scenes – and even a rhinoceros!

Pages 218-219
Sikar (5): In the *Sheesh Mahal* (glass palace) of the palace of the Raja of Sikar are paintings by a Jaipur artist. This section of the wall bears a beautiful map-picture of the town as seen from the north. On the right the Raja appears with his court and (extreme right) he is shown in conversation with a British official. (painted 1861).

Opposite page, bottom
Sikar (14): The Madan Mohan Temple stands just outside Chand Pol, the western gate of the newer part of the walled town. A shop at the entrance deals not only in holy pictures but also in sandals and biscuits. The temple was built at the close of the 19th century by the Biyani family of merchants.

Sikar (5): Pathans were familiar in North India as horse-dealers. Here one such man leads a stallion. The glass that once covered many of these paintings has been broken leaving them unprotected. At the edge of this picture the blue and white porcelain tiles which gave the Chini Mahal (China Palace) its name can be seen. They are only painted imitations! (1861).

Singhana

Singhana had considerable importance from Mughal times as the centre for smelting copper derived from nearby mines. The industry still survives, based around a new colony called, appropriately, Copper. The town was founded during the reign of Akbar, in the late 16th century, and it was a particularly Muslim town until Partition when many left for Pakistan. Presumably on account of its important industry, it was shared between the brothers after Sardul Singh died. Even British travellers coming here 150 years ago described it as being rather rundown. It is much more so today. Mosques and tombs, some dating back to the early 17th century, small and unpretentious, remain, often in a sad state of decay. Many of the stone *havelis* are collapsing. The town is dominated by a hill some 200 m high, topped by a little temple. When Col. Lockett came here in 1831 there was a saint's tomb on the lower slopes which was lit up each night. Only rubble remains.

1) *Dargah and Mehfilkhana*. These stand in the centre of the town along with a mosque dated 1763 and some small tombs. Fine buildings with non-figurative murals.

2) *Dokania Haveli*. c1845. A handsome *haveli* with two courtyards standing at the eastern edge of the town up against a vast pile of waste from copper smelting. There are good paintings in the courtyard, mostly of religious subjects. On the facade there are floral and geometric designs.

3) *Khakhiji ka Koond*. A remarkable step-well situated near the Ganga Temple and dating from around 1900.

4) *Chhatris near Teej Talab*. A short distance north east of the town lies a tank, Teej Talab. Beside it are two *chhatris*, one of which is painted. Built in 1768, the year after the Battle of Maonda, it contains a picture of that battle as well as scenes from the *Ramayana*.

Surajgarh

Originally known as Oreecha, this place fell in the portion of Keshri Singh, fifth and youngest of the five brothers. His son, Surajmal, raised its status and built a fort here in 1778. As a result the town took his name. The fort is now in the possession of a merchant family and is on the verge of total collapse. Surajgarh is some 40 km north-east of Jhunjhunu.

1) *Satyanarayan Temple.* On entering the town from the main road there is a handsome Satyanarayan temple on the right, built by Pali Ram Rora in 1889. It contains some good paintings, mostly on religious subjects. A well, also built by Pali Ramji, stands opposite.

2) *Pokarmal Khaitan Haveli.* Stands a little to the west of the north-west bastion of the fort and dates from around 1845. Most of the murals are of a later date.

3) *Lalchand Kaya Haveli.* This stands in the centre of the town, some 35 m north of the north-east corner of Gandhi Chowk, and dates from 1843. There are some interesting paintings. The footings of the building are in a chronic state of decay. A good row of contemporary shops stand to the south of the *haveli*, towards the *chowk*, the square.

4) *Narayan Das Kaya Haveli.* This mansion ranks high amongst the buildings of Shekhawati and is rich in good murals. On the facade a prince is seated and women play Holi. In the porch, Krishna dances with the *gopis*. In the forecourt a tailor tries clothes on a Rajput, carpenters saw and a *bhishti*, water-carrier, plies his trade. In the courtyard a tailor is at work, and in a scene from the folk tale, Sultan-Nehalde, the lover puts his shield over her head. Built between 1875 and 1885, this *haveli* stands on the west side of a road running north from the bazaar.

Taen

This region fell to Zorawar Singh, Sardul Singh's eldest son. The town was founded by his son, Salim Singh, in 1761 and the fort was completed in 1769. The descendants of Zorawar Singh, many in number, were notorious as bandits. The Rajputs of Taen were no exception, falling within the orbit of Thakur Shyam Singh of Bissau. The fort, a four-bastioned square redoubt, was among those slighted by the Shekhawati Brigade in 1837. The Bissau Thakur took away the great gates for his own fort and the walls were never rebuilt. Only two bastions remain, and the gateway which, probably as a result of the explosions, is in a very dangerous state. The Rajputs still build their houses on the site where the ruins of the fort stand. The exception is the Kothi, built by Thakur Moti Singh in 1846. This has some good paintings, but the building is in a very poor state. Balji and Bhoorji, two bandits who became something of folk heroes, originated from this town. They were eventually hunted down and shot near Bissau by the Bikaner State Forces around 1930. Taen, briefly quite a prosperous little town in the early 19th century, has long been eclipsed by Mandawa and Bissau. Only very recently has a metalled road reached the place.

Taranagar

I always feel a soft spot for this town for it was here, in November 1972, that I first came across the painted *havelis*. Traditionally called Reni, it is comparatively ancient. The Jain community, whose written records are usually good, claim that their local temple was founded in 942 AD. In 1842, Maharaja Ratan Singh of Bikaner decreed that the name of the town be changed to Taranagar in memory of Tara Singh, who died in battle here in 1748. The original date of the fort is uncertain. Beside the gateway there are 'hand-marks' in memory of the Ranis of Anand Singh, who committed *sati* after he too was killed in 1748. It is known that Maharaja Surat Singh largely rebuilt the place around 1800. Today it merely contains government offices and a small temple.

1) *Anand Singh's Chhatri.* Built in 1842 on orders from the Maharaja, it contains some murals. It stands not far from the bus stand, to the north-west.
2) *Tara Singh's Chhatri.* Also built in 1842 and containing some painting. This stands in front of the gate of the fort.
3) *Sadasukh Puranmal Dugar Haveli.* Built 1885 to 1897. A good painted *haveli* on the western fringe of the town. On the facade a barber cuts hair, two ladies sit in chairs. Krishna applies *tilak* to the forehead of a raja, the equivalent of coronation. On the south wall are a train and a procession. There are also pictures in the *baithak* on the south side of the forecourt.

There are several other painted *havelis* in the town, particularly in Sarda Marg. One small room beside a grain store owned by Mohanlal Sagtani contains some nice early 20th century pictures in a good state of repair.

Udaipurwati

The suffix "*wati*" differentiates this town from a number of others in the country, but it is generally known locally as Udaipur. It is an old town commanding a gap in the wall of hills. It came into the possession of Rao Bhojraj, ancestor of Sardul Singh and of many other Shekhawat rulers west of the Aravallis, who are thus known as Bhojrajka. The Sikar family, however, descend from his brother, Tirmalji. In 1608 he gave the town its name and his son, who inherited it in 1640, fortified it. Little remains of the old walls, but several of the bastions survive as does Todarmal's Mahal. There are some painted *havelis*, temples and *chhatris* in the town but mostly they are not spectacular. The murals in the Gopinath Temple were largely obliterated by whitewash in the 1960s, as was the inscription. Those in the Raghunath Temple are in a very poor state. There are several 17th and 18th century temples in the town. The *bowri*, towards the west of the town near the higher secondary school, is said to have been built by Mohan Saha, an Aggarwal merchant who was minister here in the mid-17th century. Near it is a memorial *chhatri* to Jokhi Ram Saha, dated from 1702. Amongst the subjects a Muslim ruler, surely the Emperor Aurangzeb, watches an elephant fight.

Not far from Udaipur are three small holy places – Lohargal, Kirori and Shakambari, each marking the site of a spring. The first is certainly the most impressive.

Other Places Of Interest

There are several other sites in the three districts of Churu, Jhunjhunu and Sikar which are worth a visit. The hill-top forts are only for the more energetic, although that above Khetri now has a jeep track to it. These forts include Baghor, near Khetri; two little redoubts above Kot, on the track to Shakambari; Kotri, on the way from Udaipurwati to Khandela; Shyamgarh, beyond Khandela; Kho Fort or Lohargarh on the hilltop between Raghunathgarh and Lohargal and a little stronghold on the ridge above Rewasa. Perhaps most handsome is Deogarh, built by Devi Singh of Sikar at the close of the 18th century. It stands on an isolated hill about 10 km south-east of Sikar and could be coupled with a visit to the ruins of the 10th century temple of Harsnath. This stands on a neighbouring hill and is the only monument in Shekhawati under Archaeological Survey of India protection. Some of its best sculpture and inscriptions lie locked within the old palace in Sikar.

Apart from the three holy springs around Udaipurwati, there are several religious sites in the region. Most important are Salasar, near Sujangarh in Churu district, the temple sacred to Hanuman; Khatu, near Ringus, Sikar district, dedicated to Shyamji; Jeen Mata, near Rewasa in Sikar district, holy to the goddess Jeen Mata, where there is a much-altered 10th century temple. Of the urban sites the modern Rani Sati Temple at Jhunjhunu is most important. There are several Muslim holy places, including *dargahs* at Narhad; Ked; Jhunjhunu; Fatehpur and Singhana.

Wildlife has been decimated by the extension of agriculture coupled with the retreat of jungles, since Independence no longer protected by the feudal barons. A fair selection of birds can still be seen. It is mammals which have suffered most severely. Boileau, when describing his visit to Shekhawati in 1831, gave a long list of local mammals, including lions, boar, tigers, leopard, bears and hyena. All have gone. There is a sanctuary at Chhapur, near Sujangarh, in Churu district, which is famous for its beautiful black and white Blackbuck. Two other antelope species which you might well see in Shekhawati are the Nilgai – the large Blue Bull (the male is blue-grey) and the little Chinkara.

Bibliography

Adams, A.
The Western Rajputana States. Junior Army and Navy Stores, London, 1899.

Agarwal, B.
Rajasthan Gazetteer - Sikar District. Government of Rajasthan, Jaipur, 1978.

Aggarwal, G.
Churu Mandal ka Itihas. Lok Sanskriti Shodh Sansthan, Churu, 1974.

Aggarwal, G.
"Poddar Sangreh se prapt kuchh navin itihasik sakshya" in *Maru Sri,* Churu, 1980.

Aggarwal, G.
"Vanijya vyapar men munim gumashtonki bhumika – Poddar sangreh" in *Maru Sri,* Churu, 1981.

Aggarwal, S.
"Shekhawati ke bhitti chitre" in *Maru Sri,* Churu, 1980.

Aggarwala, R. A.
Marwari Murals. Agam Prakashan, New Delhi, 1977.

Agrawal, O. P.
"A study of Techniques of Indian Wall Paintings" in *Journal of Indian Museums,* Vol. XXV–XXVI, New Delhi, 1969-70.

Archer, M.
Indian Popular Painting. Her Majesty's Stationary Office, London, 1977.

Archer, W. G.
Indian Miniatures. New York Graphic Society, New York, 1960.

Bayly, C. A.
Rulers, Townsmen and Bazaars. Cambridge University Press, Cambridge, 1983.

Bhattacharya, S.
The Rajput States and the East India Company. Munshiram Manoharlal, New Delhi, 1972.

Blake, M.
Report. Unpublished, 1835.

Boileau, A. H. E.
Personal Narrative of a Tour through the Western States of Rajwara. Baptist Mission Press, Calcutta, 1837.

Boileau, A. H. E.
Miscellaneous Writings in Prose and Verse. Thacker & Co. and Ostell & LePage, Calcutta, 1845.

Burton, Capt.
Shoojanghur Agency Report, in *Reports for 1872-73.* Government of India Foreign Department, Calcutta, 1873.

Chand, Dr. H.
"Conservation of Wall Paintings of Mughal Gate, Virat Nagar" in *Conservation of Cultural Property in India,* Vol.111, New Delhi, 1975.

Compton, H. E.
European Adventurers in India. T. Fisher Unwin, London, 1892.

Contractor, R.
Murals of Chandod and Bhillapur. Unpublished, 1983.

Coomaraswamy, A.
Rajput Paintings. Hacker Art Books, New York, 1975.

Cooper, I. A.
"Easy Riding Indian Style" in *Yatri.* New Delhi, July 1973.

Cooper, I. A.
"Wall Paintings in Rajasthan" in *Illustrated Weekly of India,* Bombay, 25th July, 1976.

Cooper, I. A.
"The Painted Houses of Shekhawati." in *New Delhi,* New Delhi, December 1979.

Cooper, I. A.
"The Painted Walls of Churu, Jhunjhunu and Sikar Districts of

Rajasthan" in *South Asian Studies*, Vol.II, London, 1986.

Cooper, I. A.
(Assisted by Sharma, R.)
Survey of the Monuments of Churu, Jhunjhunu and Sikar Districts of Rajasthan. Pending publication by INTACH.

Cooper, I. A.
The Guide to Painted Towns of Shekhawati. Arvind Sharma, Churu, 1987.

Das Gupta, A.
Indian Merchants and the Decline of Surat. 1700-1750, Franz Steiner, Weisbaden, 1979.

Elphinstone, M.
An Account of the Kingdom of Caubul. Richard Bentley, London, 1842.

Erskine, K. D.
"Western Rajputana States, Residency and Bikaner Agency", in *Rajputana Gazetteer Vol.111A,* Allahabad, 1909.

Francklin, W.
Military Memoirs of Mr. George Thomas, The author, Calcutta, 1803.

Garrick, H. B. W.
Report of a Tour of Punjab and Rajputana in 1883-84. Archaeological Survey of India Reports, Calcutta 1884.

Gray, B.
Treasures of Indian Miniatures in the Bikaner Palace Collection, Bruno Cassirer, Oxford, 1951.

Gupta, S.
Rajasthan Gazetteer – Jhunjhunu District. Government of Rajasthan, Jaipur, 1984.

Hauff, G.
"The Techniques of the Wall-Paintings of Rajasthan, India" in *Zeitshrift fur Konservierung Heft/Worms* am Rhein 1991.

Hendley, T. H.
Memorials of the Jeypore Exhibition of 1883, Vol.1, W. Griggs, London, 1883.

Keene, H. G.
Hindustan under Free Lances 1770-1820. Brown, Langham and Co., London, 1907.

Khedwal, D. N.
Fatehpur Guide, Lakshminath Press, Fatehpur, 1976.

Lockett, Lt. Col. A.
Report Unpublished, 1831.

Powlett, Capt.
Bikaner Gazetteer. Office of the Superintendent of Government Printing, Calcutta, 1874.

Prinsep, G. A.
Steam Navigation in British India. From the Government Gazette Press, by G. H. Huttmann, Calcutta, 1830.

Randhawa, M. S. and Galbraith, J. K.
Indian Painting. The Scene, Themes and Legends Houghton Mifflin Company, Boston, 1968.

Sarkar, J.
The Fall of the Mughal Empire. Orient Longman, Calcutta, 1950.

Sarkar, J.
History of Jaipur. Orient Longman, Hyderabad, 1984.

Satya Prakash
"Wall Paintings – Technique of their Execution and Preservation" in *Journal of Indian Museums,* Vol. XIII, New Delhi, 1957.

Saxena, R. K.
Maratha Relations with the Major States of Rajputana, (1761-1818) S. Chand & Co., New Delhi, 1973.

Sehgal, K. K.
Rajasthan Gazetteer –Churu District. Government of Rajasthan, Jaipur, 1970.

Seth, M.
Wall Paintings of the Western Himalayas. Publications Division, Government of India, New Delhi, 1976.

Sharma, J.
Sikar ka Itihas. Rajasthan Agencies, Calcutta, 1922.

Sharma, J.
Khetri ka Itihas. Rajasthan Agencies, Calcutta, 1927.

Sharma, U. & Jangid, A.
Bissau Digdarshan. Tarun Sahitya Parishad, Bissau, 1988.

Singh, F.
Autobiography of a Chief of Khetree. Calcutta, 1870.

Singh, H.
Shekhawats and their Lands, Rajasthan Educational Printers, Jaipur, 1970.

Singh, Karni.
Relations of the House of Bikaner with the Central Powers 1465-1949, Munshiram Manoharlal, New Delhi, 1974.

Singh, N.
Thirty Decisive Battles of Jaipur. Electric Works, Jaipur, 1939.

Singh, R.
Jhunjhuna Mandal ka Itihas. Sri Sardul Shekhawati Itihas Shodh Sansthan, Jhunjhunu, 1981.

Singh, R.
Sardul Mans Prakash. Sri Sardul Shekhawati Itihas Shodh Sansthan, Jhunjhunu 1977.

Singh, S.
Nawalgarh ka sankshit itihas. Sardul Education Trust, Jhunjhunu, 1984.

Sleeman, S.W.
Rambles and Recollections of an Indian Official. Archibald Constable & Co, London, 1893.

Srivastava, A. L.
The Mughal Empire. (1526-1803) Shivlal Aggarwal & Co, Agra, 1964.

Thoresby, Major
Report Unpublished 1841.

Timberg, T.A.
The Marwaris: From Traders to Industrialists. Vikas, New Delhi, 1978.

Tod, Col. J.
Annals and Antiquities of Rajasthan. Oxford University Press, Oxford, 1920.

Wacziarg, F. and Nath, A.
Rajasthan: The Painted Walls of Shekhawati. Croom Helm, London, 1982.

Wills, C.U.
A Reply to the Report on the Land Tenures and Special Powers of Certain Thikanedars of Jaipur State. I.M.H. Press, Jaipur, 1933.

Other titles of interest:

Arts and Crafts of Rajasthan
Aman Nath & Francis Wacziarg

Mud, Mirror & Thread
Folk Traditions in Rural India
Edited by Nora Fisher

Threads of Identity
Embroidery and Adornment of the
Nomadic Rabaris
Judy Frater

Victoria and Albert Museum • Indian Art Series
Company Paintings
Indian Paintings of the British Period
Mildred Archer

Pleasure Gardens of the Mind
The Jane Greenough Green Collection
of Indian Paintings
Pratapaditya Pal, Janice Leoshko
and Stephen Markel

For a complete catalogue of books on
Indian art & culture, please write to:
Mapin Publishing Pvt. Ltd.
Chidambaram, Ahmedabad 380 013